Law Essent

EMPLOYMENT LAW

Law Essentials

EMPLOYMENT LAW

Jenifer Ross, LL.B.(Hons); M.A. (Criminology)
Solicitor;
The School of Law, University of Strathclyde

DUNDEE UNIVERSITY PRESS
2010

First edition published in Great Britain in 2010 by
Dundee University Press
University of Dundee
Dundee DD1 4HN

www.dundee.ac.uk/dup

ISBN 978 1 84586 058 5

No natural forests were destroyed to make this product; only farmed timber was used and
replanted.

British Library Cataloguing-in-Publication Data
A catalogue record for this book is available on request from the British Library

Typeset by Waverley Typesetters, Warham, Norfolk
Printed and bound by Bell & Bain Ltd, Glasgow

CONTENTS

TABLE OF CASES

Page

TABLE OF STATUTES

1 INTRODUCTION

NATURE OF EMPLOYMENT LAW

Employment law is concerned with the relationship between employer and employee. This relationship is based legally on contract. There is generally an imbalance of power between the employer and employee, and one way in which this imbalance has been dealt with is by employees acting collectively, usually through trade unions. Although there is a great deal of law governing collective matters, including the rights of trade union members, collective bargaining between unions and employers, and industrial action, the principal focus of this book is on the relationship between employer and employee and the employment rights which the law gives to employees.

For much of the 20th century the law was seen as playing a minimal role in employment and industrial relations. This was viewed as "legal abstention" or "voluntarism" (employers and employees arranging matters voluntarily themselves). The tradition was that collective resolution of employment relations was the most effective way of proceeding, so that collective agreements would be the most important source of employee rights and obligations. There has been some erosion of this, although collective bargaining still remains important.

Since the mid-1960s there has been an expansion in the amount of statutory regulation in employment, concerned with the rights of employees, and control of trade unions and industrial action. The influential Donovan Commission (1968) advocated in its Report a greater role for law in regulating both collective and individual relations. Since then, although different governments have had different priorities and approaches, there has been a general trend to increase regulation of employment and industrial relations. At the same time there has been an increasing emphasis on individual rights, partly associated with the European Union and the European Convention on Human Rights.

SOURCES OF EMPLOYMENT LAW

Common law

Since the basis of the employment relationship is the contract of employment, the common law principles of contract apply. There are some particular aspects of the contract which are specific to employment, in particular the duties of the employer and employee that are implied into the contract. So far as health and safety is concerned, the common law of both contract and delict apply.

Since the employment relationship is one which continues over time, in probably a majority of cases indefinitely, what happens on a day-to-day practical basis can often be of more importance than legal rights. In some cases, legal rights may be affected by what happens in practice. This will be discussed in connection with the implication of terms into the contract of employment. In other cases, what happens in practice may be overruled by legal rights when a legal dispute arises.

Statute

Statute is an important source of employment law. There are many statutory employment protection rights and the protection against discrimination in employment is entirely based on statute. There are Acts of Parliament, such as the Employment Rights Act 1996 (ERA 1996), and statutory instruments, such as the Working Time Regulations 1998.

Most of these statutory rights operate independently of the contract. However, in many cases the statutes have emphasised the importance of contract and the common law rules. For example, a contract of employment is defined in ERA 1996, s 230 as a "contract of service". This is a common law concept which is interpreted according to the common law approach of the judges in the appropriate cases. Also under what is now ERA 1996, the courts had to decide what sort of behaviour by the employer would entitle an employee to terminate the contract without notice, and so be treated as having been dismissed when he had resigned. (This is usually called "constructive dismissal".) In *Western Excavations (ECC) Ltd* v *Sharp* (1978) it was held that the employer's behaviour had to be a material breach of contract.

Codes of Practice

As well as statutes, there are also Codes of Practice applicable in employment law. Statutory Codes of Practice are issued under the authority of a statute and do not have legal effect in the same way that Acts and statutory instruments do. In any legal proceedings, such as an Employment Tribunal action, where there is a Code of Practice relating to the subject matter in issue, the Code is admissible as evidence in the proceedings. The Tribunal will take the Code into account, and whether it has been complied with, in deciding whether there has been a breach of the relevant law. However, failure to comply with a provision of a Code of Practice does not in itself mean that there has been a breach of the law. This will be explained further in the chapter on unfair dismissal where the ACAS Code of Practice on Disciplinary and Grievance Procedures (2009) will be discussed.

The law of the European Union and the European Convention on Human Rights

Since the UK joined what is now the European Union in 1972, EU law has been a very important influence on employment law. It is explained further below.

The UK's obligations under the European Convention on Human Rights have become increasingly important since the Human Rights Act 1998. This is explained further below.

INSTITUTIONS OF EMPLOYMENT LAW

Employment tribunals

Employment tribunals (called industrial tribunals until 1998) (ETs) were first established in 1964. Their primary function is to hear cases brought by individuals to enforce their employment rights under various statutes, principally the ERA 1996 and the anti-discrimination statutes. The constitution and conduct of employment tribunals is governed by the Employment Tribunals Act 1996 (ETA 1996) and the Regulations made under the Act.

Constitution

A standard tribunal hearing is heard by three people drawn from three panels: a legal panel of judges appointed by the Lord President whose members chair the hearings; and two other panels drawn up by the Secretary of State, one in consultation with organisations of employers, and the other in consultation with organisations of employees. With the consent of both parties, a hearing may be heard by a judge and one other, and in certain specific cases or where both parties agree in writing, or where the case is no longer contested, by a judge alone.

The importance of tribunals increased when the right not to be unfairly dismissed was created in 1971 and they were given jurisdiction to hear unfair dismissal cases. The Donovan Commission (1968) which had recommended such a right stated that the purpose of having a separate tribunal for employment rights was to encourage informality, speed and accessibility, and to provide specialist knowledge. "A specialist court of great expertise" is how the ET was described by the House of Lords in *West Midlands Co-op* v *Tipton* (1986).

Jurisdiction

The jurisdiction was originally entirely statutory, and this remains the principal jurisdiction, hearing claims arising under specific statutes. Most cases heard by ETs are claims from employees or workers under employment protection or discrimination statutes. In addition, the tribunals also hear appeals by employers against enforcement notices under certain statutes, such as the National Minimum Wage Act 1998 or the Health and Safety at Work etc Act 1974. The Employment Tribunals Extension of Jurisdiction (Scotland) Order 1994 extended the jurisdiction of ETs to include some common law claims. Common law claims can be raised for damages for breach of, or money due under, a contract of employment or any other contract connected with employment, so long as the claims could have been raised in the ordinary courts. However, the claims can only be raised on termination of the contract of employment. Certain claims cannot be raised in an ET and must go to the ordinary courts: these include claims relating to living accommodation, or intellectual property (eg copyright, patents, trade marks), or imposing obligations of confidence or covenants in restraint of trade.

In *Secretary of State for Scotland and Greater Glasgow Health Board* v *Hannah* (1991) it was established that actions based on EC law may be brought before ETs.

Scottish tribunals can deal with cases where the respondent (the employer) resides or carries on business in Scotland or if the proceedings relate to a contract of employment to be carried out in Scotland. English jurisdiction is similar. If the respondent resides or has business in one country and the contract is performed in the other, both countries have jurisdiction. The claimant may choose whichever individual tribunal is convenient within the country.

Legal aid

There is a limited right to legal advice and assistance for claimants in an ET, and no right to legal aid to be legally represented there: the theory is that to encourage legal representation at tribunals would work against the aims of informality, speed and accessibility. However, some cases are extremely complex and difficult for a claimant to conduct on his own. Additionally, some employers can afford to employ legal representation, perhaps through an insurance policy or in-house, so that an imbalance can arise. Trade unions may decide to help an individual member in a tribunal case, while the Equality and Human Rights Commission has legal power to provide assistance in key cases.

Time limits

One of the most important procedural requirements governing claims to ETs is that any claim must be submitted within a specified time limit. Any claim made late, however well merited on the facts, will not be heard. Broadly, unfair dismissal claims must be made within 3 months of dismissal unless it is not reasonably practicable to do so. The ET can admit a claim if it considers that it has been made as soon as was reasonably practicable. Claims for statutory redundancy pay must be made within 6 months of dismissal, or within another 6 months if the tribunal considers it just and equitable to allow the claim to go ahead. In discrimination cases, claims must be made within 3 months of the date of the act complained of unless the tribunal considers it just and equitable to hear it out of time. Common law claims must be made within 3 months of termination of the contract of employment. Equal pay claims must be raised within 6 months of leaving employment, unless the employer had deliberately concealed a key fact from her (a "concealment case"), in which case the time runs from when she discovered, or could have discovered, the fact in question.

Employment Appeal Tribunal

It is possible to appeal against a decision of an ET to the Employment Appeal Tribunal (EAT). From there, in Scotland an appeal can go to the Inner House of the Court of Session (its English equivalent being the Court of Appeal) and from there to the Supreme Court. A reference could be made to the European Court of Justice for a ruling on a point of EU law if relevant at any stage. Like the ETs, the EAT sits with three members: one being a Court of Session judge and the other two people with special knowledge or experience of industrial relations as either employers' representatives or workers' representatives.

Appeal to the EAT is on a point of law only, and it is not competent to appeal against a finding of fact by a tribunal. A point of law is usually considered to fall into three categories. First, that the tribunal misdirected itself as to law: it might have applied the wrong law perhaps, or interpreted the correct law wrongly. Second, that there was insufficient evidence to support a particular finding in fact (not simply that the tribunal should have believed one witness rather than another). Third, and most difficult to interpret, is the ground that the decision of the tribunal was perverse: that no reasonable tribunal could have arrived at such a decision on the evidence. It is not enough for an appeal simply to state that a decision was perverse: the way in which it is perverse must be identified. A number of different ways of describing when a decision is perverse have been used in the courts, including "not a permissible option" or "a conclusion which offends reason" or "one to which no reasonable (employment) tribunal could have come" or "so very clearly wrong that it just cannot stand" or "so outrageous in its defiance of logic or all accepted standards of industrial relations that no sensible person who has applied his mind to the question with the necessary experience could have arrived at it" (*East Berkshire Health Authority* v *Matadeen* (1992)).

The EAT may affirm a tribunal decision, but if it allows an appeal it may either substitute its own finding if there are sufficient findings in fact to allow it to do so, or it may remit (send) the case back to the tribunal (or a differently constituted one) to make more findings in fact, this time applying the law correctly. If the EAT finds that the tribunal misdirected itself in arriving at a decision that a dismissal was unfair it should remit unless it is satisfied that no tribunal properly directing itself could have come to the conclusion that the employee was unfairly dismissed (*Morgan* v *Electrolux Ltd* (1991)). If the ET's reasons are unclear the EAT can remit to it to provide further reasons (*Burns* v *Consignia* (2004); *Barke* v *Seetec Business Technology Centre Ltd* (2005)).

ACAS (Advisory Conciliation and Arbitration Service)

This is an independent publicly funded body, established in 1975, whose broad remit is to assist in the resolution of disputes at work. It does this, as its name suggests, through offering a variety of services, aimed at preventing or resolving individual and collective disputes. It provides advice, either relating to specific questions, or of a general nature. A conciliation service is offered in both individual and collective disputes. One of its key roles is to offer conciliation in individual cases. Where a claim is made to an ET, the tribunal offices forward it to ACAS so that it can get in touch with the parties in order to offer conciliation. If both parties request the intervention of a conciliation officer, or if an officer thinks there are reasonable prospects of success, he will try to promote a settlement between the parties to avoid the claim going forward to a tribunal hearing. Around two-thirds of cases do not reach a tribunal, with around half of those being resolved through ACAS.

ACAS also offers a statutory Arbitration Scheme. This can be used as an alternative to an ET in unfair dismissal and flexible working claims. If both parties agree in writing, so long as the agreement has been reached through a conciliation officer, or after a Compromise Agreement which complies with the ERA 1996, the dispute can be resolved by arbitration, and cannot be taken before a tribunal.

ACAS also issues statutory Codes of Practice, subject to parliamentary approval. It has issued three Codes: ACAS Code of Practice 1 – Disciplinary and Grievance Procedures (2009); ACAS Code of Practice 2 – Disclosure of Information to Trade Unions (1997); and ACAS Code of Practice 3 – Time Off for Trade Union Duties and Activities (2010).

Equality and Human Rights Commission (EHRC)

The EHRC was established in 2007 by the Equality Act 2006, and replaced the previous commissions, the Equal Opportunities Commission (EOC, dealing with the Sex Discrimination Act 1975), the Commission for Racial Equality (CRE, dealing with the Race Relations Act 1976) and the Disability Rights Commission (DRC, dealing with the Disability Discrimination Act 1998). The EHRC deals with all discrimination strands. It has a number of duties which require it to work towards a society which is free from discrimination and prejudice and where there is respect for human dignity and human rights. The EHRC also has statutory powers to assist it in carrying out its duties. These include: conducting investigations into organisations where discrimination is suspected; providing legal assistance in certain cases; monitoring and enforcing the equality duties imposed on public authorities.

The EHRC also issues Codes of Practice, subject to parliamentary approval. The Codes of Practice issued by its predecessor commissions are still in force. These are: the EOC Code of Practice on Equal Pay (2003); the EOC Code of Practice for the Elimination of Discrimination on the Grounds of Sex and Marriage and the Promotion of Equal Opportunities in Employment (1985); the CRE Code of Practice on Racial Equality in Employment (2005); and the DRC Code of Practice on Employment and Occupation (2004).

EUROPEAN UNION

There are two important principles of EU law applying in relation to employment law. First of all the doctrine of "subsidiarity" places the responsibility on the Member State to implement legislation to give effect to EU Directives. In principle, once this has been done, it is the national legislation which is the source of law in the Member State. Thus, the Working Time Regulations 1998 were introduced in order to implement the Working Time Directive 93/104. Anyone who wishes to establish what their rights are in relation to working time should look in the first instance to the 1998 Regulations.

However, the doctrine of "supremacy of EU law" gives the underlying EU Directive a continuing relevance. National law must be interpreted so as to comply with the EU law so far as is possible, even if this may not be the most obvious reading of the words in the national law. This may be done by the national courts themselves. In *Litster* v *Forth Dry Dock and Engineering Co Ltd* (1989) the House of Lords read words into reg 5(3) of the Transfer of Undertakings (Protection of Employment) Regulations (TUPE) in order to secure compliance with the Business Transfers Directive 77/187. It may be the result of a decision of the ECJ in relation to the interpretation of a Directive in a case coming either from the UK or a Member State. In *Sindicato de Medicos de Asistencia Publica (Simap)* v *Conselleria de Sanidad y Consumo de la Generalidad Valenciana* (2000), the ECJ gave a decision on what amounted to working time for the purposes of the Working Time Directive 93/104 that applied not just in Spain but throughout the EU.

In addition, certain parts EU law may be of direct effect so that they can be relied on directly in the national court or tribunal. It has been established that Art 157 (previously 141, and, before that, 119) of the Treaty of Rome, the equal pay Article, has "horizontal" direct effect, so that those employed by private as well as state employers may rely on it, as was the case in *Barber* v *Guardian Royal Exchange Assurance Group* (1990). In those cases where a (part of a) Directive is of direct effect, it will be "vertical" only and thus only those who are employed by state employers may rely on it, as was the case in *Marshall* v *Southampton and SW Hampshire Area Health Authority* (1986).

European Convention on Human Rights (ECHR)

Under the Human Rights Act 1998, public bodies have a duty to ensure that the "Convention rights" made enforceable by the Act are complied with. This means that employees of these bodies may raise an action against their employer for breach of a Convention right, but employees of private employers may not. However, the Act also provides that courts and tribunals have to interpret the law in such a way as to be consistent with the Convention rights. This means that, although only employees of public authorities may raise an action against their employer under the Act, indirectly the Act affects the way all employment law is interpreted, both common law and statutory.

The ECHR rights are civil, not social, rights and do not apply explicitly to the workplace. However, a number of rights are relevant to employment. For example, Art 8, which provides for the right to respect for private and family life, has been found to be relevant in cases of workplace surveillance, as in *Halford* v *UK* (1997). However, like many of the ECHR rights, Art 8 is qualified and interference with it may be justified in certain circumstances so long as it is proportionate and in pursuit of a relevant interest, such as the prevention of crime, as was the case in *McGowan* v *Scottish Water* (2005). Other relevant rights include Art 9 (freedom of thought, conscience and religion), Art 10 (freedom of expression), Art 11 (freedom of assembly and association, which includes the freedom to belong to a trade union) and Art 14 (prohibition of discrimination), although this Article is not free-standing and can only be relied on along with another Article.

2 THE EMPLOYMENT RELATIONSHIP

THE PARTIES TO THE EMPLOYMENT RELATIONSHIP

Not everyone who is in employment is an employee. A person may be "employed" under a contract of employment, but may also be employed on a more casual basis, or may be employed by an agency, working for an end-user or may be working for themselves, contracting out their labour. Some of these individuals, and also those who employ them, may consider that they are "casual workers" or "agency workers" or "self-employed"; others may feel that they are in fact employees. While the terminology used by the parties to a contract is a strong indication of what their intentions were, it will not override other factors, if the overall contract and practice show otherwise.

It is important to identify what sort of contract a person is employed under. Many statutory employment protection rights, such as the right to redundancy pay and the right not to be unfairly dismissed, only apply to people who are employed as employees under a contract of employment; some others, such as the right to the national minimum wage, extend to those who fit the statutory definition of "worker". Those who are employed under a contract of employment are taxed under Schedule E of the Income Tax (Earnings and Pensions) Act 2003, employers being obliged to deduct tax at source, while self-employed workers are taxed under Schedule D and are responsible for their own payment of tax. Employers are responsible for paying national insurance contributions for those employed under a contract of employment (in addition to paying the employee's own contributions at source), while self-employed workers are responsible for paying their own contributions, under the Social Security Contributions and Benefits Act 1992. An employer's common law vicarious liability for the wrongful acts of those employed by them, acting in the course of their employment, extends only to those employed under a contract of employment. An employer owes specific common law and statutory health and safety duties to employees which are more extensive than those owed to others.

So far as the common law is concerned (and taxation and social security statutes), there are only two ways of categorising contracts to carry out work: either as contracts of service or as contracts for services. The parties to these contracts are respectively the employer and employee (formerly "master" and "servant"), and employer, or principal, and independent contractor. This broadly is a distinction between an employee and a self-employed person. Common law and the taxation statutes do not make any finer distinction than that. Employment protection statutes, however, do make finer distinctions. While some rights only apply to those employed under a contract of employment/service, other rights apply to those who are classified as "workers". ERA 1996 contains 12 Parts which create a range of substantive rights, 11 of which apply only to employees. Only Pt II, relating to unauthorised deductions from wages, applies to workers more broadly. Other rights, such as the right to the national minimum wage, to working time protection and equal pay, also extend to workers as more broadly defined. There is a further even broader category, those who are "in employment", who receive protection under the anti-discrimination legislation.

HOW TO IDENTIFY A CONTRACT OF EMPLOYMENT

Both at common law and statute an employee is someone who is employed under a contract of service. This is the common law concept which has been adopted without further definition in employment statutes. At common law a contract of service is distinguished from a contract for services. The former is a contract between an employer and an employee, while the latter is a contract whose parties are known at common law as employer (or principal) and independent contractor. While the concept of employee at common law is the same concept as is used in the employment statutes, the concepts of "worker" and "in employment" are not directly equivalent to the contract for services: both will be employed under forms of contracts for services, but this is not part of their statutory definition.

The difference between a contract of service and a contract for services was expressed in *Stagecraft Ltd v Minister of National Insurance* (1952) as follows:

"In the contract of service the person hired agrees to place his services under the direction and control of the hirer. In the contract for services the person hired agrees to perform a specific service for the hirer, the manner of the performance being left to the discretion of the person hired."

In this case a comedian, contracted to appear for a season in "resident variety" in theatres in Britain, was held to be employed under a contract of service. The most important factor taken into account in determining the question was the degree of control exercised over the employee by the employer. The importance of control is such that the approach to determining the question of whether a contract was one of service was at one stage based entirely on control and known as the "control test". In this case, this was expressed as follows: "A servant is a person subject to the command of his master as to the manner in which he shall do his work." There is no longer a "control test" for determining who is an employee, but control is still an important criterion in the modern approach.

At another stage in the development of this area of law another "test" was adopted, often referred to as the "integration test". This was partly developed to deal with situations where highly skilled people were employed by organisations, such as surgeons by the National Health Service, and where, for example, there had been negligence by a surgeon, the question arose as to whether the NHS was liable. This test concentrated on whether, looking at the contract between the employer and worker, the person concerned could be said to be an integral part of the organisation. This was applied in *Whittaker* v *Minister of Pensions and National Insurance* (1967) in a claim by a trapeze artiste and usherette for industrial injuries compensation for a trapeze injury.

The modern approach

There is no one element that is decisive in determining whether a contract is one of service or not, although there are essential elements. It is necessary to look at the contract as a whole to determine if it is an employment contract. The most influential formulation of the modern approach has proved to be *Ready Mixed Concrete (SE) Ltd* v *Minister of Pensions and National Insurance* (1968) in which the decision of the Minister that a lorry driver was employed under a contract of service was overturned on appeal. Three conditions were identified as necessary for a contract of service: agreement by the employee, in consideration for a wage, to provide his own work and skill to perform service for the employer; agreement by the employee to be subject to a sufficient degree of control by the employer; and the other terms of the contract being consistent with its being a contract of service. This definition is often referred to as the "multiple" or "multi-factor" test. As a definition it leaves a lot of room for interpretation, not least the third condition where there is no prescribed list of factors which are consistent and inconsistent, but it is a matter of common sense in each case.

A different emphasis can be seen in the contemporaneous case of *Market Investigations Ltd* v *Minister of Social Security* (1969) in which the Minister's decision that a market research interviewer was employed under a contract of service was upheld. It identified a fundamental difference between an employed person and someone who was self-employed through the key question "Is the person who has engaged himself to perform these services performing them as a person in business on his own account?" Although this was in the context of confirming the move away from the single "control" test, control was still an important, but not the sole, factor. This approach concentrates on issues relating to dependency, and is sometimes described as the "entrepreneurial", "small businessman" or "economic reality" test. The question to be asked was phrased in down-to-earth terms by the EAT in *Withers* v *Flackwell Heath Football Supporters Club* (1981) as "Are you your own boss?" In that case the EAT felt that the claimant, a bar steward, would certainly have answered "No", and that he was an employee.

Although the "economic reality" approach seems closer to identifying the essence of a contract of employment, it is the "multiple" test which has been the more influential, particularly in the context of employment protection rights.

Is the question of whether or not someone is employed as an employee a legal or a factual question? This matters because, if it is factual, it is entirely up to the ET to decide on its interpretation of the relationship between the parties whether the contract is one of service or not. Since *O'Kelly* v *Trusthouse Forte plc* (1983) it has been accepted that the question is primarily legal in that a contract of service has a specific legal definition. However, the same case also found that it is up to a tribunal to determine qualitatively what the contract is on the basis of the facts, so that it must decide whether there is "sufficient" control and whether the terms of the contract are consistent or inconsistent with it being one of service.

The generality of the "multiple" test is such that different parts of it may be given more emphasis in one case rather than another, both as a matter of law and in relation to the particular contract. In some cases control has been very prominent; in others less so. This may depend on why the existence of the contract is being asserted or challenged. The "entrepreneurial" test arose in the context of tax and national insurance; the issue of control has been particularly influential in relation to vicarious liability; while in unfair dismissal and other employment protection cases the concept of mutuality of obligation, which will be discussed below, has been prominent. This may be inevitable, and is certainly confusing. According to the Privy Council in *Lee* v *Chung* (1990), a unitary approach to the question, regardless of the nature of the dispute between the parties, is what is aspired to in the courts. However, this not necessarily what happens in practice.

The intention of the parties

The label that the parties give to their contract is not conclusive. In many of the cases it is an express term of the contract that it is not one of service and the worker is not an employee. The tribunal or court may still review the contract as a whole to determine its true nature. What the parties intend and what they call it is a factor to be taken into account (*Massey v Crown Life Insurance Co* (1978)), but it should not override other indications as to the true nature of the contract (*Dacas v Brook Street Bureau (UK) Ltd* (2004)).

The "irreducible minimum"

Although the courts use a multi-factor test, not all factors have the same weight. Certain elements are essential. Before it is permissible to balance consistent and inconsistent factors and to take account of all the factors in the "multiple" test, it is necessary that the contract first of all meets certain essential requirements. These requirements have been described as the "irreducible minimum" for a contract of service. In *Staffordshire Sentinel Newspapers Ltd v Potter* (2004) the obligation to provide personal service was stated to be an irreducible minimum. In *Montgomery v Johnson Underwood Ltd* (2001) control and "mutuality of obligation" were stated to be the irreducible minimum of a contract of service, while in *Carmichael v National Power plc* (1999) Lord Irving in the House of Lords referred to "that irreducible minimum of mutual obligation".

Personal service

The element of personal service, the first of the *Ready Mixed Concrete* conditions, is an essential part of a contract of service. The contract is a personal one and the power to delegate is in general fatal to its being one of service. It is also part of the statutory definitions of a worker's contract, and of the concept of "in employment". In *Ready Mixed Concrete* McKenna J did say that "a limited or occasional power of delegation" might not be fatal, but it would have to be very limited, almost certainly restricted to a replacement approved by the employer. In *MacFarlane v Glasgow City Council* (2001) an ET had found that a gym instructor who, if she was unable to take a class, was entitled to send along a replacement from a register of instructors maintained by the council, and paid by the council, was not an employee because of the power to delegate. The EAT found that it had taken too absolute an approach to this and remitted it back for reconsideration, applying the correct test.

Control

Control is still an essential, although not the sole, element. The definition of "control" adopted in *Ready Mixed Concrete* is: "It includes the power of deciding the thing to be done, the way in which it shall be done, the means to be employed in doing it, the time when and the place where it shall be done." This can extend to the skilled worker whose employer is not capable of actually controlling the work. "It is the right of control not its exercise."

Mutuality of obligation

In this context mutuality of obligation means that the employer is obliged to offer work, and the employee obliged to perform work under the terms of the contract. This can be particularly problematic in the case of casual workers where the terms of contract provide that work will be offered "as and when required" and will be accepted "if suitable". This does not oblige the parties to each other for future performance and so would not usually provide the necessary mutuality.

Mutuality has been implied by course of dealing. In *Nethermere (St Neots) v Taverna and Gardiner* (1984) the Court of Appeal considered the position of casual part-time homeworkers, who were employed from their homes sewing pockets into trousers. There was no contractual obligation on the employer to provide or on the workers to do the work. It found that, through a course of dealing over a number of years, implied mutuality of obligation had grown up. The question of a contract growing up by implication is also an issue in the case of agency workers and will be looked at below.

It can be helpful to distinguish between a global contract and an individual contract. In the case of a casual worker there may be no global contract of service lasting between periods of actual work for the employer. However, on each occasion that work is offered and accepted an individual contract may arise. In *McMeechan v Secretary of State for Employment* (1997) a claim was made by a casual agency worker under ERA 1996, Pt XII for unpaid wages from the Secretary of State's insolvency fund, which is only open to employees when their employer has become insolvent. The claim was successful for the 4-week period for which the applicant had actually last worked for the employer. Similarly, in *Clark v Oxfordshire Health Authority* (1998) a nurse who was on a "bank" of supply nurses to fill in when required had been held not to be an employee under a contract of service when not actually engaged in work for the authority as there was no mutuality of obligation, but the Court of Appeal held that she could be considered to be an employee during the period she was actually working and sent it back to the tribunal to decide if the period of work had been long enough for her to qualify for unfair dismissal protection.

Terms not inconsistent with employment under a contract of service

If the irreducible minimum is present it is still necessary to balance the various factors in the contract to decide whether the person is an employee or in essence self-employed. The factors taken into account by the court in *Market Investigations Ltd* v *Minister of Social Security* (1969) can be useful here. These include: whether the disputed service provider provides their own equipment; whether he hires out their own helpers; what degree of financial risk he takes; what degree of financial responsibility he has; and the extent to which he can profit from sound management in performing the task. An example of the courts using the multiple test is *O'Kelly* v *Trusthouse Forte plc* (1983). The tribunal considered certain factors to be "consistent with employment" – for example, that clothing and equipment was provided for them, wages were paid in arrears after deduction of tax and national insurance, the disciplinary and grievance procedure applied, work was performed under the direction and control of Trusthouse Forte. Other factors were considered to be "inconsistent with employment" – for example, that there was no obligation to give notice to end the contract, there was a custom in the industry that the workers (casual banqueting workers) were self-employed. Certain factors were considered to be neutral – there were no regular hours, there was no sick pay or pension entitlement and there was no regular salary but payment for work actually performed. However, the fact that the employer had no obligation to provide work and the worker no obligation to accept it (that is, there was no mutuality of obligation) was ultimately the determining factor.

Agency workers

For agency workers there is a different problem from that facing casual workers. Agency workers have a contract with an employment agency, which in turn has a contract with an end-user with whom the worker is placed. The worker has a contract with the agency (who will usually be responsible for paying remuneration) but is likely to be under the control of the end-user. Thus there is no contract between the worker and the end-user. In some cases the worker may be an employee of the agency, as was considered to be the case for an individual (but not global) contract in *McMeechan* v *Secretary of State for Employment* (1997), but this is not usual.

Given that there is no contract between the worker and the end-user, there is often said to be no "contractual nexus". Without a contractual relationship at all, it is not possible for there to be a contract of employment between the parties. Thus many, if not most, agency workers are not employees of either agency or end-user.

It is possible, however, that in individual cases the reality of the contractual relationship may mean that a contract of employment has grown up between either worker and agency, or worker and end-user. The Court of Appeal in *Dacas* v *Brook Street Bureau* (2004) considered the case of a cleaner who had been working for 4 years with a local authority through the employment agency. The tribunal had found that she had no contract with the end-user and her contract with the agency was not one of service. The EAT found that her contract with the agency was one of service since it paid her wages. The Court of Appeal, however, found that the question should not have been decided without considering whether there was an implied contract of service with the end-user as employer. Since Ms Dacas had not appealed against the finding that the local authority was not her employer, this did not become a live issue. Although this decision was followed in *Cable and Wireless plc* v *Muscat* (2006) and a contract of employment implied between an agency worker and end-user, the Court of Appeal has subsequently stated that it will be exceptional for there to be an implied contract, and that mere passage of time will not be enough (*James* v *Greenwich Borough Council* (2008)). There is no consistent approach here, and in Scotland the implied contract analysis has been doubted by the Outer House of the Court of Session in *Toms* v *Royal Mail Group plc* (2006).

Agency workers are protected against being treated less favourably because of their status by the Agency Workers Regulations 2010 (due to come into force in October 2011) passed to comply with EU Agency Workers Directive 2008/104/EC. This does not in itself affect the status of agency workers but does provide protection against discrimination.

WORKERS AND THOSE IN EMPLOYMENT

Workers

While many employment protection rights only apply to employees, there are others which apply to workers. The statutory definition of a "worker", for example under ERA 1996, s 230(3), includes an employee, that is someone employed under a contract of employment/service, and also someone who contracts to perform work personally so long as the contract does not make the other party (the employer) a professional client or a client or customer of his business. The element of personal service is crucial to the definition of an employee, and this is not what distinguishes a worker and an employee. Employees are dependent on their employers economically, and in a subordinate position legally.

The object of creating an "intermediate" category between employees and the self-employed is to recognise that there are workers in a position of dependency, who though not perhaps in the same position of subordination as employees are not sufficiently independent not to require protection.

In *Byrne Brothers (Formwork) Ltd* v *Baird* (2002) the EAT found that the applicants, who were self-employed labour-only subcontractors in the construction industry, were exactly the kind of worker for whom this intermediate status was created: workers who, although nominally free to move from employer to employer, in fact work for lengthy periods for one employer, supplying no more than their own labour. In some cases such labour-only subcontractors would be employees, even although their contract may on the face of it state otherwise, if the contract as a whole is in fact one of employment, as was the case in *Ferguson* v *John Dawson & Partners (Contractors) Ltd* (1976).

In employment

The anti-discrimination legislation places duties on employers not to discriminate against those who are in employment. This is a similar but broader concept to that of worker. It includes the employee, and again anyone who contracts to perform personal service, but without the qualification that the other party (the employer) must not be a professional client or customer. Again the requirement for personal service is essential. A self-employed independent contractor whose contract was not renewed when she became pregnant could not make a claim for unfair dismissal because she was not an employee. However, she successfully claimed that she had been directly discriminated against under the Sex Discrimination Act 1975 (SDA 1975) (*Caruana* v *Manchester Airport* (1996)).

However, a claim under SDA 1975 was not successful in *Mirror Group Newspapers Ltd* v *Gunning* (1986), when a newspaper group refused to transfer an agency agreement for the distribution of newspapers from father to daughter on the death of the father. While the ET and EAT held that the agency agreement came within the definition of "employment" under s 82 of SDA 1975, because the agreement required the holder to be directly involved in the day-to-day supervision of the work, the Court of Appeal held that since this did not amount to a requirement to do the actual labour, the contract was not one of employment. They held that the "dominant purpose" of any contract must be the provision of personal work or services.

Extension of employment protection rights

The Employment Relations Act 1999, s 23 gives the Secretary of State power to amend ERA 1996 and the Trade Union and Labour Relations (Consolidation) Act 1992 (TULR(C)A 1992) to extend rights to workers in particular categories, but this power has not yet been used. The power could be used in one of two ways. First, an order under the section may confer rights on individuals of specified descriptions: this would permit the extension of any of the relevant employment protection rights to either a narrow category, such as "agency worker", or to a broader category, such as "worker". Second, an order may declare individuals to be parties to workers' contracts, or to contracts of employment and may identify who is to be regarded as the employer: thus an order could provide that an agency worker was to be considered to be an employee under an employment contract (and thus have the benefit of the rights of employees), and state who was to be considered the agency worker's employer in this context.

While there are good reasons for ensuring that employees, as dependent and subordinate workers, have protection, it is perhaps more questionable whether the full range of rights should be restricted. The form of employment contract may not be at the discretion of the worker, who may be more or less dependent and subordinate in fact even although formally not employed under a contract of employment. Where an employment relationship is in practice one in which the worker is of employee status, the courts and tribunals are able to find that it is so in law as well, but the distinction between a contract of employment and a worker's contract can be narrow, and the difference in dependency and subordination between a worker and employee scarcely enough to justify withholding job protection rights.

SPECIFIC GROUPS OF WORKERS

Crown employees

Civil servants and other Crown employees were not considered to be employees and thus the rights and duties of their relationship with their employer were enforceable not according to the law of contract but under public law. However, for most public sector employees that is in the past. For most Crown employees the relationship with their employer, like private sector employees, is governed by a contract of employment which is enforceable in the same way as any other contract of employment. Employment protection rights apply to them, and in cases where the formal position has not completely caught up with reality, statutory provisions are applied to them explicitly.

Crown employees, including civil servants, have the benefit of most of the rights under ERA 1996, but not the right to statutory redundancy pay, nor to claim on the insolvency fund (s 191). Members of the armed forces have the benefit of some rights under the Act, but fewer than Crown employees generally (s 192). The rights applicable to the staff of the Houses of Parliament are contained in ss 193–194. Police officers (but not civilian employees of the police service) are excluded from a number of rights, including the general right not to be unfairly dismissed (s 200).

As a result of the public law element in Crown employment, there is the possibility that in some disputes an employee might be able to use a public law remedy such as judicial review. However, this is not available where the true nature of the dispute is one between employer and employee, since the employee would be able to rely on the contract. In *West* v *Secretary of State for Employment* (1992) it was held to be incompetent for a prison officer to challenge a failure of the Scottish Prison Service to pay his removal expenses since it was essentially a contractual matter between employer and employee. The Inner House of the Court of Session stated as a principle that judicial review would only be competent where there had been an abuse of statutory power by a body to whom a power had been delegated in a "tripartite relationship". This has been explained as occurring where a power has been delegated to someone other than an employer. Therefore a chief executive who had been suspended by his local authority employer could not bring an action of judicial review, since the council itself made the decision to suspend (*Blair* v *Lochaber District Council* (1995)). However, a supply teacher who had been removed from a list of supply teachers by a local authority was entitled to bring an action of judicial review since there was no contractual relationship between him and the authority (*Hardie* v *City of Edinburgh Council* (2000)).

Public employees

This is a broader category, including those employed in the public sector who are not in Crown employment. It would include, for example, those employed by the National Health Service, and by local authorities. Such employees have a wider range of remedies open to them than private sector employees under EU and ECHR law.

Under the Human Rights Act 1998, s 6 it is unlawful for a public authority to act in a way which is incompatible with a Convention right. This includes public authorities and also private bodies exercising a public function. Employees of public bodies have the right to raise an action under this section based on a breach of a Convention right. Employees of private bodies do not have this right.

It is also possible for public employees to rely directly on certain provisions of EU Directives, which course is not open to private sector employees. As was seen in Chapter 1, where a part of a Directive is of direct effect, a public employee may rely on it directly. In *Marshall* v *Southampton and South West Hampshire Area Health Authority* (1986) a female health service employee was able to challenge her compulsory retirement at the age of 60, when the then compulsory retirement age for men was 65, as being contrary to the Equal Treatment Directive 76/207/EC. This is open not only to those employed directly by the state but also to those who are employed by an "emanation of the state". The ECJ held that this applied in the case of a body which had been set up by statute to provide a public service under the control of the state and which exercised special powers. The House of Lords held that this applied in the case of British Gas, in another challenge to compulsory retirement of women before men (*Foster* v *British Gas plc* (1991)).

Office holders

An office holder holds a specific office under statutory authority. Many office holders are also employees employed under a contract of employment. Other office holders are not. A part-time fee-paid recorder, a judicial office holder, was held not to be employed under a contract of employment nor under a contract to provide personal services (a worker's contract) and therefore not entitled to the protection of the Part-time Workers (Prevention of Less Favourable Treatment) Regulations 2000 (*O'Brien* v *Department for Constitutional Affairs* (2009)).

Discrimination legislation makes particular provision for office holders, apart from its application to those in employment.

Apprentices

A contract of apprenticeship is not a contract of service at common law: under such a contract the employer contracts to instruct the apprentice in a particular trade or skill and the apprentice contracts to learn. Its primary object is teaching and learning. The period of the apprenticeship will be fixed. It is expected to continue throughout its full term, so that it cannot be terminated by giving notice as a contract of service can: if it is terminated wrongly the apprentice is entitled to be compensated for the loss of wages until the end of the apprenticeship and for future prospects. As a fixed-term contract it cannot be terminated on the giving of notice. In *Wallace v CA Roofing Services Ltd* (1996) an apprentice sheet metalworker with a 4-year apprenticeship contract was dismissed because of redundancy after 19 months. The English High Court held that unless the contract specifically contained a provision allowing the employer to terminate because of redundancy, it could not.

Statutory definitions of a contract of employment, such as ERA 1996, s 230(1) in general include the contract of apprenticeship along with the contract of service. Thus apprentices receive the same employment protection rights as employees. Since apprentices are learning, and traditionally young, the standard of competence and behaviour expected of them is less than that expected from an employee. At common law dismissal would only be justified if the behaviour was so bad that it was impossible for the apprentice to learn, while under unfair dismissal law a more lenient attitude is taken towards apprentices.

While apprentices have additional protections by virtue of their status, this is not the case for those under contracts for training which do not amount to apprenticeships. This is particularly relevant in relation to those government-funded schemes whereby employers are encouraged to take on (usually young) workers for training and work experience by the relevant government department paying a substantial part of their "wages". Training contracts are not employment contracts, nor are they apprenticeship contracts. In *Daley v Allied Suppliers Ltd* (1983) it was held that a young woman who was on a government-funded Youth Training Scheme was not in employment and therefore not entitled to the protection of the Race Relations Act 1976. Under the scheme, the government department entered into agreements with employers so that they accepted young people for training and work experience, the money being paid by the employer and recovered from the government department. The EAT held that Ms Daley was not an employee or in employment because of the role of the government department in regulating the arrangement, and also because, if there was a contract, it was to receive training or work experience. Subsequently, such trainees were brought under the scope of the Sex Discrimination Act 1975, the Race Relations Act 1976 and the Health and Safety at Work etc Act 1974.

There is a question as to whether a "modern apprenticeship" is a traditional contract of apprenticeship. These apprenticeships involve the employer, the "apprentice" and a government-supported training body. The initial view was that the tripartite element meant that they could not amount to apprenticeship contracts (since the education element was primarily the responsibility of the trainer and not the employer), but might, so long as they fulfilled the multiple test, be contracts of service.

The Court of Appeal held, however, in *Matheson* v *Flett* (2006) that the tripartite element did not prevent the contract being one of apprenticeship: it was appropriate for some of the training to be done outside, and part of it did take place in employment. In that case most of the factors involved appeared to point to a contract of apprenticeship, but the Court of Appeal referred it back to the ET because the findings of fact were not entirely clear as to which training scheme rules had been used.

Directors

Company directors are not employees by virtue of being directors but may be employed under a contract of service as well as being a director. A director's employment contract is often referred to as a "service agreement". In order to decide, in a case of a dispute, whether a director's contract is a contract of employment, a tribunal will apply the same multiple test to the facts of the particular case as in other situations. People at the highest level in an organisation may be employees. The managing director, with the power to control other employees, is just as capable of being an employee as those whom he controls.

Where a director also has a controlling shareholding in a company, any arrangement is likely to be looked at closely. Employment protection rights may give an employee rights to payment in the event of insolvency of the company which a director would not have. In *Fleming* v *Secretary of State for Trade and Industry* (1997) the Inner House of the Court of Session made it clear that having a majority shareholding was not in itself a bar to being an employee, though it was one of the factors they felt it was proper to take into account in deciding the issue.

There cannot be a contract of employment if the contract is a "sham", adopted, for example, in order to give the director access to the insolvency fund. In *Secretary of State for Trade and Industry* v *Bottrill* (1999) the English Court of Appeal approved the approach taken in *Fleming* v *DTI* towards directors with controlling shareholdings. They also suggested other factors to consider, including when and why the contract came into existence (was it just before insolvency?). In *Clark* v *Clark Construction Initiatives* (2008) the EAT suggested that if the terms of the contract have not been written down, and if the alleged terms have not been followed in practice (such as provisions about holidays), this would be strongly suggestive that there was not a genuine contract of employment. On the other hand, if it was shown that the alleged terms had been followed in practice, it would be strongly suggestive that there was.

If the contract is accepted as genuine, some factors to assist in determining if the contract is one of employment would include: the extent of control and whether he was able to vote on matters affecting him (*DTI* v *Bottrill*); how he has been paid – a salary would suggest employment, fees that the role was no more than as director; whether he was actually acting as an employee or more like a director (*Neufeld* v *Secretary of State for Business Enterprise and Regulatory Reform* (2009)).

Ministers of religion

Secular appointments by religious bodies are in the same category as any other employment. However, the traditional approach of the courts towards ministerial appointments has been to regard them as being on a spiritual rather than a commercial basis. Since there was no intention to be legally bound, a minister of religion could not be an employee (nor even a worker). The position was reviewed by the House of Lords in *Percy* v *Church of Scotland Board of National Mission* (2006). An associate minister of the Church of Scotland raised an unfair dismissal and a sex discrimination action when she was counselled to resign as a minister following an internal inquiry. Both actions were dismissed by the ET and the appeal was pursued only in relation to the sex discrimination action, which required proof that she was "in employment", not that she was an employee. The House of Lords found that she was in employment. There was a personal obligation to execute work: the contract between her and the Mission gave her the right to be paid and it included the duty to enforce her performance of the duties of an associate minister. The statutory rights related to civil, not spiritual, matters. Although this decision relates to an associate minister, there is no reason why its terms should not apply to all ministers of religion.

In *Percy*, the House did not consider whether she was employed under a contract of service because it did not have to. Subsequently, the English Court of Appeal has examined this in *New Testament Church of God* v *Stewart* (2008) in which a minister of the Church raised an unfair dismissal claim. It held that *Percy* had not overruled all the previous authorities. What it had done was to establish, on its own facts, that there was intention to create legal relations, and also it had ended the presumption that there was no such intention in such cases. A tribunal must still carefully consider the spiritual as well as the commercial basis of the relationship before deciding that there was the necessary intention.

THE EMPLOYER

An employee is someone who is employed under a contract of service. The employer is the other party to that contract. In the context of the worker's contract, the contract of someone who is "in employment" or of a contract for services, it is the other party to those contracts. An employee (or a worker, or a person in employment) must always be an individual human being, since the essential element is that of personal service. This is not the case for the employer. In large-scale employment it is unlikely that the employer will be an individual human being: it is more likely to be a company, a partnership or a public authority. All of these have their own separate legal personality from their members or directors or shareholders. In all circumstances where a duty is placed on an employer, it is placed upon the legal entity of the employer.

Companies and other legal persons can only operate through the agency of individuals, and as employers they will be vicariously liable for the actions of employees acting in the course of their employment, including high-level managerial employees. Companies are also bound by the acts of their directors, firms by the acts of their partners. In cases where an employee wishes to sue their employer, the appropriate respondent will be the legal person in ownership of the business.

In the case of some employment rights, it may be possible to sue someone other than the employer. A negligent worker who causes injury is responsible under the law of delict for the consequences of his negligence, and may therefore be sued. Under discrimination legislation it is also possible to sue, in addition to the employer on whom the primary duty not to discriminate rests, someone who has instructed another to discriminate (perhaps a supervisor), or who has knowingly aided discrimination (including the person who actually committed the discriminatory act), or who has induced another to discriminate (perhaps a trade union).

Essential Facts

• Definitions of employee, contract of employment and worker are set out in the Employment Rights Act 1996, s 230.

- Provisions relating to particular types of employment are found in the Employment Rights Act 1996, Pt XIII.
- Power to extend employment protection rights is given to the Secretary of State by virtue of the Employment Relations Act 1999, s 23.
- Protection of agency workers against discrimination is provided by the Agency Workers Regulations 2010.
- EC Directive on protection of agency workers: Agency Workers Directive 2008/104.

Essential Cases

Ready Mixed Concrete (SE) Ltd v Minister of Pensions and National Insurance (1968): a lorry driver buying his lorry on hire purchase from the company was found to be employed under a contract for services, not a contract of service. The case is authority for the threefold multiple test to determine whether there is a contract of service: personal service, control and consistent terms.

Market Investigations Ltd v Minister of Social Security (1969): a market researcher was found to be employed under a contract of service, not a contract for services. This case identified the underlying element of being in business on one's own account in relation to the multiple test.

Ferguson v John Dawson & Partners (Contractors) Ltd (1976): a building worker whose contract described him as a "labour only subcontractor" was held to be in reality an employee employed under a contract of service. This case is authority for the proposition that while the parties' intention, and label, is relevant it is not conclusive in determining the nature of the contract.

Carmichael v National Power plc (1999): a casual worker was found not to be employed under a contract of service. This case found that mutuality of obligation was an "irreducible minimum" of a contract of service.

Dacas v Brook Street Bureau (UK) Ltd (2004): an agency worker failed in her unfair dismissal claim against both the agency and the end-user who had asked for her to be withdrawn. The Court of Appeal said that the ET should have addressed the possibility that an implied contract of service had grown up between the end-user and the claimant.

Percy v Church of Scotland Board of National Mission (2006): an associate minister was found to be "in employment" for the purposes of the Sex Discrimination Act 1975. This provided statutory rights which were civil and not spiritual matters.

3 THE CONTRACT OF EMPLOYMENT

FORMATION

The contract of employment is governed by the general law of contract. While the formal common law position that a contract is a voluntary agreement entered into by two consenting (and equal) parties may not reflect the realities of economic power, it does reflect the legal status. The formation of a contract of employment is subject to the same principles as any other contract. Since the Requirements of Writing (Scotland) Act 1995, which abolished the common law rule requiring fixed-term contracts of a year or more and contracts of apprenticeship to be in writing, there is no requirement for writing in any contract of employment. An employment contract may therefore be formed in writing, verbally or by actions.

Once the contract has been formed it is binding on the parties, even although the employee has not started work. In *Sarker* v *South Tees Acute Hospital NHS Trust* (1997), where a job offer was withdrawn after it had been accepted, the EAT held that there was a contract in existence which had been terminated by the employer. The claimant was entitled to raise an action for breach of contract.

CAPACITY

The general rules about contractual capacity apply to contracts of employment. The age of full contractual capacity is 16. Under the Age of Legal Capacity (Scotland) Act 1991, s 2 someone under 16 can enter into a contract "of a kind commonly entered into by persons of his age and circumstances". This is capable of including a contract of service.

Controls are placed on the employment of children by the Children and Young Persons (Scotland) Act 1937. In order to comply with the EC Young Workers Directive 94/33 it was amended by the Children (Protection at Work) Regulations 1998. The Act prohibits the employment of children aged under 14 and restricts the hours of work of children aged between 14 and 16 (s 28). There are some exceptions to these rules, and local authorities have the power to introduce byelaws which permit 13-year-olds to do light work. Any contract made in breach of these provisions would be an illegal contract.

Workers under the age of 16 are covered by their own legislation, both in the UK and the EU, while the Working Time Regulations 1998 (WTR 1998) and the EC Working Time Directive 93/104 (WTD) provide for adults (18 years and over) and young workers (aged 16 to 18); therefore, it has been held that workers under the age of 16 are not covered by the WTR 1998. In *Addison* v *Ashby* (2003) a 15-year-old paper boy was held not to be entitled to 4 weeks' paid holiday under the WTR 1998.

LEGALITY

The usual common law *pactum illicitum* rule applies: an illegal contract is unenforceable. A contract which is entered into for a criminal or immoral purpose is illegal. A person employed under such a contract would not be employed under a valid contract and would not therefore be able to take advantage of statutory employment rights.

A distinction is made between a contract which is entered into for an illegal purpose, and one which is entered into for a legal purpose and was intended to be carried out lawfully, but which has been performed by unlawful means. The former will always be unlawful, whereas the latter will not be so long as the unlawful means were not intended when made. In *Coral Leisure Group* v *Barnett* (1981) a public relations executive who claimed that he had been asked to procure prostitutes for clients was allowed to proceed with his unfair dismissal claim since the contract had not been entered into for that purpose or with that intention.

A frequent concern has been where the agreed method of payment of wages under a contract has involved failure to disclose all or part of the sum to the Inland Revenue (now HM Revenue and Customs). A contract formed on that basis would be illegal (*Tomlinson* v *Dick Evans U Drive* (1978)). The distinction must be made between tax avoidance, which is a legal method of minimising the amount of tax which is due to be paid, and tax evasion which is an illegal method of arranging not to pay tax which is due. While the latter would render a contract unenforceable, the former would not. In *Lightfoot* v *D and J Sporting Ltd* (1996) the employee gamekeeper had renegotiated his contract with his employer so that he was paid less, and his wife (who assisted him and who previously received no payment) received a wage. While the amount paid by the employer remained the same, the amount paid in tax on the wages was reduced, since her personal tax allowance as well as his was set off against the payment. In an action of unfair dismissal raised when he was subsequently dismissed, the ET held that the change in payment had made the contract illegal as it was an attempt to defraud the Inland Revenue. The EAT, however, referred the matter back to consider whether it was a legitimate tax avoidance scheme which had been or would be disclosed to the Inland Revenue, in which case it would be lawful.

As it is a rule of public policy, in cases where it would not be in the public interest, a court will not apply it. In *Hewcastle Catering Ltd* v *Ahmed and Elkameh* (1992) the employees had assisted the employer in VAT fraud. They subsequently advised Customs and Excise and were dismissed. It was held that their contracts should not be held to be illegal, because the fraud had benefited the employer alone, and it would affront conscience if the *pactum illicitum* rule was used to allow the employer to profit from the illegality.

UNFAIR CONTRACT TERMS ACT 1977

Although it had been accepted in lower courts that the Unfair Contract Terms Act 1977, s 3 was capable of applying to contracts of employment, without actually applying it on the facts in these cases, the Court of Appeal has held that it cannot apply to a contract of employment since an employee does not contract "as a consumer" with the employer (*Commerzbank AG* v *Keen* (2007)).

SOURCES

The contract of employment is made up of a number of sources. It is an ongoing contract which may therefore be varied throughout its life. The principal sources are: express terms (written or verbal); implied terms (general principles); incorporated terms; implied terms (common law duties). Even where there is a written contract of employment it is likely that other sources will be relevant.

Although there is no requirement for the contract to be in writing, there is a statutory requirement for there to be a written record of the terms of employment. This should be a good practical source of the terms of the contract, although it is not in itself contractual.

DUTY TO PROVIDE WRITTEN STATEMENT OF EMPLOYMENT PARTICULARS

Employees who have 1 month's service are entitled under ERA 1996, ss 1–7 to receive, within 2 months of starting employment, a written statement of employment particulars. The statement must specify:

- name of employer and employee;
- date when employment began;
- date when continuous employment began, if different;
- scale or rate of pay or method of calculating it;
- intervals when paid;
- terms and conditions of hours of work;
- terms and conditions of holidays and holiday pay;
- job title or brief description of work;
- place of work, or, if various, indication of that, and employer's address.

This information must all be given in one note. The following information must also be given but not necessarily in the same note:

- terms and conditions relating to sickness, including sickness pay;
- terms and conditions relating to pensions and pension schemes (this information could be given by referring to a reasonably accessible document);
- the notice the employee is entitled to receive and obliged to give; (this information can be given by referring to statute or a collective agreement);
- if the job is not permanent, the period for which it is expected to continue or the date when it is expected to end;
- any collective agreement directly affecting terms and conditions;
- if the employee is required to work outside the UK for over a month, information about work outside the UK.

If there are no particulars about any of the matters in this list, the statement must say so. The employee must also be given a note specifying:

- any disciplinary rules (this information can be given by referring to a reasonably accessible document);
- any discipline or dismissal procedures (this information can be given by referring to a reasonably accessible document);
- a person the employee can apply to if dissatisfied with a disciplinary decision;
- a person the employee can apply to with a grievance;
- any procedures relating to such applications (this information can be given by referring to a reasonably accessible document).

A document is reasonably accessible if the employee has reasonable opportunities of reading it in the course of employment, or it is made reasonably accessible in some other way (s 6).

If the employer has given the employee a written contract of employment covering all the required particulars, this document will count as fulfilling this obligation (ss 7A, 7B). Any changes in any of the particulars must be notified to the employee within 1 month of the change (s 4).

Enforcement

Enforcement is sought by making a complaint to an ET, either for failure to provide a written statement at all, or for including incomplete or inaccurate information (s 11). The ET has the power to amend or declare the relevant terms. This will involve the ET investigating what the contractual terms were and declaring particulars which conform to that. An ET can identify what the terms are, but cannot invent terms where there has been no agreement (*Eagland* v *British Telecommunications plc* (1992)).

Additionally, if an employee succeeds in another claim against the employer at an ET but is awarded no compensation, and the employer had not issued a written statement, the ET must award compensation for that failure of between 2 and 4 weeks' pay (Employment Act 2002, s 38).

Legal status of the written statement

It is important to distinguish between a statutory written statement and a contract of employment. The written statement is not of itself contractual. It is a unilateral document drawn up by one party only: the employer. Though this is likely to reflect the contractual terms, it may not. A contract, on the other hand, is bilateral: it is the product of the agreement of employer and employee. If there is a conflict between the contractual agreement and the written statement, it is the contract which will prevail. In *Robertson* v *British Gas Corporation* (1983), where employees relied on a contractual letter which gave a right to a bonus, and the employer relied on a written statement which stated it was a qualified right, the contractual terms prevailed.

Although the written statement is not contractual, it is strong, that is persuasive, evidence of the terms of the contract. If it is the employer who is trying to argue that the written statement does not reflect the terms of the contract, there will be a heavy burden on the employer (whose unilateral statement it was) to prove that the contract provided otherwise. In *Trusthouse Forte (Catering) Ltd* v *Adonis* (1984) an employee was dismissed for smoking in a no-smoking area. A notice had been displayed by the employer stating that dismissal would be the penalty for such an offence. Ten days later the written particulars were reissued, in which the offence was stated to be one which merited dismissal on repetition after a warning. The dismissal was held to be in breach of contract: the employer could not convince the ET that the written particulars, issued after the notice, did not reflect the contract.

An employee who believes that a written statement does not reflect the terms of the contract but does not challenge it runs the risk that its terms will become accepted as reflecting the contract. However, failing to object does not amount to acceptance in itself, so that if there is a term in the written statement which does not come into immediate practical effect (such as sick pay), not objecting will not be of great importance; but if it does have immediate practical effect (such as place of work), failure to object combined with accepting the position will be likely to mean that the employee has accepted the terms in the written statement by implication.

AGREED TERMS

The primary source of the terms of any contract is the terms agreed between the parties. This is the case with a contract of employment. The agreement may be verbal or written. Agreed terms take precedence over any other term, and written terms (so long as the writing is contractual) take precedence over any other agreed terms. A contractual source could be an offer of appointment, so long as it has been accepted.

IMPLIED TERMS

An implied term may arise from the nature of the work which the employee is employed to do, or through the words and conduct of the parties. An implied term reflects an implied agreement between the parties, and can only arise where the conduct of the employer and employee demonstrate that the alleged term was intended to be obligatory. In *Lotus Cars Ltd v Sutcliffe* (1982) a provision in the staff handbook for "normal extra time" of 5 hours over the basic agreed 40 hours was found not to reflect a contractual term that there was a normal 45-hour week, since the evidence showed that in practice it was not considered to be obligatory to work the additional 5 hours.

An implied term cannot contradict an express term, but it may be an additional term. It may supplement an ambiguous or partial provision, or fill a gap in a contract. In *Tayside Regional Council v McIntosh* (1982) an employee who had been dismissed from his job as a garage mechanic when he was disqualified from driving claimed that his dismissal was unfair since there had been no term in his contract requiring that he possess a clean driving licence. This had been mentioned in the advertisement for the job, the application form and at interview, but not in the contractual letter. The EAT held that, while an implied term could not have contradicted an express term, it could supplement or clarify: in this case it was, it said, an essential term because of the nature of the work the employee had to do.

Tests for implied terms

Business efficacy

An influential test is the general test in commercial contracts, the "business efficacy" test. Where it is necessary to imply a term into a contract to make it workable, such a term should be implied. This is essentially what happened in *Tayside Regional Council* v *McIntosh*. As a mechanic, it would be necessary for the employee to move, or test drive, vehicles and thus a valid licence would be required. The contract of employment, it could be argued, would be unworkable without it.

In *Marshall* v *Alexander Sloan and Co Ltd* (1981) a commercial traveller was dismissed for having left company products overnight in her company car, contrary to an express term in her contract. She was off work ill and had left the products in her car during her illness. She argued that there was an implied term that her obligations were suspended during periods of ill health. It was accepted by the EAT that there must be an implied term which suspended some obligations during illness, but it was not necessary to imply any more than those which she would be incapable of carrying out. In this case she should have been able to arrange for someone else to bring the products in for her.

Obvious

Another approach has been to imply into a contract a term which is so "obvious" that it must be assumed that the parties would have agreed to it if they had consciously addressed it. This is sometimes called the "officious bystander" or "oh, of course" test – if a bystander had suggested to the parties that they include a certain term in the contract, they would both have said "oh, of course", that it was obvious it should be included. The Court of Appeal applied this approach in *Lake* v *Essex County Council* (1979) in the case of a part-time teacher on a 19½-hour contract, 3½ hours of which were allocated to preparation time (at a time when it was necessary to work for 21 hours a week to qualify for unfair dismissal protection). She claimed that she actually worked more than 3½ hours on preparation and corrections. The Court of Appeal, overturning the EAT which had found in her favour, said: "If the officious bystander had asked Mrs Lake and Essex County Council this question: 'Is Mrs Lake contractually required to work such hours outside school time as may be necessary to prepare her work so that if she does not do so she can be dismissed?' neither would have replied either testily or otherwise 'of course'." What this approach emphasises is that the implied term must be something which both parties agree (or would have agreed) should be obligatory.

Conflict between tests

There is a possible conflict between the business efficacy and the obvious tests. Something which may be necessary, or reasonably necessary, to make the contract work, may not be so obvious that the parties must have agreed to it when made. It is more likely to be the employer's interests which would be allied with that of the business, so that a "business efficacy" test of some sort is more likely to help the employer's interpretation. In *Aparau v Iceland Frozen Foods* (1996) there had been no express mobility contract in the employee's contract of employment. When the employing company was taken over, employees were asked to agree to a new written statement which stated that employees could be transferred to any store owned by the company. Mrs Aparau did not agree and, on transfer a year later to another branch, she resigned. Her resignation would only allow her to raise an unfair dismissal claim if it was a constructive dismissal, that is a legitimate response to a material breach of contract by her employer. While the ET had found that she had agreed to the new term by working on for 12 months without objecting, and, using the "oh, of course" test, that a mobility clause was implied in the original contract, the EAT did not agree: it held that because this was a change without immediate practical effect, working on did not imply that she had accepted the change. Nor did it agree that a mobility clause was implied in the original contract. It did not feel it was essential to make the contract work: a place of work is essential; a mobility clause makes life easier for management, but it is not always reasonably necessary.

It is also the case that these tests, which concentrate on what the parties intended or would have intended when the contract was formed, are insufficient in the case of contracts of employment. The contract of employment is a continuing contract and therefore it may be appropriate to take account of what the parties do subsequently. This may be more than simply evidence of what they must have meant when they formed the contract, but may also be in itself a source of implied terms. In *Mears v Safecar Security Ltd* (1982) the Court of Appeal noted that the business efficacy and officious bystander tests were insufficient for contracts of employment: what the parties did after formation also had to be taken into account. In that case, it had to be decided whether there was a contractual provision for sick pay, either express or implied.

TERMS IMPLIED BY CUSTOM AND PRACTICE

It is possible, but not common, for a term to be implied by custom and practice. This may be a custom and practice within the workplace, or industry or locality. Such a custom would have to be so well known that anyone entering the contract would be assumed to know of it. The requirements of such a custom have been stated to be that it is "reasonable, certain and notorious". In *Devonald* v *Rosser and Sons* (1906) an employer failed to establish that there was a term of custom in the South Wales tinplate trade that would permit them to terminate the contracts of their workers who were paid by piece work (not by a wage, but by payment by results) without paying them during their notice period when there was no work to be done. Not only was it not sufficiently notorious, but it was not reasonable in its one-sided nature. It was, said the court, not a "good custom". By contrast, in *Sagar* v *Ridehalgh and Sons Ltd* (1931) an employer was successful in establishing that a custom of making deductions for bad work had been implied into the individual contract of employment, since it was found that the practice had been in effect both in the employer's business and in the Lancashire cotton weaving trade for over 30 years, and, the Court of Appeal held, was a reasonable one.

It is important that implied contractual effect is shown. An implied agreement is not the same thing as an exercise of an employer's discretion, or an employee's agreeing to accept less than he is due, on one or more occasions. In *Quinn* v *Calder Industrial Metals Ltd* (1996) a policy of making a discretionary enhanced redundancy pay which had been applied on four occasions in 7 years did not give rise to a contractual entitlement. This had been a unilateral act of the employers. The policy had not been notified to employees, and the period of its application was not substantial owing to the small number of occasions. On the other hand, in *International Packaging Ltd* v *Balfour* (2003), previous agreement to accept a reduction in workers' hours with an accompanying reduction in pay did not give rise to an implied term that employees were bound to accept it when the employer unilaterally reduced hours and pay on a future occasion. The important thing is to establish that the custom has been followed without exception for a substantial period, that the custom has been drawn to the attention of employees, and that it is possible to infer an intention to be bound contractually.

INCORPORATED TERMS

Incorporation of terms into a contract occurs when the parties agree to make an outside source into a term of the contract. The terms just considered under the heading of custom and practice are often described as being "incorporated" into the contract rather than "implied". The most important sources of incorporated terms are collective agreements.

It is important to make a distinction between outside documents which are incorporated into the contract and outside documents which are referred to in the contract but which are not in themselves contractual. The distinction, as discussed above, depends on whether there has been a bilateral agreement and whether it is intended to be legally binding. An employer, for example, may draw up documents which explain how certain aspects of employment operate, but such a document, like the written statement of particulars, may be no more than a unilateral act of the employer. The following statement appeared in the relevant contract of employment in *Cadoux* v *Central Regional Council* (1986): "Your terms and conditions of employment will be in accordance with the agreement made between the Authority and (Trade Union)/National Council for Conditions and Terms of Authority Employees, as supplemented by the Authority's Rules as amended from time to time". The Authority had introduced a non-contributory pension scheme under the Rules, but subsequently withdrew the benefit. A judge in the Outer House of the Court of Session held that the Rules were unilateral (being strongly influenced by their being called "the Authority's Rules"), and not contractual. The employer was therefore contractually entitled in this case to change them without consent.

Collective agreements

A collective agreement is an agreement between an employer and a trade union or trade unions, or a group of employers and trade unions. It may cover a single issue, such as pay, or it may relate to a number of different issues. These issues may relate to individual employment terms; others may be more general and some may in particular set out procedures to be followed in particular cases, such as discipline matters or redundancies.

These latter are usually called "procedure agreements". For many years the tradition of "voluntarism" meant that there was a consensus that the true determinant of employment rights was collective bargaining, rather than the individual contract or the law. While there was a move away from this consensus in the 1980s and 1990s, there are still large numbers of workers whose employment terms are governed by collective bargaining. When it comes to legal enforcement, however, it is the individual contract that will be relied on.

Legal status of collective agreements

A collective agreement is not a legally binding contract in itself between the employer and the union. Its importance contractually usually comes from its relationship to individual contracts of employment. Although, as its name suggests, it is an agreement, it is usually not intended to be legally enforceable, an essential condition of any contract. The common law position is reflected in the provision of s 179(1) of the Trade Union and Labour Relations (Consolidation) Act 1992 (TULR(C)A 1992), which states that a collective agreement is conclusively presumed not to be a legally enforceable contract unless it is in writing with an express provision that it is intended to be legally enforceable. Most collective agreements do not contain such a provision and therefore are not legally enforceable. This does not make them contracts which are unenforceable, but means that they are not contracts at all.

The words which displace this presumption have to be very clear indeed. In *National Coal Board v National Union of Mineworkers* (1986) the parties had in 1946 agreed to be "bound by" their agreement which gave the NUM exclusive negotiating rights in respect of the consultation which was required by statute under the Coal Industry Nationalisation Act 1946 (CINA 1946). The NCB had revoked the agreement in order to be able to negotiate with a breakaway union, the Union of Democratic Mineworkers. The High Court held that the phrase "bound by" was not specific enough to overcome the presumption against legal enforceability. It is interesting to note that some years later, in *R v British Coal Corporation, ex parte Vardy* (1993), the two unions united to challenge a decision by the successor to the NCB to close a number of collieries without consultation, as they were required to under the agreed procedure agreement. This time the unions were successful. The High Court held that BCC had ignored its obligations under CINA 1946, and the legitimate expectations of their employees that they would be consulted. It therefore quashed the decision to close the collieries pending consultation.

Effect of collective agreement on the individual contract of employment

Although the collective agreement itself creates no legal rights between the parties to it, the employer and the trade union, its terms, or certain of them, may nevertheless become part of an individual contract of employment through the process of incorporation. The collective agreement will not be enforceable by the parties to it, but its terms may be enforceable by the employer or employee as between each other under the contract of employment.

The collective agreement involved in *Marley v Forward Trust Group* (1986) stated that it was to be binding "in honour only". Contracts of employment, including Mr Marley's, incorporated the terms of the collective agreement. The collective agreement contained a provision allowing people transferred where there had been a redundancy situation 6 months to decide whether to take a redundancy payment rather than transfer. When Mr Marley tried to exercise that right, his employer said that the term was unenforceable because of the "honour only" term in the collective agreement. The Court of Appeal held that, although the collective agreement could not be enforced in itself by the union or employer, since it had been incorporated into the contract of employment its terms could be enforced as part of the contract by either employer or employee. Thus Mr Marley was entitled to the benefit of the redundancy payment as a term of his contract of employment.

In *Burke v Royal Liverpool University Hospital NHS Trust* (1997) a covering letter with the written contract of employment incorporated collective agreements between the employer and the union into the contract of employment. The domestic services of the employer by law had to be put out to competitive tender, and the existing department put in a tender to keep the services. To help make the department competitive in the bidding, the union agreed to a reduction in wages through an exchange of letters. After success in the bidding, the employer implemented the reduction in wages. This was held to be enforceable as part of the individual contract of employment, as the exchange of letters amounted to a collective agreement, and the original contract of employment had incorporated all collective agreements into it.

Method of incorporation

The evidence must show that there is a contractual intent between the employer and employee that the terms of a specific collective agreement or of collective agreements in general are part of the individual contract of employment. In *Alexander v Standard Telephones and Cables Ltd* (1991) the English High Court laid out its suggested approaches: first, examine the contract of employment in order to identify the intention of the employer and employee and interpret any written contractual terms; second, if there is no written contract, infer from all the other available materials, including the written statement of particulars and the collective agreement itself, what the intention must have been; third, some parts of a collective agreement may be incorporated and others not.

Express incorporation

The terms of a collective agreement can be incorporated into the individual contract expressly. There may be a term to that effect in a written contract of employment, or there may be a separate contractual document (as in *Burke* (1997)), or there may be a verbal agreement to that effect. In any case, whether it is expressly or otherwise incorporated, it is one of the required particulars that must be recorded in the written statement, discussed above, which the employer must give to the employee. A classic example of express incorporation can be seen in *NCB v Galley* (1958), where the contract of employment contained an express term that the terms of the deputies were to be governed by collective agreements negotiated from time to time. In a new agreement about shift working, it was provided that workers could be asked to work reasonable overtime on Saturdays. Mr Galley refused to work on a Saturday, arguing that his contract of employment did not contain a term requiring him to do so. It was held, however, that the collective agreement, in accordance with the express term, had been incorporated into each contract of employment, and accordingly this term had become part of his individual contract.

Implied incorporation

The terms of a collective agreement can be incorporated into the individual contract by implication. This refers to the conduct of the parties. In general this will arise when there is a custom to that effect in the relevant workplace. A "reasonable, certain and notorious" practice (see the section on custom and practice above) of implementing collective agreements can evidence contractual intent. In *Henry v London General Transport Services Ltd* (2002) there had not been express incorporation, but there had been a tradition of negotiation between the employer and the recognised union and the application of collective agreements to employees' terms and conditions. As a lead in to a proposed management buy-out, the employer and union agreed to changes in terms and conditions, including a pay reduction which was put into effect after the buy-out. Mr Henry and a number of others worked for 2 years under protest on the new terms before starting ET proceedings. The ET found that there had been a custom or tradition of collective agreements being considered to be legally binding. The Court of Appeal found this finding in fact to be incompatible with their further finding that for fundamental changes the custom might not apply to incorporate them into individual contracts of employment. It also held that the 2 years working under the changed terms before raising the action amounted to an implied acceptance.

Agency

The principle underpinning incorporation is that of identifying contractual intent on the part of employer and employee. Where it applies, it does not matter whether an employee is a union member or not. In certain cases, where a union or union representative enters into an agreement with an employer on behalf of a named employee or group of employees, the agreement will take effect on the basis that the representative was acting as an agent for the members. The agreed terms will be binding between the employer and employee. In *Edwards* v *Skyways Ltd* (1964) a trade union negotiated a redundancy package for four pilots including an *ex gratia* payment, which the company later refused to pay. It was held that the union had acted as the agent for the individual pilots and had created a binding obligation between employer and individual employee.

Terms suitable for incorporation

Not all terms of a collective agreement may be considered as suitable for incorporation. This will usually arise in relation to two sorts of terms: first, where the agreement is primarily a procedure agreement regulating dealings between the union and the employer such as dispute resolution; second, where the agreement is an expression of policy or aspiration on the part of the employer and union. In both cases it would be considered that there was no intention that such terms would be enforceable as part of contracts of employment. The union and employer in *British Leyland (UK) Ltd* v *McQuilken* (1978) had agreed that in the event of redundancy employees would be interviewed to ascertain if they wished retraining or redundancy. Subsequently, the employer decided to give employees the option of transfer or retraining and did not conduct interviews. It was held that the company was not in breach of contract. The agreement was in the nature of a long-term plan dealing with policy not individual rights, and it was not intended to be legally enforceable as part of the individual contract of employment. In *Kaur* v *MG Rover Group Ltd* (2005) the phrase "There will be no compulsory redundancies" was held not to be appropriate for individual incorporation. On the other hand, a provision in a collective agreement which had provided that selection for redundancy would be made on a "last in first out" basis was held to be legally enforceable by an employee in *Anderson* v *Pringle of Scotland Ltd* (1998). It may not always be easy to distinguish between the agreement concerned with aspiration and policy and the agreement concerned with legally enforceable individual terms.

IMPLIED DUTIES: TERMS IMPLIED BY COMMON LAW

Both employer and employee have duties implied into the contract by the common law. These duties were developed in the 19th century and reflect the subordination inherent in the relationship of employer and employee. At the same time there was a growing paternalism which is also reflected there. There have also been more recent developments expanding the employer's duties. The duties can be seen as underpinning the essential nature of the contract whereby the employee agrees to provide work for the employer in return for a wage (the "wage/work bargain").

The common law duties of the employee are: the duty to give personal service; the duty to obey orders; the duty to take reasonable care; the duty of loyalty. The common law duties of the employer are: the duty to pay wages; the duty to pay expenses; the duty of care for health and safety; the duty of trust and confidence.

The duties are mutual duties: that is they are owed in exchange for each other. Not every duty is the counterpart of another duty, but, where they are, if one party is in breach of their duty they cannot sue for breach of the counterpart duty by the other. The counterpart of the employee's duty to pay wages is the employer's duty to give personal service and the duty to obey orders. The counterpart of the employer's duty of trust and confidence is the employee's duty of loyalty. (The employer's duty is usually referred to as the "mutual" duty of trust and confidence, which emphasises this reciprocity.) In *Macari* v *Celtic Football & Athletic Co Ltd* (2000) it was held that the employer's breach of the mutual duty of trust and confidence did not justify the employee in failing to obey orders, and thus his dismissal for this failure was legitimate. On the other hand, in *Aberdeen City Council* v *McNeill* (2010), an employee who was in breach of the duty of loyalty was not entitled to terminate the contract of employment on the basis that the employer was in breach of the duty of trust and confidence since he himself was already in breach of the reciprocal duty.

Like all implied terms, these duties are subordinate to the express terms of the contract of employment. However, express terms will be interpreted so as to comply with the implied duties wherever possible. In *Johnstone* v *Bloomsbury Area Health Authority* (1991), a case which pre-dated maximum working time regulations, it was held that a hospital doctor's contract, which provided for a basic 40-hour working week and a requirement to be available for up to 48 hours of additional overtime, had to be interpreted so that the doctor could not be required to work for such hours as it was reasonable to foresee could damage his health. In other words, the duty of care was taken into account.

The implied duties of the employee

Duty to be willing to give personal service

The contract is one of *delectus personae*. This means that the identity of the employee is essential to the contract. It was seen that personal service is part of the "irreducible minimum" of a contract of employment: its essence is that the employee agrees to provide his own personal services to the employer. At common law this principle applies to the employer's identity as well, so that a contract of employment cannot be transferred from one employer to the other. Although this has been to an extent altered by the Transfer of Undertakings (Protection of Employment) Regulations 2006 (see Chapter 9), the employee still retains the right to opt out of any transfer (reg 4).

As it is personal, performance cannot be delegated to another, although (as was discussed above) a limited ability to send a substitute with the employer's approval may not change the nature of the contract.

Duty to obey lawful and reasonable orders

Just as personal service is an essential part of the contract, so is the element of control by the employer. The employer's prerogative is to give orders to the employee which the employee must obey. However, these orders must be within the scope of the contract, and must be lawful and reasonable. An employee need not obey an order to do something which is unlawful, nor something which is unreasonable.

An example of an unlawful order which it was appropriate for an employee to disobey can be seen in *Morrish* v *Henlys (Folkestone) Ltd* (1973). A garage employee refused to obey an order from his manager to falsify the record of petrol he had used, in order to correct deficiencies in the records. His consequent dismissal was held to be unfair, since he was fully entitled to disobey such an order. An example of an unreasonable order which it was appropriate for an employee to disobey can be seen in *Ottoman Bank* v *Chakarian* (1930), a decision of the Privy Council. The employee, a

Turkish subject sent to work in Constantinople, told the bank that his life was in danger and he fled from Constantinople. His dismissal was held to be wrongful, since he was entitled to refuse to remain where his life was in danger in spite of his employer's otherwise legitimate orders.

These two concepts came into conflict in *Buckoke v Greater London Council* (1971) with (in that case) reasonableness taking precedence. An instruction to firefighters to cross red lights when driving to an emergency, while driving carefully in doing so, was found to be reasonable, and, although at that time technically unlawful, one which the employee should have obeyed.

At common law, failure to obey a lawful and reasonable order justifies dismissal without notice (summary dismissal) if it is sufficiently serious. At common law an employer can dismiss without notice only where it is justified by a material breach of contract by the employee. This is often described as a repudiatory breach: that is, a breach so serious that it indicates that the employee does not intend to be bound by the contract.

Two contrasting actions of wrongful dismissal (see Chapter 4) demonstrate the application of the principle. In *Laws v London Chronicle* (1959) the summary dismissal of a secretary who walked out of a meeting with her immediate boss despite having been told to remain by her managing director was held to be wrongful, since the disobedience was not sufficiently serious to be considered repudiatory. On the other hand, in *Pepper v Webb* (1969), the wrongful dismissal action by a gardener who was summarily dismissed when he told his employer that he "couldn't care less about your ... greenhouse and your ... garden" was unsuccessful since his action was repudiatory of the contract.

Duty of loyalty

This duty is also referred to as the duty of trust and confidence (the employee's side of the mutual duty of trust and confidence), or the duty to give faithful service, or the duty of fidelity, and comprises a number of headings.

Employees do not generally owe a fiduciary duty to their employer simply by virtue of being an employee. A fiduciary duty would impose a wide-ranging duty to act in the employer's interests at the expense of his own. A fiduciary duty extends beyond the terms of the contract itself. A director of a company has a fiduciary duty towards the company, and a senior employee may have a fiduciary duty in relation to certain aspects of the contract. In *Nottingham University v Fishel* (2000) the employee was the Director of a University clinic. Without the knowledge of the University he also held clinics abroad, involving some of his staff at the University in some of those. After his employment with the University ended they sought payment of the profits he had made from these clinics abroad. The University was only partially successful. It was held that in relation to the clinics themselves there was no conflict between his work for the University and that work, so that no order should be made in relation to that. However, he owed a fiduciary duty in relation to the employees of the University for whom he was responsible. By involving them in work which was outside their duties he was in breach of duty, and an order was made in relation to that.

Duty of honesty   A contract of employment is not a contract *uberrimae fidei* (of the utmost good faith), so there is no duty to disclose material facts. The employee's duty is to be honest, but not necessarily to disclose prejudicial information if it is not asked for. In general an employee does not have to tell the employer of any wrongdoing he has committed. In *Bell* v *Lever Bros* (1932) the company discovered, after agreeing to the early resignation of senior employees in exchange for £30,000, that they had been involved in secret speculation in conflict with the company's interests, which would have justified their summary dismissal. The company sued for return of the money on the basis that the agreement to pay was voidable because of misrepresentation. The House of Lords held that since there was no duty to disclose, simple failure to disclose could not amount to misrepresentation.

There may be special circumstances in which there is a duty to disclose. It may be part of the employee's contractual duty (express or implied, perhaps as a supervisor) to report others' wrongdoing, which might also involve their own. In *Sybron Corporation* v *Rochem Ltd* (1983) the European Zone Controller, a senior employee, received his full pension when he retired. The company had paid into it on the basis that if he were dismissed for fraud or serious misconduct he would only be entitled to the benefit of his own contributions. Some years after his retirement the company discovered that while employed by them he had been working with other employees to set up a company which had worked in competition with them. They argued that the payment of their contributions had been made because of misrepresentation, his failure to disclose his misconduct. The Court of Appeal held that, although there was no duty to disclose his own misconduct, nevertheless he had a duty by virtue of his responsibilities to report the misconduct of his subordinate employees (even although this would mean also disclosing his own), and his failure to do so had been a misrepresentation. His failure to disclose was therefore a misrepresentation which made their agreement to pay voidable.

The duty of honesty is not simply a duty not to be dishonest. It is a duty to be honest in dealings with the employer. In *Sinclair* v *Neighbour* (1967) a betting shop manager borrowed money from the till, even although he knew this was prohibited, leaving an IOU. His action for wrongful dismissal consequent on his summary dismissal was unsuccessful. The Court of Appeal ruled that, even although he had not acted dishonestly, nevertheless his behaviour was inconsistent with the duty of good faith owed to an employer.

Duty not to make a secret profit   An employee should not make any personal gain from his employment, without the knowledge and consent of the employer. This includes not just taking a bribe but gaining any advantage or payment from the employment. In *Tesco Stores Ltd* v *Pook* (2004) the employers were entitled to recover a £300,000 bribe paid to the employee.

Duty to act in the employer's interests   While working for the employer, the employee must act in the employer's interests. Once an employee has left an employer's employment there is nothing to stop competition with the employer. However, while still in employment, even in the employee's own time, competing with the employer would be a breach of duty. The duty to act in the employer's interests can be further broken down.

Duty to co-operate   This aspect of the duty of loyalty as a duty to co-operate with or not to disrupt the employer's business emerged in the case of *Secretary of State for Employment* v *ASLEF (No 2)* (1972). A "work to contract" by train drivers, whereby they obeyed the employer's rule book to the letter, was held to be in breach of contract since it was done with the intention of disrupting the employer's business.

Duty not to work for rivals   While an employee must work for the employer during working time, this duty does not extend past the employer's time. An employee may work for himself or for someone else in his own time. However, where there is a potential conflict between the interests of the employer and a secondary employer, there would be a breach of duty if there was a danger that confidential information might be revealed. In *Hivac Ltd* v *Park Royal Scientific Instruments Ltd* (1946) a manufacturer of hearing aids successfully obtained an order prohibiting five of its employees from working with a competitor outside working hours, because it was able to show that the employees had access to confidential information (although there was no evidence that they had actually disclosed any of it). The employees had a duty not to place themselves in a position where their interests might conflict with their employer's.

Duty not to benefit personally An employee should not take advantage of his position in order to benefit their own interests for the present or the future, such as canvassing customers for a future business. In *Adamson v B and L Cleaning Services Ltd* (1995) the dismissal of a foreman of a company of cleaning contractors for putting his own name as an individual on a tender list which the employer was on while still in its employment was held to be fair.

Duty not to disclose confidential information An employee must not disclose confidential information of the employer. An example of the enforcement of this duty can be seen in *Camelot v Centaur Communications Ltd* (1998). Camelot, the operators of the National Lottery, applied for an order that the publishing company reveal the source of a leak of information which it had published, about the proportions of money which were going to good causes and to the directors and shareholders. The order was granted, the court holding that disclosure fell within one of the provisions of the Contempt of Court Act 1981, s 10, which withheld journalistic immunity where it was in the interests of justice to do so. This was because the leaks were in breach of the duty of loyalty, and could seriously damage the ability of the company to operate effectively because of the climate of suspicion which would exist within the company.

There is a difference in the implied duty between what an employee may not disclose while still an employee and what may not be disclosed after employment ends. The common law duty does have an impact after employment, but in a more limited way. In *Faccenda Chicken v Fowler* (1986) three categories of confidential information were distinguished: easily accessible information (which it would not be breach of contract to disclose); information which was told in confidence or which it was obvious was confidential but was part of the skill or memory of the employee (which it would be breach of contract to disclose during employment but not afterwards); and "trade secrets", information so confidential that it should never be divulged even after employment ended. Thus, using information in the second category, gained while an employee (such as the names of customers), would not be a breach of the implied term, but recording the information while an employee for use afterwards would be.

An employee might seek to justify or defend disclosing confidential information by relying on a common law "public interest" defence (*Initial Services Ltd* v *Putterill* (1968)). More likely an employee might seek to rely on the "whistleblower's" protection from dismissal or detriment introduced by the Public Interest Disclosure Act 1998. It does not give a blanket protection: it provides for the setting up of procedures within a company to deal with disclosures of confidential information in the public interest. Where an employee has made a disclosure following the procedures, he will have protection from unfair dismissal and from being subjected to a detriment, under ERA 1996, ss 47B and 103A. The protection against detriment applies not just to employees, but also to workers, with an extended definition of worker (s 43K).

In general, simply going public, such as by contacting a newspaper, will not be protected. The disclosure first of all must be a "qualifying disclosure". A qualifying disclosure exists where the person disclosing has a reasonable belief that one of the following is happening or is likely to happen: a criminal offence has been committed; a person is failing in a legal obligation; there has been a miscarriage of justice; an individual's health and safety is endangered; the environment is being damaged; or that any of these is being concealed (s 43B). The employee must have a reasonable belief that the disclosure qualifies, even if it turns out this is not the case. In *Babula* v *Waltham Forrest College* (2007) the Court of Appeal held that the belief of the person disclosing, a lecturer who believed that his predecessor had been inciting hatred against non-Muslims and accordingly that he would have committed the crime of inciting racial hatred (when it would not), had been reasonably held. His disclosure of the information to the FBI and CIA was therefore held to be qualifying.

A qualifying disclosure is a "protected disclosure" so long as it is made in accordance with the provisions of ERA 1996, ss 43C–43H. This includes disclosure: in good faith to the employer, or, if the failure is someone else's, to that other person (s 43C); or if made while obtaining legal advice (s 43D); or, where the employer is appointed by statute or government minister, in good faith to a UK Minister or a member of the Scottish government (s 43E); or in good faith to prescribed persons (such as members of regulatory bodies like the Health and Safety Executive) (s 43F); or in circumstances where the employee reasonably believes the employer would subject him to detriment, or would not take any action, so long as it is in good faith and not for personal gain (s 43G); or where there is an exceptionally serious failure and the disclosure is made in good faith and not for the purpose of gain (s 43H). Any agreement between an employer and employee to restrict this right is void (s 43J).

Any court or tribunal considering this issue would also have to take account of Art 10 of the ECHR (freedom of expression), which is a qualified right, and also Art 8 (private life), which is also qualified. If the material is journalistic, literary or artistic, HRA 1998, s 12 requires a court to take into account whether it would be in the public interest to disclose it.

Restrictive covenants An employer may seek to prevent an employee from revealing confidential information after he has stopped working for the employer by including an express term in the contract of employment preventing the employee from taking the same kind of work for a period in the local area. Such terms are usually called restrictive covenants. An employer is not entitled to protection against competition from an ex-employee, so that such a term is presumed to be unenforceable as being in restraint of trade unless the employer can prove that it is required to protect its legitimate interests and is reasonable. The legitimate interests are trade secrets and customer connection (not competition). The legitimacy of customer protection depends on the nature of the business, the position of the employee in the organisation and the extent of the covenant in terms of area and time covered. The legitimacy of trade secret restraints depends on these factors and also the extent of the secrecy. In *Bluebell Apparel Ltd v Dickinson* (1980) the employer, a manufacturer of jeans, applied for an interdict to prevent an ex-manager taking up a post with a rival firm which manufactured jeans in breach of a term in his contract of employment that he should not disclose trade secrets, nor work for a competitor for 2 years anywhere in the UK or the world. The order was granted: given the employee's position in the company and the worldwide nature of the jeans market, the restriction was found to be reasonable.

Ownership of inventions At common law an invention which is connected with the employee's employment is the employer's as the employee must work in the best interests of the employer. However, this position has been ameliorated by the Patents Act 1977 so that the employer has ownership only where the invention was made in the course of the employee's duties; or was made in the course of specifically assigned duties from which the invention might reasonably be expected to result; or was made in the course of the employee's duties, and the employee's responsibility gives him a duty to further the employer's interests.

Duty to show reasonable skill and care

An employee must show reasonable care and skill in carrying out work for the employer. If an employee does not exercise reasonable care and skill, he may be required to indemnify the employer for loss caused by the failure. The House of Lords in *Lister* v *Romford Ice and Cold Storage Co Ltd* (1957) allowed the employer to recover the damages it had had to pay out because of the death of an employee from the employee whose actual negligence had caused the death when reversing one of the company's lorries in the company yard. Similar recovery of compensation from an employee whose negligence had caused loss to his employer was allowed in *Janata Bank* v *Ahmed* (1981).

The implied duties of the employer

Duty of trust and confidence

This is a duty which has developed relatively recently. Its origins are sometimes traced in a common law duty on the employer to treat the employee with courtesy. It is often viewed as the employer's counterpart to the employee's duty of loyalty: the employer must be worthy of that loyalty and do nothing to destroy the basis of the relationship of trust between employer and employee. Hence it is often referred to as the mutual duty of trust and confidence. It has had the effect of placing a greater requirement for fair and reasonable treatment of the employee on the employer.

The duty has been developed by the courts, particularly because of the development of the concept of constructive dismissal in unfair dismissal (see Chapter 7). A resignation because of a material breach of contract by the employer can amount to a dismissal: this can include breach of the common law duties. Early cases were concerned with possible breaches of the duty of mutual trust and confidence. The classic formulation of the duty, approved subsequently by the House of Lords, comes from *Woods* v *WM Car Services Ltd* (1982) where an employee failed in her unfair dismissal action since it was not accepted that there had been any breach by the employer of either an express or an implied term, including the term that the employers "would not without reasonable and proper cause conduct themselves in a manner calculated or likely to destroy or seriously damage the relationship of confidence and trust between the parties".

The duty, and this formulation of it, was recognised by the House of Lords in *Malik* v *Bank of Credit and Commerce International* (1997). Two managers of the bank, which had gone into liquidation following fraudulent trading, claimed that they were unable to obtain subsequent employment because of their association with the bank, even though they had not been involved in the corrupt practices. The House of Lords held that the behaviour of the bank, in conducting its business in a dishonest and corrupt manner, amounted to a breach of the duty of trust and confidence.

The employer does not have to have intended to damage the relationship with the employee: the question is to be decided objectively, looking at whether the behaviour was likely to have that effect, as it did in *Malik*. Nor is it necessary for the employee to be aware of the employer's behaviour while an employee, which the employees in *Malik* were not.

The sort of behaviour caught by this duty is varied. It extends to bullying and harassment (*Horkulak* v *Cantor Fitzgerald International* (2003)), failing to take a complaint seriously (*Bracebridge Engineering Ltd* v *Darby* (1990)), and insulting an employee (*Isle of Wight Tourist Board* v *Coombes* (1976)). The duty may require positive action from the employer where necessary. In *Transco plc* v *O'Brien* (2002) the company's predecessor, British Gas, had not sent the employee information, sent to all employees, about enhanced redundancy terms because they did not think he was a permanent employee. The ET found that he was a permanent employee and the Court of Appeal agreed that the failure to inform him of the package was a breach of the duty of trust and confidence, since it did not treat him in a fair and even-handed manner.

Given that the duty is not to do anything which is likely to destroy or seriously damage the relationship of trust and confidence, a breach of it will inevitably be a material breach of contract (which may justify resignation without notice if the employee resigns in response without delay, and thus mean that such resignation is a constructive dismissal for unfair dismissal). In *Morrow* v *Safeway Stores plc* (2002) the ET had held that the public ticking off an employee had amounted to a breach of the duty but was not so serious as to be a repudiatory (or material) breach. The EAT remitted the case back, since the finding that there had been a breach of the duty must inevitably mean there had been a repudiatory breach.

In a controversial decision, *Johnson* v *Unisys Ltd* (2001), the House of Lords held that the duty did not apply to the manner of dismissal as this does not refer to the carrying out of the contract itself. The effect of this decision has been mitigated by further decisions that the duty does apply in the steps leading up to the dismissal (*McCabe* v *Cornwall County Council*; *Eastwood* v *Magnox Electric* (2003)).

The emergence and importance of this duty is such that it has been argued that it is an "overarching" duty, in the sense that there is a unitary duty, with the other duties being sub-sets of the principal duty. The overarching duty would be the mutual duty, encompassing the employee's duty of loyalty as well as the employer's duty.

Where the courts have implied terms into the contract it can be difficult to determine whether the term is being implied under the rules of business efficacy or obviousness, or as an implied common law duty, perhaps as part of the mutual duty. In *Scally* v *Southern Health and Social Services Board* (1991) the House of Lords held that the employer had a duty to inform doctors of a limited time right to additional pension entitlements to get the benefit of which they had to take steps and of which the employees were unaware.

Duty to pay wages

The employer's duty is to pay wages. Thus, if the employer pays wages, the primary duty is fulfilled: there is no general duty to provide work. As a judge said over 60 years ago in *Collier* v *Sunday Referee Publishing Co Ltd* (1940): "Provided I pay my cook her wages regularly, she cannot complain if I choose to take any or all of my meals out." Thus, an employer who suspends an employee on full pay will not usually be in breach of contract. Suspension without pay, however, is a different matter and would be a breach unless there is a contractual term permitting it. The term may be express or implied, and, if the contract does not permit otherwise, the obligation to pay wages continues until the contract is terminated.

There are limited circumstances in which an employee can demand work as well as wages. There can be an implied duty to provide work where the failure to provide the work as well as wages could lead to a loss of reputation or publicity, usually applying in the case of actors, as was the case in *Herbert Clayton and Jack Waller Ltd* v *Oliver* (1930) when an actor who was removed from a leading role successfully obtained damages since his reputation would suffer as a result.

Where wages are dependent on work, as in the case of piecework where there is no wage, but payment by amount of work completed, there is a duty to provide sufficient work (*Devonald* v *Rosser and Sons* (1906)). This applies to payment by commission (*Turner* v *Goldsmith* (1891)), but not necessarily where commission supplements a basic wage (*Turner* v *Sawdon* (1901)).

Where the employee is also an office holder there is a suggestion that such an employee is entitled to work unless there is good cause to prevent it (*Collier* v *Sunday Referee Publishing Co Ltd* (1940)). There is also authority for the proposition that some forms of employment may require an employee to be given work in order to keep up a level of skill. The Court of Appeal stated in *William Hill Organisation Ltd* v *Tucker* (1998) that the nature of the work of the employee, a senior dealer involved in setting up spreadsheet betting, was so specialised that he required to be provided with work. In addition, in this case, there was a contractual provision that the employer would give him every opportunity to develop his skills.

So long as the employee is ready and willing to work the employer must continue to pay wages unless the contract allows the employer to withhold wages. This may be a contractual term allowing an employer to lay off employees if there is no work, or it might be a term allowing an employer to suspend without pay as a disciplinary measure. An employer may wish to lay off employees for a number of reasons, mainly financial. If the employer does not terminate the contract by giving notice or summary dismissal, the obligation to pay wages should continue. In *Jewell* v *Neptune Concrete Ltd* (1975) workers were laid off without pay when there was no contractual right to do so. When Mr Jewell resigned and claimed redundancy pay it was held that he had been constructively dismissed because the employer was in material breach of contract.

Duty to indemnify

The employer has a duty to indemnify or reimburse an employee for losses or expenses incurred in the course of employment.

Duty to take reasonable care for the employee's safety

At common law an employer has a duty to take reasonable care for an employee's safety and to protect him from foreseeable risks. It is both contractual and delictual. This duty will be examined in more detail in Chapter 12.

Duty to ensure a reference is accurate

There is no duty to provide a reference for a current or ex-employee. An employer may refuse to do so. However, if the employer decides to do so, the reference must be accurate.

An employer will have the defence of qualified privilege to an action for defamation. This means that so long as the reference was given to a prospective employer without malice in the genuine belief that it was true, an employer will not be liable in damages for defamation.

The employer also owes a duty to the employee to take reasonable care in writing a reference. An employer who gives an opinion about an employee or former employee which he would not have given if he had taken reasonable care to check the facts may be liable in damages to the employee, so long as it can be proved that it was the bad reference which caused him not to get the new job (*Spring* v *Guardian Assurance* (1994)).

Essential Facts

- Provision for the employment of school age children is given in the Children and Young Persons (Scotland) Act 1937 (as amended.)
- An employee's entitlement to employment particulars are detailed in the Employment Rights Act 1996, Pt I.
- Provisions relating to protected disclosures are set out in the Employment Rights Act 1996, Pt IVA.
- The legal status of collective agreements is governed by the Trade Union and Labour Relations (Consolidation) Act 1992, s 179.
- Ownership of employee inventions is regulated by the Patents Act 1977.

Essential Cases

Robertson v British Gas Corporation (1983): employees were found to be entitled to a bonus provided for in the contract of employment. The statutory written statement of employment particulars is not contractual in itself and cannot override the contract.

Devonald v Rosser and Sons Ltd (1906): an employer did not succeed in arguing that there was a custom which allowed it not to pay wages to employees when there was no work. A custom, to be contractually binding, must be "reasonable, certain and notorious".

Marley v Forward Trust Group Ltd (1986): a collective agreement containing redundancy terms which was incorporated into the employee's contract of employment stated that it was not legally binding. It was held that the terms were enforceable as part of the contract of employment even although the collective agreement could not be enforced in itself.

Faccenda Chicken v Fowler (1986): employees who set up in competition with their former employer and canvassed its customers were not in breach of the implied duty of loyalty. This case clarified the circumstances in which the implied duty not to reveal confidential information continues after employment has ended.

Johnstone v Bloomsbury Area Health Authority (1991): a hospital doctor whose contract provided that his working hours were 40 hours a week, with another 48 hours on call, was held to be entitled to an order declaring that he could not be asked to do so many hours that it would foreseeably damage his health. The express contractual terms were interpreted in the light of the employer's duty of care.

Malik v Bank of Credit and Commerce International (1997): former employees of an employer which had traded fraudulently were entitled to raise an action for damages because their employment prospects had been damaged by the bank's breach of the implied mutual duty of trust and confidence. The House of Lords recognised and defined the duty.

4 VARIATION, TERMINATION AND ENFORCEMENT

VARIATION OF THE CONTRACT OF EMPLOYMENT

A contract of employment is, like all contracts, a bilateral agreement between the parties to it. The general principle is that a contract can only be varied by the bilateral agreement of the parties to it. A unilateral act cannot vary a bilateral agreement.

This general principle means that it is not possible for either employer or employee to vary the terms of the contract without the agreement of the other party. This is a point that is likely to have more relevance for the employer, who might wish to change the contractual terms and may find it difficult to obtain employee agreement to change. Therefore a letter from an employer, a notice by an employer or the issuing of a fresh written statement cannot in themselves vary the contract.

An employer who unilaterally changes the terms of the contract is in breach of contract. As there had been no contractual term, either when the contract was made, or subsequently implied by custom permitting the employer to reduce hours and wages unilaterally, in *International Packaging Corporation (UK) Ltd* v *Balfour* (2003) it was held that the reduction in wages by the employer was an unauthorised deduction.

It will be a question of interpretation whether certain unilateral measures by an employer are contractual or an exercise of the employer's managerial prerogative. A staff handbook, laying out procedures, may be contractual if there is an express or implied term in the contract of employment incorporating the handbook or the policies within it. On the other hand, such a document may be a unilateral statement by the employer as to the procedures which it intends to follow in certain circumstances. In *Wandsworth London Borough Council* v *D'Silva* (1998) the Court of Appeal found that the terms of a sickness absence policy in a staff handbook were too vague to have contractual effect and were intended to act as guidance to managers as to how to manage such situations. As a legitimate unilateral document, the employer was entitled to amend it (changing the review period for long-term absence from 12 months to 6 months).

Variation by agreement

An employer must obtain the agreement of the employee to a change in the terms of the contract. The primary way of obtaining such agreement would be by express agreement, written or verbal. An employee may agree individually to a change in terms. In *Hepworth Heating Ltd* v *Akers* (2002) the employer wished to change the method of paying wages to cashless pay. To those employees who did not agree to this, a notice was sent that they should agree to the change or be dismissed. The employees signed in agreement, but stating that they were signing "under duress". The EAT found that the employer had been entitled to issue the notice of termination so that there had been no duress affecting their agreement to the change. They had not, therefore, been dismissed and were not entitled to claim unfair dismissal.

In cases where it is a contractual term that collective agreements made from time to time with a recognised trade union will be incorporated into the individual contract of employment, the mechanism of incorporation of the terms of a fresh collective agreement will effectively vary the contract.

Variation by implied agreement

Just as contracts can be formed by conduct or implication, so they can be varied in the same way. The employee who acquiesces in a change announced by an employer may be found to have agreed to the change if his actions (or failure to act) are held to amount to agreement. This may depend on the nature of the change. Where the purported change has immediate practical effect, such as change in hours or pay, carrying on working without objection is likely to amount to implied agreement. On the other hand, where the purported change does not have immediate practical effect, such as sick pay or holidays, working on will not give rise to the same implication.

The case of *Jones* v *Associated Tunnelling Co Ltd* (1981) gives an example of this. Mr Jones was employed by the company to work initially in workplace A, 2 miles from his home. His written statement provided that he worked at workplace A. Five years later he was moved to workplace B, which was 12 to 13 miles from his home. A further 4 years later a new written statement was issued which said that his place of work was workplace B or such place in the UK as the employers may determine from time to time. Three years later yet another new written statement stated that he may be required to transfer to any place in the UK at the request of the employer. Four years after that he was told to work at workplace C, which was very close to workplace B and as close to his home. He did not agree to this, resigned from the company and asked for a redundancy payment which he would only be entitled to if his resignation would count as a dismissal if the employer was in breach of contract in asking him to move to workplace C. The EAT held that there was no breach of contract in asking him to move. The court dealt with this as an issue of implied terms in the contract, and did not rely on the written statement as effectively varying the contract. Using the obvious test, the court concluded that a reasonable implied mobility clause in the contract would permit transfer to any workplace within reasonable commuting distance of home. As it happened, the transfer was within that reasonable commuting distance. The EAT would not have inferred agreement to any wider mobility clause from the failure to object to previous changes announced by the employer. They did not have immediate effect and working on could not be taken to be implied agreement.

The same approach was adopted in *Aparau v Iceland Frozen Foods* (1996), but this time it worked in the employee's favour. When a new written statement was issued on the takeover by a new employer which included a clause entitling the employers to require employees to move to any store, Ms Aparau refused to sign in agreement. A year later she refused an order to transfer and resigned. As in *Jones*, her resignation would only be a dismissal if the employer was in breach of contract in requiring her to move. The EAT held that the tribunal had been wrong when it found that by not objecting she had impliedly agreed to the new terms and conditions.

Contractual provision for unilateral change

Unilateral contractual change is possible if the contract provides for it, that is if the parties have bilaterally agreed to give one party (in employment contracts, usually the employer) the right to vary certain terms. Such a power would require clear and unequivocal express provision in the contract. The Court of Appeal in *Wandsworth Borough Council v D'Silva* stated that in interpreting a contract the courts would try to avoid an interpretation which would allow unilateral variation of rights given to an employee.

In *Airlie v City of Edinburgh District Council* (1996) the employees' contracts were governed by a collective agreement, which had been incorporated into their contract of employment. The collective agreement laid down a Scheme and Code of Practice for the bonus. The Code of Practice expressly reserved the employer's right to manage, and gave it the right to review the scheme after consultation. Both union and employer were given the right to terminate the scheme on 3 months' notice. When the employers and trade union could not agree on changes, the employers introduced changes anyway. The EAT held that the terms of the Code of Practice were contractual, being part of the collective agreement which had been incorporated into the contracts of employment. The employers therefore had the contractual right to review and change the Scheme.

Similarly, in *Bateman* v *Asda Stores Ltd* (2010), a staff handbook which was incorporated into the individual contracts of employment gave the employers the "right to review, revise, amend or replace the contents of this handbook, and introduce new policies from time to time reflecting the changing needs of the business". The EAT held that this was clear and unequivocal and gave the right to the employer to introduce changes to the work and pay structure which it had been unable to get all of its employees to agree to.

Variation without agreement

If one of the parties to the contract of employment (in practice usually the employer) wishes to change any term of the contract, there are two legal alternatives. Preferably the employer should obtain the agreement of the employee(s) to the proposed change. An employer who cannot obtain this agreement and wishes to proceed with the change regardless must terminate the original contract lawfully (by giving the required notice) and offer re-employment under a new contract with the change in terms. Since this is a dismissal by the employer it will open up the termination for possible scrutiny in an action for unfair dismissal.

In *Kerry Foods Ltd* v *Lynch* (2005), the employee, who had been given notice of termination of his contract under which he worked a 5-day week together with the offer of a new contract for a 6-day week, resigned before the notice period expired and claimed that he had been constructively dismissed. He argued that there had been a breach of the employer's duty of trust and confidence. The EAT, however, held that the employer had acted legitimately and was not in breach of the duty. The employee, by resigning when he was not justified in doing so, had not therefore been dismissed.

TERMINATION OF THE CONTRACT OF EMPLOYMENT

The way in which a contract of employment terminates can depend on the type of contract it is. At common law, contracts can be divided into four categories depending on how long they are intended to last and when they terminate.

A contract *ad vitam aut culpam* is one which is intended to last for the lifetime of the employee, or until the employee's conduct or competence justifies the employer in terminating the contract.

A contract of employment for a fixed task lasts until the particular task is completed or until the employee's conduct or competence justifies the employer in terminating the contract. The employee is also bound for the period of the fixed task unless justified in resigning by the employer's conduct.

A contract of employment for a fixed period lasts until the agreed period expires, or the employee's conduct or competence justifies the employer in terminating the contract. The employee is also bound for the fixed period unless justified in resigning by the employer's conduct.

Probably the most common form of contract of employment is the periodic contract. Such a contract is automatically renewed, by the principle of tacit relocation, unless one of the parties gives notice to terminate it. It is entered into for an indefinite period. In the Fixed-term Employees (Prevention of Less Favourable Treatment) Regulations 2002, such an employee (with whom fixed-term employees are entitled to compare themselves) is referred to as a "permanent" employee. Although there is no built-in termination, and although it is conceived as permanent, the contract of employment can be terminated by notice by either party.

Termination by notice

Termination by the employer is dismissal; termination by the employee is resignation. Either may terminate the contract by giving the appropriate notice.

Contractual notice

The appropriate notice will be the contractual notice. This may be an express or an implied term. The notice due is one of the particulars which must be included in the written statement due under ERA 1996, s 1.

Statutory minimum notice

ERA 1996, s 86 provides for minimum notice periods. While the parties cannot give shorter notice than that specified, there is nothing to stop them giving longer notice. Once an employee has been in continuous employment for a month he becomes entitled to receive 1 week's notice; after 2 years' continuous employment the entitlement becomes 1 week for every year of employment up to a maximum of 12 weeks' notice.

An employee who has 1 month's continuous employment or more must give 1 week's notice to the employer.

There is provision under ss 87–91 for minimum remuneration during the notice period, which does not apply where the employee is entitled under the contract to notice a week or more longer than the statutory period. In *Scotts Co (UK) Ltd* v *Budd* (2003), an employee who had been off on long-term sick leave had been given, as he was entitled, 13 weeks' notice, a week more than the maximum statutory provision, so these sections did not apply and he was not entitled to be paid during his notice period as he had exhausted his pay entitlement.

Enforcement of the statutory notice provisions is by means of an action for breach of contract, which can be raised in an employment tribunal.

These statutory provisions do not affect the common law right of either party to terminate the contract without notice by reason of the conduct of the other party (s 86(6)).

Reasonable notice

If there is no contractual notice period, under common law the appropriate notice period is "reasonable" notice (which could not be less than the statutory minimum). What is reasonable depends on the circumstances including the post and seniority of the employee. In *Morrison* v *Abernethy School Board* (1876), 3 months was held to be reasonable notice for the employee schoolmaster who had been dismissed without notice and with 15 days' pay. In *Hill* v *C A Parsons Ltd* (1972), 6 months was considered to be reasonable notice for the employee professional engineer who had been dismissed with only 1 month's notice.

Payment in lieu of notice

Instead of notice being given and the employee working out the period of notice, an employer might make a payment "in lieu of notice" (instead of notice). The employee is not required to work for the period of notice. This usually happens by agreement, with an employee accepting that the payment will not require service in return.

Circumstances can arise where it is not in the employee's interests to accept this. In *Morran* v *Glasgow Council of Tenants' Associations* (1998) early termination would mean that the employee did not qualify for unfair dismissal protection where giving the contractual notice of 4 weeks would have allowed him to work for sufficient weeks to qualify. In *Morrish* v *NTL Group Ltd* (2007) termination with payment of wages in lieu of the required 12 months' notice meant that the employee missed out on opportunities for bonus and other rights and suffered a decrease in pension rights. In both cases the employees sued for loss caused by the failure to allow them to work out their notice. In *Morran* no notice had been given and the employee sued not only for the amount of notice but for loss of opportunity to raise an unfair dismissal action. There was a contractual term giving the employers the right to pay wages in lieu of notice. The

Inner House of the Court of Session held that the employee had been wrongfully dismissed but was entitled to no more than the 4 weeks' notice which he should have received. The express term in the contract entitled the employers to require the employee not to work out the notice period. In *Morrish* there was no such contractual term. The Inner House held that the common law did not imply a right to pay wages in lieu into every contract, so that in the absence of such a term the employers did not have the right to require the employee not to work during the notice period. He was therefore entitled to sue for damages for loss caused by the early termination.

Where an employer fails to pay the due amount for notice, the remedy is to sue for breach of contract. There is no independent right to payment. This means that the standard rules regarding damages for breach of contract apply, in particular that compensation is for loss caused, and that the employee must mitigate his loss. In *Hardy* v *Polk (Leeds) Ltd* (2004) an employee who was entitled to 7 weeks' notice was dismissed without notice. She started to work for another employer 4 weeks later. She was successful in her unfair dismissal claim and, along with other compensation, she was awarded 4 weeks' notice. She appealed, arguing that she should have been awarded the full 7 weeks' notice amount. The EAT did not accept her argument and held that since the employers were liable for breach of contract for failing to pay notice, this could only be so far as she had suffered loss. Since she had in fact earned more in her new job than her old one, the only loss she had suffered was during the 4 weeks she was unemployed.

Expiry of term or completion of task

At common law a contract for a fixed period or a fixed task ends when the period or task comes to an end. The contract comes to an end at the expiry of the term, and neither party is required to give notice (*Robson* v *Hawick School Board* (1900)).

This is the common law form of "fixed-term contract". For unfair dismissal and redundancy law, a fixed-term contract also includes a contract which has a fixed end date but can be terminated by notice by either party before the fixed term expires (*Dixon* v *BBC* (1979)). For the purposes of both of these statutory rights, failure to renew a fixed-term contract is a dismissal (ERA 1996, ss 95 and 136).

The Fixed-term Employees (Prevention of Less Favourable Treatment) Regulations 2002 prohibit less favourable treatment of a fixed-term employee than a comparable permanent employee. In these Regulations a fixed-term employee includes someone who is employed under a contract that will normally terminate not only on the expiry of a specific term, but also on the completion of a particular task, or on the occurrence or non-occurrence of a specific event (other than retiring age). By reg 8, a fixed-term employee automatically transfers to a permanent contract after 4 years' continuous employment unless the employer can objectively justify its fixed-term nature when it was entered into or when it was renewed.

Agreement

Employer and employee may agree to end the contract: this is neither a resignation nor a dismissal. This will be considered further in the chapter on unfair dismissal (Chapter 7).

Frustration

Like any contract, a contract of employment may be terminated by the doctrine of frustration. Where it arises, the contract is terminated by operation of law. Under the doctrine a contract is frustrated when it becomes impossible to perform due to an unexpected external event, without either party being at fault. In *Condor* v *Barron Knights* (1966) the drummer of a pop group who was under contract to play for 7 nights a week was dismissed when, after a breakdown in his mental health, he was hospitalised and his doctor told the group that he would suffer a more serious breakdown if he continued to perform for more than 4 nights a week. Mr Condor wanted to continue with the contract, working for 7 nights a week and sued for wrongful dismissal. It was held that his health made it impossible for him to continue under the terms of the contract, which was therefore terminated, not by dismissal, but by frustration.

Ill health alone will not usually frustrate a contract. This is particularly so with a periodic contract which the parties may have expected to carry on indefinitely, since it must have been within their expectation that the employee might have some ill health requiring absence during the contract. Frustration by ill health is therefore not something that the courts readily apply, especially in the case of periodic contracts. There have been a number of cases where the employer has argued that there has been frustration of contract rather than an ill-health dismissal. In *Notcutt* v *Universal Equipment Co (London) Ltd* (1986) a health report on the employee who had been off work because of a coronary stated that he would never be able to work again as a result. When the employer notified Mr Notcutt that his contract was at an end, he raised an action for pay during his notice period. It was held that the contract had terminated because of frustration due to the "total incapacity" of the employee which

was outside the contemplation of the original contract. He was not entitled
to notice or notice pay in such circumstances.

Where the ill health is less catastrophic, it may still be possible to
argue that the contract may be frustrated if it looks as if the employee may
be incapable of work for an extended or indefinite period. In *Marshall* v
Harland & Wolff Ltd (1972) the court held that, in deciding whether the
contract had been frustrated, the following should be taken into account:
the terms of the contract (including the provisions as to sick pay); how long
the employment was likely to last in the absence of sickness; the nature
of the employment (whether the employee is one of many in the same
category or whether he occupies a key post); the nature of the illness or
injury and how long it has already continued and the prospect of recovery;
and the period of past employment. However, the more recent attitude
of the EAT to this issue can be seen in *Williams* v *Watson Luxury Coaches*
(1990) in which it was stated that "the courts must guard against too easy
an application of the doctrine, more especially when redundancy occurs
and also when the true situation may be a dismissal by reason of disability".
If it is found that the contract is frustrated, it takes it out of protection
from unfair dismissal and also removes the right to redundancy pay, since
there has been no dismissal. An employer is entitled in appropriate cases to
dismiss because of ill health, so long as it is reasonable (see Chapter 7).

The doctrine may arise in circumstances other than ill health. In *F C
Shepherd & Co Ltd* v *Jerrom* (1986) the Court of Appeal held that when an
apprentice with 21 months' service was sentenced to between 6 months'
and 2 years' Borstal training for an assault, the sentence frustrated his
4-year contract of apprenticeship. It was held that not all sentences of
imprisonment or equivalent will automatically frustrate a contract of
apprenticeship or employment, but that they could frustrate it, and in this
case did because the interruption to his training (in the event Mr Jerrom
served the minimum term) would leave him less well trained than he
should have been. Being sentenced to imprisonment was the frustrating
event and was therefore without fault on the part of the employee. The
employee's criminal act which led to the sentence was not.

It is central to the doctrine of frustration that the frustrating event
should not have been one contemplated by the parties when the contract
was made. If there is a contractual procedure for dealing with events of that
nature it is unlikely that the doctrine can apply. In *Four Seasons Healthcare
Ltd* v *Maughan* (2005), a mental nurse was suspended without pay for 10
months while charged with assault and bailed not to approach his place of
work where the alleged assault had taken place. He was subsequently found
guilty and sentenced to 2 years' imprisonment. He was successful in suing

for the 10 months' pay due during his period of suspension. It was held that the prison sentence frustrated the contract, but the earlier imposition of the bail conditions had not. There was a contractual dismissal procedure which provided for summary dismissal for verbal or physical abuse to the patients. The employer should have followed its own procedures for dealing with such an allegation.

Death or dissolution

The death of either party, employer or employee, frustrates the contract. The dissolution of a partnership or the winding up of a company will also terminate the contract, but if a business is acquired as a going concern the Transfer of Undertakings (Protection of Employment) Regulations 2006 (TUPE) will operate to transfer the contracts of existing employees to the new employer (TUPE, reg 4), though an employee cannot be forced to transfer if he does not wish to (TUPE, reg 4(7)). (See Chapter 9.)

Acceptance of breach of contract

Where one party materially breaches or repudiates the contract, the other is entitled to terminate the contract without notice. It is a general principle of contract law that material breach by one party gives the other (the innocent party) the right to terminate the contract. It is the action of the innocent party in accepting the breach which terminates the contract, not the breach itself. Thus, where an employee materially breaches a contract of employment and the employer says that the contract is at an end because of the breach, this is a dismissal since it is the "acceptance" of the breach by the employer which has ended the contract. The employer cannot argue that it is the breach by the employee which terminated the contract, since the party not in breach does not have to exercise the right to end the contract. In *London Transport Executive* v *Clarke* (1981) the employer's argument that the employee had ended the contract by taking 7 weeks' unauthorised leave was rejected. It was the employer's acceptance of the employee's breach which had ended the contract. However, the Court of Appeal went on to find that the employer's termination was fair.

REMEDIES FOR BREACH OF THE CONTRACT OF EMPLOYMENT

Specific implement/interdict

The contract of employment involves a personal relationship, so neither employee nor employer can be compelled to adhere to it.

Therefore an action of specific implement is not competent either to compel the employee to work or the employer to continue employing the employee. This common law rule is reinforced by TULR(C)A 1992, s 236, which provides that it is not competent for a court to order specific implement or interdict which compels an employee to work, or attend any place to carry out work. This is also the case where an employee is successful in winning an unfair dismissal case: a tribunal may order re-employment by the employer but if the employer refuses the only remedy is additional compensation (see Chapter 7). The prohibition against an interdict applies where it would effectively compel the employee to work for the employer or be completely idle (*Page One Records Ltd* v *Britton* (1968)).

There are, however, some circumstances in which it may be possible to obtain an interdict. An employer may be able to obtain an interdict to prohibit an employee working for another in breach of an express or implied contractual term. Such an order would only be granted if the employer is prepared to comply with its side of the contract, and the order is necessary to protect the employer's legitimate interests. Protection against competition from the employee is not legitimate, but protection from the danger of disclosure of confidential information or of attracting customers from the employer is legitimate. A requirement by an employer for an employee to continue in employment but remain at home and not work is often called "garden leave". It occurs usually where an employee wishes to leave before the end of the contractual notice period to work for a competitor. It is at the court's discretion whether to grant it. In *Provident Financial Group Ltd* v *Hayward* (1989) an injunction (the English equivalent of an interdict) was refused where an employee who had been placed on garden leave for the period of his 6 months' contractual notice left to work for a competitor after 2 months. Although it could have been ordered since the employee was in breach of contract, nevertheless there was no real prospect of serious damage to the employer. On the other hand, in *GFI Group* v *Eaglestone* (1994) an injunction was granted because there was a real prospect of loss, albeit the court did not feel that the full extent of the notice period was necessary for protection, restricting the injunction to 13 weeks instead of 20.

An employee might be able to obtain an interdict against an employer in order to postpone a contractually improper dismissal, for example where the employer dismissed the employee without going through the contractual procedure. This would only be granted if the employee still retained the confidence of the employer: if the element of trust and confidence had gone the interdict would not be awarded. This approach was developed in a series of cases in the English courts. In *Anderson* v *Pringle of Scotland Ltd* (1998) the Court of Session followed this practice first developed in England when it ordered an interdict to prevent the employer declaring redundancies on anything other than the contractually agreed "last in first out" basis. There was no lack of trust and confidence in the employee. In *Peace* v *City of Edinburgh Council* (1999) an interdict was granted to prevent the dismissal of a teacher using non-contractual disciplinary procedures instead of the contractual ones. The court was prepared to grant this because it was enforcing the term of a contract and was not challenging his suspension pending investigation, nor dismissal itself.

Damages for wrongful dismissal

Wrongful dismissal is the term used at common law to describe a dismissal without notice which is not justified. An employee who is dismissed in such circumstances is entitled to raise a common law action for wrongful dismissal.

Dismissal without notice is called summary dismissal, and is justified only when the employee is in material breach of contract. Not every breach of contract will justify summary dismissal, therefore. The breach must be material or repudiatory: that is, serious enough to show that the employee does not intend to be bound by the contract.

The measure of damages for wrongful dismissal will be calculated in the usual way for breach of contract, and will be sufficient to restore the employee to the position he would have been in but for the wrongful dismissal. Since the employer would have been entitled to dismiss with notice, compensation is often restricted to the amount due for notice, as it was in *Morran* v *Glasgow Council of Tenants' Associations* (1998). There have been cases in England in which damages have been awarded where a dismissal has been in breach of a contractual procedure and compensation awarded for the additional time it would have taken if it had been procedurally correct. In *Gunton* v *London Borough of Richmond* (1980) a college registrar was summarily dismissed without the contractual dismissal procedure having been followed. He was unsuccessful in having his dismissal declared void, but he was awarded damages for the loss he had suffered during the notional month that it would have taken for the contractual procedure to have been followed. The Scottish courts have followed the English approach in relation to interdicts/injunctions so that it is likely this related approach to damages would also be followed.

Withholding wages

If an employee refuses to carry out a significant part of their employment duties, this is a repudiation of contract, which would entitle the employer to terminate it. If the employer does not terminate it, the employer is entitled to withhold wages. This is an issue that will frequently arise where an employee is taking strike action. Where an employee does not work as part of strike action, no wages are due for the period during which the employee was in breach of contract by refusing to work. In a case where the employee is absent from work altogether, the amount of wages the employer is entitled to deduct is a day's pay for each strike day and not, as the employer sought to argue in *Cooper* v *Isle of Wight College* (2008), the actual loss to the employer. The employer had wished to calculate a day's pay leaving out of account not only weekends when the employee did not work and which it was agreed should be discounted, but also the employee's paid holidays.

The situation is more complicated when an employee takes industrial action which does not involve a complete refusal to work but instead a refusal to do certain duties. Where the refusal amounts to a material breach, the employer is again entitled to terminate the contract without notice. If the employer does not terminate the contract, it is not obliged to accept partial performance and pay for it: the employer is entitled to refuse to allow the employee to work at all, in effect to suspend the employee without pay. In *Laurie* v *British Steel Company* (1988) employees who refused to perform all of their normal work due to a dispute were suspended without pay after being warned that this would be the result. The Lord Ordinary refused to order payment of their wages since there had been a material breach of contract in the refusal to work normally. The argument that the employer must either accept the breach and terminate the contract or comply with the obligation to pay wages was not accepted. The employees could not insist on their wages when they were not prepared to work under the contract.

If the employer decides not to pay wages, it must have told the employee that partial performance will not be accepted. In *Wiluszynski* v *London Borough of Tower Hamlets* (1989) a housing officer took industrial action which involved non-co-operation in certain parts of his work. It was a small but important part of his duties. He worked throughout the 5 weeks of the dispute. On each day his line manager read to him a statement that the employer was not prepared to accept partial performance and that he would not be paid. He was not paid for the 5 weeks during which he worked applying the non-co-operation policy.

It was held that the employer had made clear its refusal to accept partial performance and therefore had no duty to pay him. If the employer accepts partial performance by, for example, saying nothing while the employee works in breach of contract, there is no right to withhold wages. However, if an employer accepts partial performance from an employee but makes it clear that there will be no payment in respect of the non-performance, the employer may be able to withhold part of the wages. In *Miles* v *Wakefield Metropolitan District Council* (1987) the House of Lords held that the employer was entitled to deduct the proportion of wages due to a Registrar of Births, Deaths and Marriages who, as part of industrial action, refused to perform marriages on a Saturday. The employer had advised him that if he was not prepared to work normally on a Saturday he should not attend at all. The deduction of 3/37ths of a wage, representing the Saturday hours as a proportion of total hours, was upheld.

Unlawful deductions from wages

Where an employer fails to pay what is contractually due, there is a procedure under ERA 1996, Pt II for raising an action for unlawful deductions in an ET. This procedure is available to an employee who believes that the employer has, in breach of contract, paid an insufficient amount. Many cases, including many considered in this and the preceding chapters, have been brought under this procedure, where the tribunal has had to establish the terms of the contract and apply the common law principles to the case.

This procedure is appropriate both where the employer has consciously made a deduction from wages, and also where the employer is simply in breach of contract in failure to pay or in the amount paid. In the former case a deduction is lawful only where it is required or authorised by statute or the contract of employment, or the worker has given prior agreement in writing to such a deduction (ERA 1996, s 13). The provisions governing deductions from wages will be considered along with other statutory provisions in the following chapter.

Essential Facts

- Minimum notice periods are set out in the Employment Rights Act 1996, Pt IX.

- The procedure for raising an action for unlawful deduction from wages is set out in the Employment Rights Act 1996, Pt II.

- No remedy of specific implement or interdict is available to compel adherence to a contract of employment: Trade Union and Labour Relations (Consolidation) Act 1992, s 236.

- Fixed-term workers are protected from discrimination by virtue of the Fixed-term Employees (Prevention of Less Favourable Treatment) Regulations 2002.

Essential Cases

Jones v Associated Tunnelling Co Ltd (1981): in this case, while the EAT found against the employee and held that there was an implied term allowing the employers to require him to move workplace, it emphasised that the contract cannot be varied without agreement. Simply issuing a fresh written statement will not in itself vary the contract. Failure to object to a new written statement will in particular not imply acceptance if the change relates to a matter which does not have immediate practical effect.

Williams v Watson Luxury Coaches Ltd (1990): an employee who was off work due to ill health for over 6 months was told her contract of employment was frustrated when she tried to return to work. The EAT reviewed the principles by which a contract could be frustrated and warned against too easy an application of the doctrine, especially when redundancy occurs.

London Transport Executive v Clarke (1981): the employer argued that an employee who was in material breach of contract when he returned late from holiday had terminated the contract. The Court of Appeal held that it was the acceptance by the employer of the employee's repudiation of the contract which ended it, and not the breach by the employee.

Anderson v Pringle of Scotland Ltd (1998): an employee obtained an interdict to stop the employer implementing a redundancy procedure which was different from the procedure which had been incorporated into his contract of employment.

Laurie v British Steel Corporation (1988): employees who refused to work as normal due to a dispute were unsuccessful in an action to be paid for the work they had done. The Outer House of the Court of Session held that the employees could not enforce payment of wages where they were refusing to work normally.

5 TERMS AND CONDITIONS

Previous chapters have been primarily concerned with the contract of employment and its common law basis. This chapter turns to statutory provisions affecting employment rights. It will focus primarily on provisions dealing with the basic issues of pay and working time. The national minimum wage and working time legislation lay a baseline for minimum pay and maximum hours. These, together with other rights affecting pay and working time, will be considered.

WAGES

National minimum wage

There had been minimum wage legislation since the beginning of the 20th century, but that applied only to specific low pay sectors of the economy through Wages Councils, which were abolished between 1986 and 1993. The National Minimum Wage Act 1998 (NMWA 1998) introduced a national minimum wage (NMW) applying to all sectors, supplemented by the National Minimum Wage Regulations 1999 (NMWR 1999).

Qualification

Although it is a national standard, not every working person is entitled to the NMW. To qualify, the individual must be over compulsory school age, must be working in the UK and must be a "worker" (NMWA 1998, ss 1 and 54). In addition to those employed either as an employee or as a worker, the Act also applies to agency workers, homeworkers and Crown employees even if they are not otherwise workers (ss 34–36). However, a number of categories of workers do not benefit. Certain classes of people have been excluded by NMWR 1999, including apprentices (for the first year), workers on certain government training schemes, students on work placement for less than a year, and workers on schemes for homeless people or those on income support who are provided with shelter in return for work (reg 2). Further exclusions include voluntary workers for charities and voluntary organisations, prisoners, members of the armed forces and people living as part of a family (NMWA 1998, ss 37–44; NMWR 1999, reg 2).

The Act gives the Secretary of State power to add to the list of those who are excluded, but qualifies that by stating that any exclusions cannot be made on the basis of different areas; different sectors of employment;

undertakings of different sizes; different ages over 26; or different occupations (s 4). To that extent it is a national minimum wage.

Rate of NMW

There is a single hourly NMW (NMWR 1999, reg 11). Although this is the headline rate, there are in fact two additional lower rates which apply to younger workers. The Act permits differentials up to the age of 26 (s 4), but entitlement to the full NMW currently starts at 22. The existence of differential rates for the NMW is an exception to the Employment Equality (Age) Regulations 2006 (reg 27) (Equality Act 2010, Sch 9, para 11). The current rates are as follows: for those aged 22 and over (the "single hourly rate of the national minimum wage") £5.93; for those aged between 18 and 21, £4.92; for those aged 16 and 17 (but not apprentices), £3.64.

The rate is set by the Secretary of State on the advice of the Low Pay Commission, an independent statutory public body. It is reviewed annually and any increases usually occur in October.

Calculation of the rate

To calculate whether the NMW has been paid, a worker's hourly rate is calculated by dividing the total remuneration (TR) received by the worker during the pay reference period (PRP), less certain reductions, by the number of hours of work during that period (NHW) (reg 14). This can be expressed as (TR in PRP)/NHW must be no less than NMW. The NMWR 1999 contain detailed provision as to calculation of all of these elements. Only an outline of the broad principles involved is given here.

Total remuneration This is determined by adding together all money payments paid by the employer to the worker in and relating to the PRP in question whether paid in that PRP or the subsequent one (reg 30). This does not include any advance of wages, any pension, any redundancy pay, any tribunal award or any award under a suggestion scheme (reg 8). Nor does it include any payment in kind with the exception of the provision of accommodation (reg 9). Certain payments are deducted from the total, including payment made when the employee was absent from work or engaged in industrial action, payment relating to an earlier PRP, overtime or shift premiums, allowances other than an allowance attributable to the worker's performance carrying out the work, and any tips or gratuities paid by customers (reg 31). Until October 2009, if customer tips were administered by the employer and paid through the payroll they could be attributed by the employer to the NMW. However, in order to stop employers using customer tips in this way, the law was amended so that all tips, however administered, cannot count. Allowances are defined as payments attributable to a particular aspect of the worker's working arrangements which is not consolidated into his standard pay (reg 2). The EAT in *Smith v Oxfordshire Learning Disability Trust* (2009) held that a "sleep-in" payment paid to an employee in addition to his basic salary as a flat rate for sleeping overnight was not an allowance since it was not separate from his work. They distinguished between that and an additional payment to which the employee would be entitled if he had a disturbed night (which he had never had), which would be an allowance and deductable.

Pay reference period   The PRP is one month, or, if pay is paid by reference to a period of less than a month, that period (reg 10). Therefore, while the PRP for monthly workers is one month, the PRP for weekly paid workers would be one week, and so on.

Number of hours of work   How the hours of work are determined depends on the category of work, whether it is time work, salaried hours work, output work or measured hours work. These categories only refer to the way in which pay is calculated: they do not relate to the type of work the worker carries out. The NMWR 1999 explain how the hours are to be calculated for each category of work.

Time work   This is work paid for on the basis of the time worked (reg 3). The time work is the number of hours worked in the PRP in question (reg 20). A worker who is "on call", that is available to do time work when required at or near the place of work is engaged in work unless the worker's home is at or near the place of work and he is entitled to spend the time at home (reg 15(1)). If the worker is provided with somewhere to sleep by the employer at or near the place of work, time spent there will only be time work when he is awake for the purpose of working (reg 15(1A)). These provisions come into operation only when the worker is not required to work during the "on call" periods. If, for example, he is expected to be ready to respond to emergencies on the spot, in effect the worker is on duty, even although permitted to sleep for part of this period, and the whole time will count as time work. In *Wright* v *Scottbridge Construction Ltd* (2003) a nightwatchman who was employed 7 nights a week from 5 pm to 7 am claimed that he was not being paid the NMW since his pay divided by the hours he worked was lower. The employer argued that only hours when he was actually awake should be taken into consideration. The Inner House of the Court of Session held that since he had to be ready throughout the whole period to respond to circumstances he was paid for the whole period and accordingly was entitled to the NMW for all of the hours worked. The EAT confirmed that the amendment of NMWR 1999 to introduce reg 15(1A) had not altered the basic definition of time work, holding in *Burrow Down Support Services Ltd* v *Rossiter* (2008) that a night-sleeper in a care home who was required to respond to emergencies during the night but could otherwise sleep was working throughout the period. The provisions of reg 15 came into play only when the worker was not actually required to work but simply to be available in case he was required to work.

Salaried hours work   In this category the worker is entitled to be paid an annual salary for working certain basic hours in the year, with the salary being paid at weekly or monthly intervals regardless of the amount of work done in each period, and with no additional payment for these hours, apart from a performance bonus (reg 4). The hours in this case would be basic hours plus any additional hours worked for which the worker was paid divided by 12 if the PRP is a month, or 52 if it is a week, and so forth (reg 21). There are similar provisions to time work in relation to "on call" hours (reg 16).

Output work   This form of work is often called "piece work". This is work where payment is not based on time but on what is produced or processed, or some other measure of output such as sales (reg 5). The output work will be the number of hours spent by the worker in the PRP to produce the pieces or perform the tasks (reg 22). Alternatively, the employer may decide to pay not on actual hours but according to "rated output work". The employer must conduct tests to find the mean hourly rate at which the objects etc are produced, and must give written notice of the rate (regs 24–25). The number of hours worked by the worker to produce the objects will be taken to be 120 per cent of the number of hours someone working at the mean hourly rate would have taken (reg 26). This means that someone who works a little slower than the mean hourly rate will still earn the NMW.

Measured hours work   This is work which is none of the previous three, and includes work where there are no specified hours and the worker is required to work when needed or when work is available (reg 6). The hours of work will be the actual number worked in the PRP, unless there is a daily average agreement (reg 27). This is a written agreement, agreed before the start of the PRP by which the employer and worker agree the average number of daily hours the worker is likely to spend on contractual duties (reg 28).

Enforcement

Employers are required to keep records where they employ anyone who qualifies to be paid the NMW sufficient to show that the NMW is being paid and keeping records of any relevant agreements made (reg 38). Workers have the right of access to these records under a statutory procedure (NMWA 1998, s 10), and may complain to a tribunal if the employer fails to comply (s 11).

The NMW is enforceable as a contractual right by the individual worker. Any worker who is paid less than the NMW is contractually entitled to be paid the difference between his wage and the NMW (s 17). This can be done by an action under Pt II of ERA 1996 (see below), and those workers who would not qualify as workers under that Act but do under NMWA 1998 are given the right to use this process (s 18).

In addition to enforcement by the individual worker, HM Revenue and Customs has enforcement powers. Where an officer believes that an employer has not paid the NMW he may serve a notice of underpayment requiring payment of the outstanding amount within 28 days (s 19). The notice must also require the employer to pay a financial penalty to the Secretary of State within the 28 days, of 50 per cent of the total amount of underpayment in respect of all workers, subject to a minimum of £1,000 and a maximum of £5,000 (s 19A). The Act also creates a number of criminal offences where an employer wilfully fails to comply with the Act either in respect of paying the NMW or in complying with the records provisions or co-operating with enforcement (s 31).

Sick pay

There may be a contractual term, either express or implied, providing for payment of wages while absent due to ill health. The contract may provide for full pay, or part pay, for all or part of the duration of the absence. The written statement must state any terms relating to incapacity for work due to sickness or injury, including any provision as to sick pay. There does not have to be a contractual provision for sick pay, and if there is none the written statement must say so.

Statutory sick pay

Although there may not be a right to contractual sick pay, there is, however, a right to statutory sick pay (SSP) under the Social Security Contributions and Benefits Act 1992 (SSCBA 1992) and the Statutory Sick Pay (General)

Regulations 1982 (SSP(G)R 1982) (as amended). An employee whose pay is at least the lower earnings limit for National Insurance contributions (currently £95 per week) can claim SSP from his employer when sick and incapable of work. SSP is not due for the first 3 days of a period of sickness, but is due from 4 days. A 4-day period of sickness is a "period of incapacity for work". If there is a break between periods of incapacity for work of less than 8 weeks the periods make one "linked" period of incapacity for work (and therefore the 3-day qualification period is not necessary in the subsequent periods). SSP is payable for a maximum period of 28 weeks for any one period of entitlement (including linked periods of incapacity for work), with the maximum period of entitlement being 3 years. SSP is payable at a flat rate (currently £79.15) and does not depend on the level of pay.

When SSP was introduced the employer was able to recover what was paid out in SSP by receiving a rebate on national insurance contributions. In 1994 this ended and only employers who have several people off sick at one time are able to obtain a rebate. An employer can recover the amount of SSP paid in a month which is more than 13 per cent of its total national insurance contributions in that month (the "percentage threshold scheme").

The employee or an agent must notify the employer that he is unfit to work. SSP(G)R 1982 allows the employer to set a time limit for notification, so long as it is not earlier than the first qualifying day and so long as reasonable publicity is given to it. Otherwise, it must be given within 7 days, with a possible extension of between a month and 90 days if good cause is shown. The employer may specify a procedure for notification for SSP purposes but this cannot require that the notice is given personally, or in the form of medical evidence, or more than once every 7 days, or on a document supplied by the employer or on a printed form (SSP(G)R 1982, reg 7,).

Any agreement to exclude payment of SSP is void, as is any agreement for an employee to make a contribution towards it (SSCBA 1992, s 151). Where an employee is entitled to contractual sick pay, payment of SSP discharges the contractual pay for that amount, and vice versa (SSCBA 1992, Sch 2, para 2). Whatever the terms of the contract, the payment received by the employee from the employer cannot be less than the amount due for SSP. An employer cannot terminate a contract of employment in order to avoid paying SSP. If an employer does so, entitlement to SSP continues as long as it would have continued if the employee was still employed by the employer (SSP(G)R 1982, reg 4).

Deductions from wages

At common law it was open to the parties to agree contractual terms which might regulate the right of an employer to deduct money from the wages due to an employee or worker. As a result of widespread use of this by early capitalists – for example, by requiring workers to spend their money in company shops or to accept payment in kind as wages – deductions from wages were regulated by statute from the early 19th century. These were the Truck Acts (1831–96), which applied to manual workers only and provided that they must be paid in cash, and also gave protection against certain deductions from wages including for "fines". The application of the Truck Acts lasted until the passing of the Wages Act 1986 when the distinction between manual and other workers was ended. The relevant legislation is now the ERA 1996, Pt II. The Truck Acts were repealed: the law applies to all workers, manual or otherwise, and not just employees; it permits cashless pay; and it prohibits unauthorised deductions. While the provisions in the Truck Acts constrained the nature of the deductions which an employer could make, including a requirement of reasonableness, the law now only requires authorisation of deduction and does not regulate the nature of the right to make a deduction.

Deductions from wages can only be made by an employer as permitted by ERA 1996, Pt II. They can only be made if they have been authorised in one of three ways (s 13). First, a deduction may be authorised by a statutory provision, such as deduction of tax or national insurance contributions. Second, it may be authorised by a provision in the worker's contract. In this case the provision must be either a written term in the contract of which the worker has been given a copy before the deduction in question is made; or an express or implied term (if express, either oral or written) of which the employee has been given written notice (including both existence and effect of the term), again in advance of the deduction in question being made. Thus there must be both contractual agreement and written notice. Third, the worker may have previously signified agreement in writing to the making of a deduction.

If the authorisation is based on a contractual term it is not necessary for the worker to have given written consent separately, but it is necessary for the worker to be given notice individually. In *Kerr* v *The Sweater Shop (Scotland) Ltd* (1996) the employer refused to pay the employee his holiday pay when he was dismissed for gross misconduct, claiming that this was authorised by a change to the company rules (a variation of contract) which had been intimated to all employees by a notice on the company notice board. The EAT held that, although there was a contractual term permitting deduction in these circumstances, there had not been proper notification since the Act required individual notice.

If there is a contractual variation to permit deductions, or if the worker agrees in writing to deductions, this does not authorise any deductions relating to the conduct of the worker or any other event which occurred previous to the variation or agreement. In *Discount Tobacco & Confectionery Ltd v Williamson* (1993) stocktaking in March revealed deficiencies of over £3,000 and the employee signed an agreement giving the employers permission to deduct £3,500 from his wages over 175 weeks. When more deficiencies were revealed in the May stocktaking he was dismissed and the employers withheld all money due to him to set off against the deductions. The EAT held that since the written agreement was made after the stocktaking deficiencies which the deductions related to, it was ineffective. They pointed out that the purpose of the provision was to prevent employers putting undue pressure on workers to agree to deductions, and thus it was necessary for any consent to be given in principle before the source of the deductions occurred.

For the purposes of this part of the Act, ERA 1996, s 27 defines "wages" as any sum payable to the worker in connection with his employment, including any fee, bonus, commission, holiday pay or other emolument referable to the employment, whether payable under the contract or otherwise, and vouchers which have a fixed monetary value and can be exchanged for money, goods or services. It is specifically stated (s 27(3)) that where payment is made of a non-contractual bonus it is to be treated as wages. The argument that such a bonus only became wages once it was paid has been rejected by the EAT. In *Farrell Matthews & Weir v Hansen* (2005) the employer told the employee that she was to receive a discretionary bonus, but refused to pay the outstanding balance due when she resigned due to the employer's breach of contract. The EAT held that this amounted to an unlawful deduction of wages. In the case of a non-contractual discretionary bonus as in this case, until the bonus is declared no bonus is payable, but once it has been declared there is a legal obligation to pay it.

Also included in the statutory definition of wages are statutory sick pay, statutory maternity pay, statutory paternity pay, statutory adoption pay, guarantee pay, payment for time off under statutory rights, payments on suspension on medical grounds and certain payments ordered by employment tribunals. Specifically excluded from the definition are advances under an agreement for a loan, expenses incurred by the worker in carrying out employment, pensions or any allowance in connection with retirement or loss of office, payment in connection with redundancy, or any payment other than in the worker's capacity as worker. In *London Borough of Southwark* v *O'Brien* (1996) a car allowance paid to a trade union organiser by the employer, which the employer subsequently stopped paying, was held not to be wages as it was for expenses in connection with employment. Any dispute about non-payment of these would have to be dealt with under the common law, and could only be taken to an ET if employment has ended. Otherwise an action would have to be raised in the sheriff court.

Unauthorised deductions from wages are the stated subject matter of these provisions but this includes non-payment. The latter is not expressly referred to in the legislation, and over-literal interpretation of the word "deduction" initially led to the view that total non-payment would not be covered as deduction implied partial payment. The Court of Appeal rejected this view in *Delaney* v *Staples (t/a De Montfort Recruitment)* (1992). If the deduction is total and results in a failure or refusal to pay anything, the provisions of Pt II of ERA 1996 apply.

Retail transactions

As well as the general protection against unauthorised deductions, retail workers have additional protection. Because they hand over stock and receive money from customers on behalf of the employer, problems are more likely to arise in relation to stock deficiencies and cash shortages. The additional protection applies not just to those who work in the retail sector, but to workers who carry out a retail function, whether or not they do so on a regular basis. Retail employment means the carrying out of "retail transactions" (the supply of goods and services) directly with members of the public or with fellow workers or other individuals personally, or the collection of money in connection with such transactions (ERA 1996, s 17).

The first additional protection concerns the form and timing of any deduction arising from cash shortages or stock deficiencies. Any deduction must be made within 12 months of the employer establishing the need to make the deduction. If there is to be a series of deductions the first must be made within the 12-month period (ERA 1996, s 18). If the employer seeks to recover money not by deduction but through a payment from the worker, the general provisions relating to authorisation of deductions apply to this method, and in addition the worker must be notified in writing of the total liability for the cash shortage or stock deficiency. The employer must issue a written demand for payment, the demand being issued on a pay day, which must occur after the notification but before the end of the 12-month period (ERA 1996, s 20).

The second additional protection concerns the amount of any deduction. The amount must not exceed one-tenth of the total amount of wages payable to the worker on the pay day in question, except in the case of a final instalment of wages (ERA 1996, ss 18 and 20). Deductions may therefore have to be made in instalments.

Suspension on medical grounds

As previously discussed, an employer cannot suspend an employee without pay unless there is a contractual term to that effect. There are circumstances in which health and safety legislation may require that an employee does not do particular work because of exposure to risk. In such a case it might be argued that the operation of the contract has been frustrated under the principles discussed in Chapter 4. ERA 1996, s 64 provides for a right to suspension with pay in these circumstances for up to 26 weeks. The right arises when the employee is suspended because of a requirement under particular statutes or a recommendation in a Code of Practice issued under s 16 of the Health and Safety at Work etc Act 1974 (HSWA 1974). These are specified in s 64 and the list can be added to by the Secretary of State. They are: Control of Lead at Work Regulations 1980, reg 16; Ionising Radiations Regulations 1999, reg 24; and Control of Substances Hazardous to Health Regulations 1988, reg 11.

This is a preventive measure, designed to stop employees becoming ill as a result of exposure to the processes involved. If the employee is ill, whether as a result of the processes or otherwise, this right does not apply (ERA 1996, s 85). He would fall to be treated under any sick pay arrangements, contractual or statutory.

Similarly, if the employer offers suitable alternative work during the necessary period of suspension, whether or not it is work which the employee was contracted to perform, the employee will lose the right if he unreasonably refuses to perform that work. This is also the case if the employee does not comply with any reasonable requirements imposed by the employer to ensure the availability of his services (s 85).

To qualify for the right the employee must have worked continuously for a month for the employer. The amount of pay to be received is a week's pay, up to a maximum of 26 weeks. Any contractual arrangements will still apply, and payments under the contract will be set off against payments due under the statutory arrangements and vice versa (s 69). This right can be enforced by making a claim to an employment tribunal within 3 months (s 70).

Guarantee pay

If an employer has no work for his employees to do, but considers this to be seasonal or otherwise temporary, rather than terminate employment the employer may decide to lay them off. There may be a contractual entitlement to a certain amount of guaranteed pay, or there may be a contractual entitlement on the part of the employer to lay off in particular circumstances without pay. In some industries there are collective agreements (incorporated into contracts of employment) governing this. If an employee is laid off without pay there is an entitlement to a statutory guarantee payment under ERA 1996, s 28.

An employee who has worked for a month for the employer is entitled to receive payment for any "workless day", that is a day during which the employee would normally be required to work but where there is no work because of a diminution in the requirements of the business for the work the employee does or any other occurrence affecting the normal working of the business in relation to the work. There is no entitlement if the situation is caused by a strike or other industrial action, nor if the employer has offered suitable alternative employment and the employee has unreasonably refused, nor if the employee has refused to comply with a reasonable requirement imposed with a view to making sure his services are available (s 29).

Guarantee payment is due on the basis of the employee's normal hourly rate for each workless day (s 30). However, there is a cap on the daily rate, with a prescribed maximum (currently £21.20). There is also a cap on the number of days, with a maximum entitlement of 5 days in a 3-month period (s 31). The right can be enforced by making a claim to an ET within 3 months (s 34).

An entitlement to contractual guarantee pay can also be enforced. In *Davies v Hotpoint Ltd* (1994) a collective agreement (which was incorporated into contracts of employment) provided for payment for a guaranteed 39-hour week, and also permitted short-time working if "approved". When the employer felt that short-time working was necessary, the trade union did not agree. The employer introduced short-time working and refused to pay the guaranteed 39 hours. It was held that approval by the union was necessary to effect approval of short-time working: the employer could not unilaterally vary the arrangement. The failure to pay the guaranteed 39 hours was therefore an unlawful deduction from wages.

Payments of contractual guarantee pay are set off against any entitlement to statutory guaranteed pay and vice versa. (s 32). In *Cartwright v G Clancey Ltd* (1983) the employee had already received 5 days' guaranteed pay under the government short-term working scheme within the previous 3 months. His claim for statutory guarantee payment for a further 4 workless days was refused since he had already received the maximum payment from his employer.

WORKING HOURS

Working Time Directive

The EC Working Time Directive 93/104 (WTD) was passed as a health and safety measure under the EC Health and Safety Framework Directive 89/391. The WTD is intended to lay down minimum safety and health requirements for the organisation of working time. It provides for rights to minimum periods of daily and weekly rest, rest breaks and paid holidays, introduces special provision for night workers and establishes the maximum working week. The scope of the WTD was extended in 2000 to cover workers previously excluded, including non-mobile works connected with road and sea, junior doctors, rail and offshore workers and aviation workers not covered by a dedicated Directive. Road transport, aviation and seafarer workers have their own Directives.

The original UK Working Time Regulations had to be amended as a result of a decision by the ECJ in *R v Secretary of State for Trade and Industry, ex parte BECTU* (2001) that a requirement for a 13-week qualification period for holiday pay did not comply with the Directive. However, it was held in *Gibson v East Riding of Yorkshire Council* (2000) that Art 7 of the Directive was not directly effective and so could not be relied on by a Council employee to claim paid holiday leave before the UK Regulations became effective. More recently the relevant government department (currently Department for Business, Innovation and Skills (DBIS)) had to amend its guidance to employers as to the taking of rest breaks. In *Commission of the EU v UK* (2006) the ECJ held that the UK did not comply with the WTD since the then guidance about rest breaks said that "employers must make sure that workers can take their rest, but are not required to make sure they do take their rest". As a result, the second half of the quoted sentence has been removed from the guidelines.

Working Time Regulations

The Working Time Regulations 1998 (WTR 1998) were introduced to comply with the WTD and, when the WTD was extended in 2000, the WTR 1998 were subsequently amended to comply. (Unless otherwise stated, the following references are to provisions of WTR 1998.) Following the scope for derogation in the Directive, many of the provisions of the

WTR 1998 can be varied so long as the employer obtains a "relevant agreement": in some cases a collective agreement or workforce agreement; in others individual agreement. Contracting out of the obligations under the WTR 1998, other than as expressly allowed, is void (reg 35). As will be noted below, the only part of the WTR 1998 (or WTD) which permits contracting out is in relation to maximum weekly working time. There are also exclusions or variations. For example, reg 21 excludes a number of "special cases" from the operation of the regulations governing night working, daily rest and rest breaks. These include offshore work, security work and situations where continuous service or production is required in specified work such as hospitals, the press, urban transport, or where there is a seasonal "surge" in areas such as tourism. Where the exclusions apply the employer is obliged wherever possible to allow an equivalent period of compensatory rest and, exceptionally, if that is not possible, to take appropriate steps to safeguard the worker's health (reg 24). Here the broad rules will be considered rather than the detailed provisions.

The WTR 1998 lays down minimum terms, and greater protection may be provided by agreement. Like the NMWA 1998, the WTR 1998 apply to workers, not just employees.

Working time

Working time is defined as any period during which a worker is working at the employer's disposal and carrying out his activities or duties. This includes time when receiving training related to work, and any other time agreed under a "relevant agreement" (reg 2). On-call time, where a worker is on call and during the on-call period is required to be present at a place determined by the employer, counts as working time, even if the worker is permitted to sleep. So held the ECJ in *Landeshauptstadt Kiel v Jaeger* (2003) in the case of a doctor who was required to be on call at a place determined by the employer, and was involved in working time for the whole period he was on call, including the period he was asleep. The EAT similarly held in *MacCartney v Oversley House Management* (2006) that a resident manager worker who was required to be on duty for 24 hours in the accommodation provided by the employer and was required to respond to emergencies, was involved in working time throughout the whole period. She had therefore been deprived of her entitlement to rest breaks.

Maximum weekly working time

The maximum weekly number of working time hours is 48 hours in each 7 days, including overtime (regs 4–5). This is calculated not on a weekly basis but as an average over a reference period. The basic reference period is 17 weeks; special classes of worker (such as seasonal workers) have a 26-week reference period; and a reference period of up to 52 weeks could be agreed by a collective or workforce agreement. For young workers, that is those over compulsory school age but under 18, the maximum working time is 8 hours a day and 40 hours a week, aggregating hours worked for more than one employer (reg 5A). It is the employer's duty to take reasonable steps to ensure that each worker complies with this limit.

Individual opt-out   Unlike many other EU countries, the UK has included a provision whereby the employer can obtain a worker's agreement in writing so that the 48-hour limit does not apply. The reference period may be varied by collective or workforce agreement, but the complete opt-out from the limit requires the individual worker's written agreement (reg 4). The EU has been attempting to restrict the use of this opt-out, but, in spite of the health and safety arguments, the UK Government has continued to argue for the retention of this flexibility.

Daily and weekly rest

Adult workers are entitled to at least 11 hours' consecutive rest in each 24-hour period; young workers to 12 hours (reg 10). Adult workers are entitled to an uninterrupted weekly rest period of at least 24 hours in each 7-day period; young workers to 48 hours (reg 11).

Rest break

An adult worker is entitled to a minimum of 20 minutes' break where more than 6 hours a day are worked; a young worker to a minimum of 30 minutes for over 4.5 hours (reg 12). For monotonous or other work patterns that might put health and safety at risk, rest breaks must be "adequate" (reg 8). This could be no less than the minimum periods otherwise specified and is likely to be greater.

The requirement is for one 20-minute break where more than 6 hours are worked, no matter how far over 6 hours the working time is. If one of the reg 21 exclusions applies, under reg 24 the employer must provide an equivalent period of compensatory rest, or exceptionally, if not possible, give protection to safeguard the worker's health. In *Corps of Commissionaires Management Ltd* v *Hughes* (2009) the EAT confirmed that the entitlement was to only one 20-minute rest break and went on to consider how reg 24 should apply when it was not possible to give a compensatory rest break.

Night working

A night worker is someone who normally works at least 3 hours at night, night being 11 pm to 6 am unless agreed otherwise by a collective or workforce agreement (but the period must include midnight to 5 am) (reg 2).

A night worker's normal hours of work cannot exceed an average of 8 hours for each 24 hours, calculated either according to the 17-week reference period, or for workers involved in special hazards or heavy mental or physical strain their actual working hours cannot exceed 8 in any 24-hour period (reg 6). Workers cannot be required to work at night without having had the opportunity to undergo a free health assessment, and should have regular assessments. There is a right to be transferred to day work if certified by a doctor that it is necessary (reg 7).

An employer must ensure that young workers do not work during the "restricted period", that is 10 pm to 6 am (or 11 pm to 7 am, according to contract) (reg 6A).

Holidays

The WTR 1998 provide for a minimum of 4 weeks' paid annual leave (reg 16) and an additional leave period (reg 16A). The 4-week period as originally provided included public holidays and the additional leave period is intended to allow the 4-week minimum in addition to public holidays (or equivalent). The additional leave rose in three phases to 1.6 weeks' leave from April 2009. Thus the minimum paid annual leave is 5.6 weeks.

The dates on which holiday leave is taken would normally be agreed between the employer and worker. If it cannot be agreed, the procedures in reg 15 must be used. The worker must give notice of the chosen dates which is twice the length of the period of holiday that the worker is seeking. The employer can give the worker notice requiring him to take leave or not to take leave on specific dates. The worker's notice is subject to any requirements of the employer.

Offshore workers who have specified periods working offshore throughout 52 weeks may not be entitled to any additional holiday time than the onshore time. In *Craig* v *Transocean International Resources Ltd* (2009) an offshore worker failed in a claim for additional time for holiday. The EAT held that so long as time onshore ensured the statutory rest periods and holiday time, there was no reason why it could not also be holiday since the employee was not required to work during that period.

Rolled up holiday pay   A question to which the Scottish and English courts gave different answers was whether "rolled up" holiday pay was permissible. This is where a worker is not paid when he takes his holiday, but the pay for hours worked includes an element for holiday pay. The Scottish answer was that this was impermissible (*MPB Structures Ltd* v *Munro* (2003)); the English that it was permissible (*Marshalls Clay Products* v *Caulfield* (2004)). The ECJ has given its ruling on the question in a number of cases referred from the English Court of Appeal (*Robinson-Steele* v *RD Retail Services Ltd* (2006)). The answer may be described as impermissible, with qualifications. Formally, it is contrary to the WTD since it may militate against workers taking holidays if they do not get paid at the time they are due to take them. However, if the situation is transparent – that is, the precise proportion paid as holiday pay is made clear when it is actually paid – it may be permissible.

Sickness   A worker who is off sick is still entitled to holidays. Sick leave has a different purpose from holiday leave: the former is to get well, the latter is to rest. On a reference from the UK the ECJ held in *Stringer* v *HM Revenue & Customs* (2009) that while the legislation may preclude a worker taking holidays (and thus receiving holiday pay) while off sick, it cannot preclude the worker taking the relevant leave when he returns to work. If a worker's contract is terminated during or after a period of sick leave, he is entitled to be paid for the holidays that could not be taken because of the sickness.

Termination   A worker who leaves without using any or all of his statutory annual leave is entitled to receive compensation (reg 14). If a worker leaves having exceeded the proportion of leave for the year, the employer may obtain compensation from the worker for the excess period, but only if there is a "relevant agreement" to that effect.

Enforcement

The working time and night work provisions are enforced by the Health and Safety Executive using a range of administrative and criminal sanctions (regs 28–29) The individual worker may enforce the rest period and holiday provisions at an ET (reg 30). An action for holiday pay may be raised either under reg 30 or as a claim for unlawful deduction of wages (*Stringer* v *HM Revenue & Customs* (2009) (HL)).

The complexity of WTR 1998 can be gauged by the decision in *Miles* v *Linkage Community Trust* (2008). A care worker who had not received compensatory equivalent rest period did not succeed in obtaining any compensation from a tribunal. Part of the reason for the decision not to award any compensation was that the employer had taken legal advice and the Regulations were so complicated that it was unsurprising if an employer did not understand them.

Rights to time off

There are a number of statutory rights to time off, some with pay and some without pay. Some of the more important ones are outlined here. Provisions relating to maternity or parental rights will not be dealt with here but with other maternity and parental rights in Chapter 11. These rights apply to employees, apart from the final one, which applies to workers.

Trade union duties and activities

Trade union duties An official of an independent trade union recognised by the employer has a right to reasonable paid time off for carrying out duties as an official (TULR(C)A 1992, s 168). This includes negotiating with the employer, or attending TUC approved courses, on the range of matters by which collective bargaining and collective agreements are defined under TULR(C)A 1992, s 178: terms and conditions, hiring and firing, work allocation, discipline, trade union membership, facilities for union officials, and negotiation and consultation procedures. It also includes consultation and negotiation concerning redundancies and transfers of undertakings. The official is entitled to receive the pay he would ordinarily have received, unless it varies with the amount of work done, in which case payment will be by reference to average hourly earnings (s 169).

Union learning representatives A member of an independent recognised trade union who is a union learning representative is entitled to reasonable time off without pay to deal with the training needs of other union members (s 168A).

Trade union activities A member of an independent recognised trade union is entitled to reasonable time off without pay to take part in trade union activities and also to act as a representative of the union (s 169). All of these rights can be enforced by a claim to an ET within 3 months.

ACAS Code of Practice In each case the amount of time off to be allowed is what is reasonable in all the circumstances having regard to the ACAS Code of Practice. This is ACAS Code of Practice No 3, "Time off for trade union duties and activities" (2010), which gives guidance on the law and what is appropriate for compliance. Like all Codes of Practice failure to follow it does not in itself mean that the employer is in breach of law, but the Code is relevant evidence for a tribunal considering whether the law has been complied with.

Employee representatives

Where there is no recognised trade union, there is provision for employee representatives to be elected in order to consult about mass redundancies and transfers of undertakings (see Chapters 8 and 9). These are employees who are elected as representatives, and they are entitled to reasonable paid time off for the elections for the post, and to carry out the functions once elected (ERA 1996, ss 61–63). This right can be enforced by making a claim to an ET within 3 months.

Safety representatives

Employees who have been appointed by an independent recognised trade union as safety representatives have the right to necessary paid time off to carry out the functions of a safety representative and to undergo training (Safety Representatives and Safety Committees Regulations 1977, reg 4). This right can be enforced by making a claim to an ET within 3 months.

Public duties

Employees who are Justices of the Peace and those who are members of certain public bodies are entitled to reasonable unpaid time off (ERA 1996, ss 50–51). The public bodies include local authorities, statutory tribunals, police authorities, certain NHS bodies, certain education bodies, the Scottish Environment Protection Agency or Scottish Water. The right in the case of a JP is to perform the duties of the office, in the case of the others to attend meetings and carry out approved functions of the body. The amount of time off depends on how much time is required to perform the duties generally and how much for the particular duty, how much time off has already been permitted, and the circumstances of the employer's business and the effect of the employee's absence on the running of the business. This right can be enforced by making a claim to an ET within 3 months.

In case of redundancy

An employee who has been continuously employed by the employer for 2 years and who has been given notice of dismissal for redundancy is entitled to reasonable paid time off before the end of the notice in order to look for new employment or to make arrangements for training for future employment (ERA 1996, ss 52–54).

To accompany to a disciplinary or grievance hearing

Where a worker is required or invited to attend a disciplinary or grievance hearing, he is entitled to be accompanied by a trade union employee or official who has been certified as experienced in acting in this capacity, or by another of the employer's workers. The employer must permit a worker to take paid time off for this purpose (Employment Relations Act 1999, s 10(6) and (7)). This right can be enforced by making a claim to a tribunal within 3 months.

Essential Facts

- Provisions regulating the national minimum wage are set out in the National Minimum Wage Act 1998.
- Provisions governing statutory sick pay are found in the Social Security Contributions and Benefits Act 1992.
- Working time protection is provided under the Working Time Regulations 1998.
- The EC Directive on working time, Working Time Directive 93/104, lays down minimum health and safety requirements for the organisation of working time.
- Deductions from wages are regulated by the Employment Rights Act 1996, Pt II.
- Statutory entitlement to guarantee pay is set out in Employment Rights Act 1996, Pt III.
- Provisions relating to suspension from work are found in the Employment Rights Act 1996, Pt VII.
- A number of statutory rights to time off are set out in the Employment Rights Act 1996, Pt VI.
- Statutory provision for time off for trade union duties and activities is contained in the Trade Union and Labour Relations (Consolidation) Act 1992.

Essential Cases

Kerr v The Sweater Shop (Scotland) Ltd (1996): authorisation of deductions from wages requires individual written notification as well as being a term of the contract of employment. Notice on the company notice board was not individual notification.

Burrow Down Support Services Ltd v Rossiter (2008): an employee who was required to respond to emergencies at night in a care home but who could otherwise sleep was engaged in time work throughout the period under reg 3 of NMWR 1999. Regulations 15 and 15A only came into play when the employee was sleeping at home or at work to be available for work rather than working.

MacCartney v Oversley House Management (2006): a resident manager who was required to be on duty for 24 hours a day was working throughout that time, and had therefore been deprived of her entitlement to rest breaks under WTR 1998.

Robinson-Steele v R D Retail Services Ltd (2006): the ECJ held that in principle the Working Time Directive requires holiday pay to be paid when the holiday is taken. However, this was qualified by a statement that if the situation is transparent and when rolled up holiday pay is paid the precise proportion relating to holidays is made clear, it may be permissible.

Stringer v HM Revenue & Customs (2009): the ECJ held that the Working Time Directive requires workers who are off sick to be given the benefit of their holiday entitlement on their return to work. If the contract of employment ends during sickness, the worker is entitled to pay for the holidays missed.

6 CONTINUITY OF EMPLOYMENT

CONTINUOUS SERVICE

For some employment rights it is necessary that the claimant is an employee, and also has a minimum period of continuous employment with the employer from whom the right is claimed. In such cases, absence of the necessary qualifying period is an absolute bar to exercising the right in question, regardless of the merits of the case. This applies particularly in the case of two of the most important employment protection rights: unfair dismissal and the right to statutory redundancy pay where the qualification periods are 1 year and 2 years respectively.

Although the issue of continuous service appears to be a technical legal matter, it has proved to be an issue of some political importance, with practical impact. The length of a qualification period is one way of barring access to the right in question. Over the years one of the contested issues in relation to unfair dismissal has been the changing qualifying period. When first introduced in 1971 the qualifying period was 2 years. On a change of government, the right not to be unfairly dismissed was re-enacted and the qualifying period reduced to 6 months. On a further change of government it was increased, first in 1979 to 1 year, then in 1980 to 2 years in the case of employers who employed less than 20 employees and in 1985 to 2 years universally. The increase of the qualifying period to 2 years was subsequently challenged in *R v Secretary of State for Employment, ex parte Seymour-Smith and Perez* (1999) on the basis that it amounted to indirect sex discrimination in that fewer women than men would be able to satisfy it, and thus was contrary to Art 5.1 of the Equal Treatment Directive 76/207 (now replaced by Directive 2006/54). Indirect discrimination will be explained in Chapter 10. That case was referred to the ECJ, which held that a small and persistent difference between the numbers of men and women able to qualify (as the workplace statistics showed in this case, the difference being around 10:9) could amount to prima facie evidence of indirect sex discrimination. However, on its return to the House of Lords (2000), the challenge was unsuccessful as the increase to 2 years was found to be justified by the then employment policy of the government of encouraging employment. Nevertheless, before the decision of the House of Lords in 2000, in the preceding year the qualifying period was reduced back down to 1 year (ERA 1996, s 108).

This case followed an earlier, successful, challenge to another of the requirements of continuous service. Before 1995 a key element of the continuity rules was that the employment concerned had to be for a minimum number of hours per week. To qualify for unfair dismissal protection or for the right to statutory redundancy pay, the employee had to have worked for 16 hours a week for 2 years, or for between 8 and 16 hours for 5 years. At under 8 hours the employee could never qualify. In *R v Secretary of State for Employment, ex parte Equal Opportunities Commission* (1994) the House of Lords held that this requirement amounted to indirect sex discrimination since fewer women than men would be able to fulfil it. In this case the House of Lords did not find the government's justification convincing, largely because the argument went not much further than simply stating what it was without supporting evidence, that withholding the rights would increase job opportunities, or granting the rights diminish them. As a consequence of this decision the hours requirement was removed.

Although standard unfair dismissal rights and the right to redundancy pay require a qualifying period of continuous employment, most employment protection measures do not require such a period. All of the employment protection measures under ERA 1996, except the protection regarding deduction from wages, apply only to employees. Deduction from wages protection and certain other rights, such as the right to equal pay, apply to the broader category of workers, and protection against discrimination extends to the even broader category of those "in employment" (see Chapter 2). In addition, although the standard right not to be unfairly dismissed applies to employees with 1 year's continuous employment, there are many types of unfair dismissal which do not require any qualifying service (see Chapter 7).

STATUTORY RULES

The general rule is that the employee must have been continuously employed for the relevant period with the same employer, working backwards from the relevant date, in the case of unfair dismissal "the effective date of termination" (s 97). If the Transfer of Undertakings (Protection of Employment) Regulations 2006 (TUPE 2006) apply, the period of employment with the transferor employer will count together with the subsequent period with the transferee employer in a claim against the latter. (TUPE 2006 will be explained in Chapter 9.)

Whether or not there is an unbroken period of employment is calculated according to the rules in ss 210–219 of ERA 1996.

The total period of qualifying service is to be computed in months and years (s 210). Thus, a person whose effective date of termination (dismissal) is 31 March will have 1 year's qualifying employment if he has been continuously employed by the relevant employer from 1 April of the previous year.

The total period must be made up of qualifying weeks with no break. In general, weeks which do not count in computing employment break continuity. Employment is presumed to be continuous unless it is shown to be otherwise (s 210(5)). Thus if the employer argues that, although the employee has been employed between 1 April in one year and 31 March in the next, there was a break in continuity during the year, the burden of proving this rests with the employer.

Continuity of weeks

Each week during which there is a contract of employment in existence between the employer and employee counts in computing the employee's service (s 212(1)). The important thing is that there is an unbroken continuity of weeks as an employee of the employer. It is not necessary to have been employed in the same job continuously. In *Wood* v *York Council* (1978) an employee who resigned one job with the Council to take up another job in a different department of the Council was held by the Court of Appeal to have been in continuous employment throughout. In *Tipper* v *Roofdec Ltd* (1989) the same conclusion was reached in the case of a lorry driver whose contract of employment was frustrated when he lost his licence (so the tribunal held) but was re-employed immediately by the employer as a cleaner. When he was dismissed because of redundancy less than a year later, the EAT held that he did have sufficient continuous employment to qualify for a redundancy payment as he was employed in successive weeks by the employer when one contract ended and the other began.

Given that continuous employment is calculated weekly and not daily, it is possible that leaving an employer's employment for a very short period will not break continuity, so long as the employee is employed in successive weeks. It does not matter what the reason was for the termination of the first contract of employment, whether by resignation, dismissal or (as in *Tipper* v *Roofdec*) frustration: if the employee was employed during one week by the employer and in the following week by that employer, continuity is unbroken. This would be so even if the break was in effect for a week or more, such as where an employee might resign on the Tuesday of one week and be re-employed by the same employer on the Thursday of the following week. In *Sweeney* v

J & S Henderson (Concessions) Ltd (1999) the EAT held that continuity had not been broken when an employee resigned on 15 February and was re-employed on 21 February since he had been employed by them in successive weeks.

Breaks in employment

The normal rule is that where the employee stops working for the employer, continuous employment ends. If there is a week during which there is no contract of employment in existence, that week does not count towards continuity and also breaks it. However, there are certain exceptions to this principle (s 213(3)).

Sickness

If the contract of employment is not in existence during a week because the employee is sick or injured, that week both counts and does not break continuity. Note that this rule does not have to come into play to preserve continuity where the contract of employment continues in existence but the employee is not at work because of sickness. It is only where the contract has been terminated because of sickness that it is necessary to rely on this exception. In *Donnelly* v *Kelvin International Services* (1992) the employee was an offshore worker who resigned when his doctor advised him he should no longer work offshore. He worked for another employer for 5 weeks, but then restarted employment with his former employer. When he was subsequently dismissed his employer argued that his continuity had been broken by the period of his resignation and working for someone else. While the ET agreed, the EAT remitted it back, directing that it was a matter of fact whether or not the employee had been incapable of work (for the offshore employer) due to sickness during each one of the weeks, and if he had been the fact that he did other work would not stop the exception applying.

This exception applies only for a break of up to 26 weeks.

Temporary cessation of work

If the break in employment is because there has been a "temporary cessation of work" the weeks will not break continuity and also count towards it. The "work" referred to is the work of the employee: the employer's work as a whole or of the type done by the employee does not have to have ceased. The House of Lords decided this in an early redundancy payment case, *Fitzgerald* v *Hall Russell* (1970), when a welder was laid off for 2 months while others were not. The 2-month break was in the middle of a 9-year period of employment and redundancy pay is assessed according to length of service. The tribunal had held that only the second part of his employment could be counted, but the House of Lords held that this approach was too narrow and technical: they should look at the whole period involved.

The intention of the parties is important: that is, whether the cessation was intended to be temporary. This does not have to have been expressed when the break occurred, but can be judged in hindsight. It is most likely to arise where an employee is laid off because of shortage of work, where it was always the intention (whether explicit or not) to re-employ when work was available.

It is difficult to know when a cessation is temporary and there is not a clear approach from the courts. Temporary has been described as "transient" or "relatively short" in relation to the period of employment. The Court of Appeal has taken two different approaches to this issue: the mathematical approach, and the broad brush approach. The mathematical approach is often seen as deriving from a comment made in the House of Lords' decision in *Ford v Warwickshire County Council* (1983) where it held that a teacher who was employed in successive years for the academic session could take advantage of this provision, since the gaps were relatively short in duration in relation to the duration of the periods of employment, or transient. Lord Diplock said *obiter* that in any seasonal employment the length of the gap would be decisive. In *Flack v Kodak* (1986) the Court of Appeal, however, took the view that it was important to look at the contract throughout its whole life (not just the past immediate year or 2 years) to see if the gap was temporary; but subsequently in *Sillars v Charringtons Fuels Ltd* (1989) it disapproved this approach in favour of looking at the ratio of employment to unemployment in the relevant period (the last 2 years of employment in this case). The employee was employed on seasonal work and in the last 2 years had worked for 27½ weeks and 31 weeks. The periods of unemployment were held to be too long to be considered temporary. It was not disputed that the intention of the parties was that employment would start again after the seasonal break, but the duration of the break was given more importance than the intention. This approach was followed by the EAT in *Berwick Salmon Fisheries Co Ltd v Rutherford* (1991) where the seasonal fishing pattern which had previously been 30 weeks on and 22 weeks off changed to 23 weeks on and 29 weeks off in the 2 years before termination. It found that the absences were too great in proportion to the employment to be seen as temporary. It is not clear that the word "temporary" necessarily incorporates the idea of "short".

Arrangement or custom

The third exception to the rule that periods of non-employment break continuity is where by arrangement or custom the employee is regarded as continuing in employment. This could arise where an employee is seconded for a period (of any length) to another employer. Usually a custom will pre-date the particular absence in question, but there are conflicting statements from the EAT as to whether it is necessary for an arrangement to pre-date the absence. In *Booth* v *United States of America* (1999), where the US army was in the habit of employing maintenance workers on fixed-term contracts of less than 2 years and then re-employing them after a break of no less than 2 weeks, it was held that there was a break, and no arrangement to treat employment as continuous (indeed it was almost certain that it was precisely to stop this happening that the employer operated the practice). It was necessary that any arrangement be in place before the break took place. On the other hand, in *London Probation Board* v *Kirkpatrick* (2005) where a dismissal was reversed 2 months later after an internal appeal, the EAT held that there had been an arrangement that the employment would continue during that period, and stated that there was no reason why an arrangement could not arise after the event. It may be that this would only arise in relation to these particular circumstances.

In *Booth* v *USA* the EAT acknowledged that its decision would provide a loophole for an employer to use who wished to avoid liability for redundancy pay and unfair dismissal, but stated that it was for Parliament to close the loophole. It seemed to regard the matter in the same light as tax avoidance (as opposed to tax evasion): a legitimate if regrettable practice.

A number of employers make provision for "career breaks" – usually for employees who have taken maternity leave and wish further time with children before returning to work. It will depend on the nature of the arrangements whether such a career break counts towards continuity. Section 213(3)(c) states that the nature of the custom or arrangement is that it should be such that the employee is "regarded as continuing in the employment of the employer for any purpose". If the career break scheme involves the employee in resigning with no involvement as an employee for any purpose during the period of the break, as was the case in *Curr* v *Marks and Spencer plc* (2002), it is not a qualifying arrangement. On the other hand, if there is some continuing involvement, as there was in *Unwin* v *Barclays Bank plc* (2003) where the employee was entitled during the 2-year period of the career break to concessionary rates for the Chartered Institute of Bankers and to staff benefits in relation to loans, the arrangement will comply with the subsection and continuity will not be broken and the period of the break will count.

Strike action

A week in which the employee takes part in a strike (whether for the whole week or part of it) does not count for the purposes of continuity of employment. However, it does not break continuity either (s 216). This is also the case where the employee is not working because of a lock-out by the employer.

Change of employer

The general rule is that continuous employment must be by one employer. However, s 218 provides for a number of exceptions.

If a trade or business is transferred, employment at the time of transfer counts as employment with the transferee. The provisions of TUPE 2006 also apply. If a contract of employment is transferred by Act of Parliament from one corporate body to another, employment at transfer counts as employment with the transferee. If the employee is employed successively by associated employers, employment with the first employer at the time of starting employment with the second employer counts as employment with the second employer. Employers are associated if one is a company of which the other (directly or indirectly) has control, or if both are companies of which a third person (directly or indirectly) has control (s 231).

If an employer dies and the employee is employed by the personal representative of the employer, employment with the employer at time of death counts as employment with the personal representative. If there is a change in partners, personal representatives or trustees who employ an employee, similarly employment at the time of change counts after the change. In *Stevens* v *Bower* (2004) this was held also to apply where one of two partners was struck off the roll of solicitors leaving the remaining partner as sole principal.

Essential Facts

• Continuous employment rules are set out in the Employment Rights Act 1996, Pt XIV, Chap 1.

Essential Cases

Tipper v Roofdec Ltd (1989): an employee who was re-employed by the same employer in a different capacity immediately following the termination of the previous contract of employment had been employed in successive weeks by the same employer. Employment was therefore continuous (ERA 1996, s 210).

Sweeney v J & S Henderson (Concessions) Ltd (1999): an employee who resigned from his employment with the respondent to work for another employer, and who subsequently reapplied for and obtained employment with the respondent in the next week, was held to have been in continuous employment as he was employed by the employer in successive weeks (ERA 1996, s 210).

Donnelly v Kelvin International Services (1992): an employee resigned from working offshore for the respondent on medical advice and worked for another employer before returning to work for the respondent. The EAT remitted the case back to the ET to reconsider its decision that there was no continuity, by considering whether he had been incapable of working for the respondent for all of the weeks between resignation and re-employment (ERA 1996, s 212).

Ford v Warwickshire County Council (1983): the House of Lords held that a temporary teacher who was employed from September to July for a number of years by the Council had been in continuous employment. The breaks were due to a temporary cessation of work. The periods of non-work were relatively short and were characterised as transient (ERA 1996, s 212).

Booth v United States of America (1999): employees who were employed on a series of contracts of just under 2 years with a 2-week break in between did not have continuous employment. There was no custom or arrangement by which they were regarded as continuing in employment (ERA 1996, s 212).

7 UNFAIR DISMISSAL

THE RIGHT NOT TO BE UNFAIRLY DISMISSED

The ERA 1996 provides a right not to be unfairly dismissed (s 94). This right should not be confused with the common law action of wrongful dismissal (see Chapter 4). Unless otherwise stated, statutory references in this chapter are to ERA 1996.

It is important to distinguish between wrongful dismissal, the common law remedy, and unfair dismissal, the statutory remedy. There are significant differences, some of which make wrongful dismissal a more valuable remedy in some circumstances, others unfair dismissal. The remedy of wrongful dismissal is universally available while there is a 1-year qualification period for the unfair dismissal remedy. However, unlike wrongful dismissal, the remedy of unfair dismissal is available when the employer dismisses with notice and also when the employer fails to renew a fixed-term contract. Damages in unfair dismissal cases are not restricted to the notice period, but there is a cap on the amount of compensation which can be awarded. For the highly paid unlawfully dismissed employee, particularly one on a fixed-term contract brought prematurely to an end, wrongful dismissal is likely to be a more lucrative remedy. For the less highly paid employee unfair dismissal is likely to give rise to greater compensation since it does not have the restriction on damages to the notice period (and possibly a period for not following contractual procedures).

QUALIFYING FOR THE RIGHT NOT TO BE UNFAIRLY DISMISSED

Qualifying service

Only employees have the right not to be unfairly dismissed. In a standard unfair dismissal the employee must have been in employment with the dismissing employer for a continuous period of a year, working back from the date of dismissal (s 108). There is no qualifying service necessary, however, in cases of "automatically unfair dismissal".

Working in Great Britain

There is no express requirement, as there used to be, that the employee does not work outside Great Britain. However, in *Lawson* v *Serco Ltd*

(2006) the House of Lords held that there is an implied principle that the right applies only to those working in Great Britain at the time of dismissal. Working means more than a casual visit: the employee must be "really working" in Great Britain, as the House of Lords put it.

Being employed by a British company is not sufficient, nor is it necessary. In the case of peripatetic employees, the relevant issue is where the employee is based. Where the employee works abroad the key question is whether the employee is working for the purpose of a British business. Examples include where the employee is posted to work abroad on behalf of a business conducted in Britain (as, for example, the foreign correspondent of a British newspaper), or where the employee is working in a social or political enclave abroad (as, for example, on a British naval base). In *Lawson* v *Serco*, applying these principles, the House of Lords found that an airline pilot working for a non-British company who flew out of Heathrow Airport as his base, a civilian employee working in a British military base in Germany and a security adviser on an RAF base in the Ascension Islands were all working in Great Britain.

DISMISSAL

An action for unfair dismissal can be raised only if an employee has been dismissed. "Dismissal" is given an extended meaning in ERA 1996 and can occur in three ways: termination of the contract by the employer, with or without notice; expiry of a fixed-term contract without renewal; termination of the contract by the employee with or without notice where the employer's conduct would have entitled the employee to resign without giving notice (s 95).

If there is a dispute as to whether the employee has been dismissed, the burden of proof lies with the employee to show that he was dismissed.

The "effective date of termination" (when continuous service will be counted back from, and time limits for application to a tribunal will be counted forward from) is usually the date when the employer's notice expires or, if no notice was given, the date the contract terminates. For the purposes of calculating continuous service, or the basic award in compensation, if the employer gave notice which was less than the statutory notice required by s 86, the effective date of termination will be the notional date when proper statutory notice would have expired. (s 97).

If the employer has given the employee notice and within the notice period the employee gives the employer notice which takes effect before the end of the employer's notice, the employee will be taken to be dismissed for the reason the employer gives for the original termination (s 95).

Termination by the employer

Usually termination by the employer will involve an explicit dismissal. However there may be circumstances in which the employee resigns, or agrees to go, where the termination is driven by the employer. Tribunals have been careful to look at the reality of the situation as well as the form of words to see if the termination was truly at the instance of the employer. If an employer gives an employee an ultimatum to resign or be dismissed, that will be an employer termination (*Robertson* v *Securicor Transport* (1972)). Similarly, if an employee is pressurised to agree to resign, that will also be an employer termination. In *Caledonian Mining Co Ltd* v *Bassett and Steel* (1987), a case involving a claim for redundancy pay (where the definition of dismissal is the same), it was found that the employer had "inveigled" employees into resigning before they had been dismissed by reaching a secret agreement with the National Coal Board to offer their employees work before dismissal by them. It was the employer's conduct which had caused the resignation by "dishonestly persuading the men to resign with the express purpose of avoiding responsibility for redundancy pay". The element of dishonesty seems crucial in this case.

Deciding whether an employee has resigned or been dismissed may not be easy simply from the words used, especially where either party has spoken in the heat of the moment. While unambiguous words (such as "I am resigning" in *Sothern* v *Franks Charlesly & Co* (1981)) will usually be given effect to, in other cases a tribunal will look at the whole circumstances to see how the words used could be reasonably interpreted. In *Kwik-Fit (GB) Ltd* v *Lineham* (1992), where an employee had walked out of the job in anger and thrown keys on the counter and the employer had taken this as a resignation, the EAT felt that the situation was sufficiently ambiguous that the employers had not been entitled to treat it as a resignation.

Non-renewal of a fixed-term contract

Even although failing to renew a contract which has a fixed end date would not normally be described as a dismissal, for the purposes of unfair dismissal (and the right to redundancy pay) a failure by an employer to renew such a contract will count as a dismissal. Otherwise an employer would be able to avoid the jurisdiction of the tribunals simply by employing employees on fixed-term contracts and not renewing them. A fixed-term contract includes both a common law fixed-term contract (which cannot be terminated by notice before the end of the fixed-term), and also a contract with a fixed-termination date which can also be terminated by notice before that date, the latter being more common (*Dixon* v *BBC* (1979)).

Resignation justified by employer's conduct (constructive dismissal)

Like non-renewal of a fixed-term contract, so resignation by an employee is not usually a dismissal: it is employee termination of the contract. However, the employer's conduct may justify resignation, in which case the resignation will count as a dismissal, and is usually known as "constructive dismissal". The statute states that this occurs where the employee "is entitled to terminate [the contract of employment] without notice by reason of the employer's conduct" (s 95). The courts have interpreted this as requiring entitlement under the common law to terminate without notice. At common law, and therefore under this provision, only a material breach of contract by the employer can entitle the employee to resign without notice. The decision of the Court of Appeal in *Western Excavations (ECC) Ltd* v *Sharp* (1978) settled that material breach by the employer was required, and not simply unreasonable behaviour. In that case the employee had been suspended without pay for 5 days (in accordance with his contract of employment) and when he asked for an advance in holiday pay to tide him over the employer refused. Both the ET and EAT had found there to be constructive dismissal because the employer had behaved unreasonably. The Court of Appeal, however, held that if the behaviour did not amount to breach of contract (which this did not as there was no obligation to advance holiday pay), the employee could not be justified in resigning. The breach by the employer may be of any term in the contract, express or implied. It can include a breach of the mutual duty of trust and confidence: indeed, it is in the context of the concept of constructive dismissal that this duty developed. As discussed in Chapter 3, any breach of the duty of trust and confidence is a material breach by definition, since it consists in conduct by the employer which is likely to destroy or damage the relationship of trust and confidence.

If an employer tries to impose changes to a contract of employment without agreement and without going through the process of giving notice and re-engagement, this will amount to a breach of the original contract and, if sufficiently serious, will entitle the employee to resign and make a claim for unfair dismissal. It may be that the change which the employer seeks to make is so fundamental to the contract that it in effect amounts not just to repudiation of the original contract but actual termination by the employer. In that case the employee will not need to resign. This will be an unusual situation but it occurred in *Alcan Extrusions* v *Yates* (1996) where the employer, after unsuccessful negotiations with the trade union, imposed changes which included change from predictable to rolling shift patterns, removal of overtime entitlement and less favourable holiday terms. The employees advised the employer that they viewed the changes as tantamount to dismissal. They continued working under the new terms but raised actions for unfair dismissal. The employer's argument that they had not been dismissed because they had not resigned in response to the breach of contract was rejected: the changes were so extreme that their imposition amounted to direct employer termination of the original contract.

The employee must resign as a consequence of the breach in order to qualify as having been dismissed in this way, and should do so without delay. There may, however, be a series of actions by the employer, leading up to a "final straw" which precipitates the actual resignation. In *Lewis* v *Motorworld Garages Ltd* (1985) an employee who was demoted continued to work, but resigned some time later after continued criticism and threats. While the ET and EAT had held that he had affirmed the contract by working on after demotion and the subsequent actions by the employer were not material, the Court of Appeal found that he could rely on the original demotion and subsequent actions cumulatively as a breach of the mutual duty of trust and confidence.

While the employee is deciding whether or not to accept the breach and resign, the employer cannot affect the legal position by trying to take back or remedy the breach. The employee has the right to terminate the contract in response to a material, or repudiatory, breach. In *Bournemouth University* v *Buckland* (2010) a professor resigned because his examination papers had been re-marked after he had marked them. Before his resignation, a University inquiry found in his favour and criticised the exam-marking process. The EAT had held that this inquiry "cured" the breach. However, the Court of Appeal overturned this decision: once a breach has been committed it cannot be undone.

REASON FOR THE DISMISSAL

There are two categories of unfair dismissal: automatically unfair dismissals for specific statutory reasons, and "standard" unfair dismissals where the reason is not one of the specified reasons. In a "standard" unfair dismissal claim the employer must show what was the reason or principal reason for the dismissal (s 98(1)). In the case of automatically unfair dismissals the burden of proof will rest with the employee to show that the dismissal was for the specified reason.

Automatically unfair dismissals

These are dismissals for specific inadmissible reasons. They differ from standard unfair dismissals in that there is no requirement for a period of continuous employment, and once the inadmissible reason has been established the dismissal is automatically unfair without any further proof of fairness or unfairness. This is a way of protecting employees from dismissals which infringe particular rights. There are a number of inadmissible reasons (ss 99–105). A few of these are highlighted here.

Leave for family reasons

It is automatically unfair for an employee to be dismissed where the principal reason for the dismissal relates to pregnancy, childbirth or one of the family leave rights available (s 99). The specific inadmissible reasons are laid out in the Maternity and Parental Leave etc Regulations (MPLR 1999) (reg 20) and the Paternity and Adoption Leave Regulations 2002 (PALR 2002) (reg 29). They include pregnancy and childbirth; taking maternity leave, ordinary or additional; taking parental leave or dependent care leave; taking paternity leave; taking adoption leave, either ordinary or additional. If an employee is selected for dismissal for redundancy for one of these reasons, even although redundancy is the precipitating factor for the dismissal, this will also be automatically unfair.

Trade union membership and activity

It is automatically unfair for an employee to be dismissed for a trade union reason. There are five such reasons: being or proposing to become a trade union member; taking or proposing to take part in trade union activities; making use of, or proposing to make use of, trade union services; failing to accept an offer which would be an unlawful inducement to leave a trade union (or other similar purposes) or disapply collective bargaining; and not being a member of, proposing to resign from, or refusing to join a trade union (TULR(C)A 1992, s 152). The employer must have the inadmissible reason in mind when deciding to dismiss. In *CGB Publishing* v *Killey* (1993) an employee was dismissed because of his behaviour at a meeting, which the tribunal found had been determined by his being a trade union member. The EAT rejected the tribunal's consequential finding that he had therefore been dismissed for a trade union reason. The test depends on the subjective reason for dismissal held by the employer.

In the case of trade union activities and using trade union services, these must take place at "an appropriate time" to qualify for automatically unfair protection. This is defined as either outside working hours, or during working hours with the agreement of the employer. In *Marley Tile Co Ltd* v *Shaw* (1980) a shop steward was dismissed because he called and attended a union meeting during working hours. He had advised the employer, which had not replied. The Court of Appeal held that in this case silence had not meant consent, so that the activity had not taken place at an appropriate time.

The trade union activity must be relevant to the dismissing employer. It was for some time believed that this meant that the trade union activity must have been with the dismissing employer after a decision in *City of Birmingham District Council* v *Beyer* (1977) that an employee, dismissed when his employer discovered that he was a well-known trade union activist, had not been dismissed for an inadmissible reason since the trade union activity was not with the relevant employer. However, in *Fitzpatrick* v *British Railways Board* (1991) the Court of Appeal held that a dismissal in similar circumstances for past trade union activity was automatically unfair if the reason for the dismissal was that the current employer was afraid that the employee would engage in similar trade union activity in his employment with them.

Official industrial action

It is automatically unfair to dismiss an employee for taking part in official protected industrial action (TULR(C)A 1992, s 238A). The position of an employee who is engaged in industrial action in relation to dismissal will be looked at more generally towards the end of this chapter when automatically unfair dismissal will be considered alongside the other provisions.

Health and safety

There are six circumstances in which a dismissal with a health and safety connection will be automatically unfair (ERA 1996, s 100). The first three relate to the carrying out of health and safety duties. First, there is the dismissal of an employee who has been designated to carry out health and safety functions by the employer for carrying out (or proposing to carry out) these functions. Second, there is the dismissal of a workers' safety representative or member of a safety committee for carrying out (or proposing to carry out) these functions. Third, there is the dismissal of an employee who has taken part (or proposed to take part) in statutory consultations with the employer, or in an election of safety representatives.

The second set of circumstances applies to employees generally. First, if there is no safety representative or safety committee or if there is one but it is not reasonably practicable to go through this avenue, it is automatically unfair to dismiss an employee for bringing the employer's attention by reasonable means to harmful or potentially harmful matters. Second, there is the dismissal of an employee who, in the case of danger which the employee reasonably believes is serious and imminent and which he could not reasonably be expected to avert, has left the workplace while the danger persists and refuses to return. Third, there is the dismissal of an employee who, in the case of danger which the employee reasonably believes is serious and imminent, took (or proposed to take) appropriate steps to protect himself or others from the danger.

What is appropriate in the last of these categories depends on all the circumstances including the employee's knowledge and the facilities and advice available to him at the time. The dismissal will not be unfair if the employer shows that the employee was so negligent in the steps that he took that a reasonable employer might have dismissed him.

The danger from which an employee may feel the need of protection by refusing to return to the workplace can include danger arising from the behaviour of colleagues. In *Harvest Press Ltd* v *McCaffrey* (1999) an employee who refused to return to work while a colleague who had abused him and left him in fear for his personal safety remained was held to be automatically unfairly dismissed, since the term "danger" had to be interpreted without limit and to cover any danger, however it arose.

An employee is entitled to take steps to protect the public as well as themselves or fellow workers. In *Masiak* v *City Restaurants (UK) Ltd* (1999) a chef was dismissed because of his refusal to cook chicken which he considered was a health hazard to customers. The EAT did not agree with the tribunal that this was not relevant to s 100 dismissals and remitted it back to consider whether the danger was "serious and imminent" as required by the section.

Asserting a statutory right

Protection is given to people who try to assert their statutory rights. It is automatically unfair to dismiss an employee for either bringing proceedings to enforce a statutory right, or to allege that the employer has breached a statutory right (s 104). If the claim or allegation is unfounded, the employee still has this protection so long as it was made in good faith.

The statutes covered by this protection include ERA 1996, TULR(C)A 1992, WTR 1998 and TUPE 2006. In addition, protection is given to those asserting rights (or having them asserted on their behalf) under NMWA 1998 (ERA 1996, s 104A).

Making a protected disclosure

It is automatically unfair to dismiss an employee for making a protected disclosure (s 103A). The circumstances in which protected disclosures arise were considered in Chapter 3.

Spent convictions

Under the Rehabilitation of Offenders Act 1974 (ROA 1974) a conviction which has become "spent" in terms of that Act is not a proper ground for dismissal (s 4(3)(b)). Whether or not a conviction is spent depends on the punishment imposed. Sentences of life imprisonment and sentences of imprisonment for over 30 months are excluded entirely from rehabilitation. The appropriate periods after which a conviction becomes otherwise spent are laid out in s 5.

Certain professions and employments are exempt from the provisions of this Act, including lawyers, accountants, police and medical, nursing and social services workers; and in these cases no convictions are ever "spent".

Reason in standard unfair dismissals

Where the dismissal is not for one of the inadmissible reasons the employer must establish that the principal reason falls within one of the potentially fair reasons specified in ERA 1996 (s 98(1)).

It is the reason which the employer actually relied on when dismissing the employee which is relevant, not any reason either discovered or elevated in importance after dismissal. A tribunal could decide that the employer actually and genuinely dismissed the employee for a reason other than that which they gave, but the tribunal cannot substitute a reason which was not in the employer's mind at the time of dismissal. In *Kuzel v Roche Products Ltd* (2008) the tribunal did not accept either the employee's assertion that she had been dismissed for making a protected disclosure, or the employer's that she had been dismissed because of a breakdown in relations, but found that the real reason was loss of temper and failure to follow procedure by the manager involved. The Court of Appeal held that it had been entitled to find as a question of fact that this was the reason.

Potentially fair reasons

The employer must establish that the reason falls into one of the potentially fair reasons and if this cannot be done, must lose. The dismissal is unfair.

The statutory fair reasons are capability or qualifications, conduct, retirement, redundancy, contravention of a statutory duty (s 98(2)); and some other substantial reason justifying dismissal (s 98(1)(b)). Capability is assessed by reference to skill, aptitude, health or any other physical or mental quality.

If the ET finds that the real reason for the dismissal was not a statutory reason, the dismissal will be unfair, even if there may have been grounds for a fair dismissal. In *ASLEF* v *Brady* (2006) a trade union had sacked its general secretary after a fight at a barbecue. The ET found that it was not the fight or what the official had said about it that had been the reason for the dismissal, but instead the wish of the Executive Committee to get rid of him because of a difference of political view. This was not one of the potentially fair reasons. Thus the dismissal was unfair.

Right to a written statement

An employee with 1 year's continuous service who has been dismissed may require a written statement of the reasons for dismissal from the employer. If the employer does not comply within 2 weeks the employee may apply to a tribunal (s 92).

FAIRNESS

Once the reason has been proved by the employer the ET will consider whether the dismissal for that reason was fair. This will be decided according to the terms of ERA 1996, s 98(4). Whether a dismissal is fair or unfair is to be judged in the light of the reason shown by the employer, and depends on whether in the circumstances the employer acted reasonably or unreasonably in treating it as a sufficient reason for dismissing the employee. The subsection requires account to be taken of the size and administrative resources of the employer's undertaking, and that the question be determined by an ET in accordance with equity and the substantial merits of the case.

Section 98(4) does not place a burden of proof on either employer or employee. While the burden is on the employee to prove there has been a dismissal, if disputed, and to prove one of the automatically unfair grounds, if that is what is alleged, and the burden is on the employer in a standard unfair dismissal to prove that it was for a potentially fair reason, there is no burden of proof in relation to fairness in a standard unfair dismissal. Like all UK statutory provisions this must be interpreted so far as possible to comply with the ECHR. It would not normally be fair for an employer to dismiss an employee for a reason which amounted to an unjustified interference with a Convention right. However, most of the relevant Convention rights are qualified. In *Pay v UK* (2009) the unsuccessful employee in *Pay v Lancashire Probation Service* (2004) took proceedings against the UK, alleging breach of Arts 8 (private life), 10 (freedom of expression) and 14 (discrimination). He had been dismissed from his job as a probation officer, which included working with sex offenders when his employers discovered that he was involved in merchandising bondage and sado-masochistic products and performing in fetish clubs. Photographs of his involvement were on the internet. The European Court of Human Rights (ECtHR) held that there had been no breach of Convention rights in UK law permitting his dismissal. While there was interference with his private life, and with his freedom of expression, these were justified by the protection of the employer's reputation: it was within the UK's margin of appreciation to take a "cautious approach" in order to ensure that employees like Mr Pay retained the respect of offenders and the confidence of the public and the victims, particularly concerning sex offences.

Reasonableness

According to the statutory language a tribunal must determine whether the dismissal is fair for the reason shown by the employer: the reason must be sufficient. This will depend on all the circumstances including the size and administration resources of the employer. The decision must take into account equity and the substantial merits of the case.

The band of reasonable responses

The tribunal has to decide whether a reasonable employer would have taken the decision to dismiss for the reason in question in the circumstances. It must not decide what it would have done had it been the employer, but must decide if the employer's decision was within the "band of reasonable responses" of a reasonable employer (*Iceland Frozen Foods Ltd v Jones* (1982)). This presumes that there is a spectrum of reasonable responses, with a harsh but reasonable decision at one end and a lenient but reasonable decision at the other. The band of reasonable responses test has been criticised for following rather than setting standards, and for in effect placing the burden of proof on the employee by making the question one of whether no reasonable employer would have decided to dismiss. The EAT decided not to follow it in *Haddon* v *Van Den Bergh Foods Ltd* (1999), but the Court of Appeal rapidly overruled this and reaffirmed the test in *HSBC Bank plc* v *Madden* (2000).

Procedural fairness

Reasonableness relates to whether there was sufficient reason to dismiss, and also whether the employer adopted a reasonable procedure in making the decision. The statute is concerned with the behaviour of the employer in deciding to dismiss.

No "no difference" rule   The House of Lords held in *Polkey* v *A E Dayton Services Ltd* (1987) that it was an error of law for a tribunal to decide, in cases where a dismissal was procedurally unfair, that the dismissal was fair because it would have made no difference if a proper procedure had been used. This is not an absolute principle: whether or not a procedural irregularity rendered a dismissal unfair or not still depends on whether in all the circumstances the employer acted reasonably or unreasonably. Nevertheless, as a general principle procedural fairness is as important as fairness of reason.

Contractual procedures   Where there is a contractual procedure, while failure to follow it in every respect may not automatically render a dismissal unfair, nevertheless the employer's failure to comply is something a tribunal should take into account. A reasonable employer can be expected to comply with the requirements of its own disciplinary procedure. The House of Lords in *West Midlands Co-operative Society Ltd* v *Tipton* (1986) held that a dismissal was unfair when an employer refused to allow the dismissed employee the appeal which his contract provided for against dismissal.

Introduction and repeal of statutory procedures   From October 2004 until April 2009 there were statutory minimum procedural requirements for employers to follow (Employment Act 2002, s 32 and Sch 2). Failure to follow them rendered a dismissal automatically unfair. These procedures had been introduced with the aim of bringing about internal agreements between employer and employee and a reduction in tribunal cases. However, it was found that in fact the procedures had led to an increase in complexity and an increase in numbers of cases. They were repealed by the Employment Act 2008.

ACAS Code of Practice When the statutory procedures were repealed the ACAS Code of Practice on Disciplinary and Grievance Procedures was revised (2009), and given more significance by a provision that failure to follow the procedures can result in an increase or reduction in compensation (an increase if the employer is at fault, a decrease if the employee is at fault) (Employment Act 2008, s 3). The Code of Practice applies primarily to conduct dismissals, but its principles also apply to competence dismissals (Code, para 1). The Code details the steps that an employer should take when handling disciplinary issues in the workplace. It is admissible as evidence at a tribunal, and while failure to follow the procedure does not in itself mean that there has been a breach of the Act, nevertheless it is evidence that it may not have been.

Statutory right to be accompanied There is a general statutory right on the part of a worker (not just an employee) to be accompanied at any disciplinary or grievance hearing by a single person, chosen by the worker, who is either a union official or certified as experienced in such matters, or a fellow worker. This person can address the hearing and confer with the worker (Employment Relations Act 1999, s 10). If an employer refuses a reasonable request to be accompanied, the worker may complain to a tribunal.

Size and administrative resources of the employer

Small employers must behave fairly no less than large employers. Nevertheless, the size and administrative resources could determine the kind of procedures which it is reasonable for an employer to adopt. The ACAS Code of Practice (para 3) states that it may sometimes not be practicable for all employers to take all the steps it sets out. For example, smaller employers may not be able to adopt the same standards of independence at all stages of a disciplinary hearing.

Equity and the substantial merits of the case

Each case must be determined on its own merits. A component of fairness is equitable, or consistent, treatment of employees. Nevertheless, each case depends on its own facts and it may be that it is appropriate to treat different employees differently for the same (mis)conduct where their blameworthiness, personal situation or record is different (*Securicor Ltd* v *Smith* (1989)).

THE POTENTIALLY FAIR REASONS

Conduct dismissals

The ACAS Code of Practice deals primarily with this form of dismissal and much of the case law has been concerned with issues of procedure. The employer's own disciplinary procedure should be followed, and if it gives clear warning of the sort of conduct which will merit dismissal, a dismissal for that reason is more likely to be found to be reasonable (*Beedell* v *West Ferry Printers Ltd* (2000)). However, a tribunal can still consider whether a dismissal is reasonable even where the employer has followed the contractual procedures. In *Ladbroke Racing Ltd* v *Arnott* (1981) three betting-shop workers were dismissed for gross misconduct, as laid down in the company rules, for placing bets for family members. The Inner House of the Court of Session held that just because dismissals were in terms of the contract, this did not in itself make them fair: they still had to be assessed to see if they were reasonable in all the circumstances. In this case the betting had been condoned by senior employees, and the ET had been entitled to find that the employer's decision to dismiss most of the staff in the office was unreasonable.

The Burchell *test*

The decision of the EAT in *British Home Stores* v *Burchell* (1980) has been very influential, and although it was challenged at the same time as the band of reasonable responses test it was also reaffirmed by the Court of Appeal (*HSBC Bank plc* v *Madden* (2000)). In *Burchell*, an employer's decision to dismiss an employee for suspected dishonesty, when there had been insufficient evidence for a prosecution and where it was now accepted that she was innocent, was held to have been reasonable. The employer had met a threefold test: there was a genuine belief in the employee's guilt; the employer had reasonable grounds for this belief; and the employer had carried out a reasonable investigation as the basis of these grounds. An employer does not have to have proof of misconduct to a criminal or civil legal standard of proof. Genuine belief is sufficient. This may not be fair to the innocent employee, but it focuses on the reasonableness of the employer's behaviour as s 98(4) requires.

What is necessary in the way of investigation will depend on all the circumstances, including the type of evidence that is available to the employer. The more circumstantial the evidence, the more that will be needed in the way of investigation (*Inner London Education Authority* v *Gravett* (1988)).

Although genuine belief in the employee's guilt is necessary where one employee is concerned, where the employer suspects two employees of misconduct but cannot decide which one is to blame, reasonable suspicion may entitle the employer to dismiss both employees (*Monie* v *Coral Racing* (1980)).

Good practice

The importance of investigation, hearing the employee and a system of appeal has been emphasised both in the ACAS Code of Practice and in many cases. The EAT has given helpful guidelines in some cases as to what makes good practice. General guidelines about conducting hearings are given in *Clark* v *Civil Aviation Authority* (1991). Guidelines as to the acceptable use of anonymous informants are given in *Linfood Cash and Carry Ltd* v *Thomson and Bell* (1989). The Code of Practice gives good practice for the conduct of investigations (paras 5–8); for informing and meeting with the employee (paras 9–16); for making disciplinary decisions including a decision to dismiss (paras 17–24); and providing an opportunity to appeal (paras 25–28).

Capability dismissals

Although these are not misconduct dismissals, so that a disciplinary approach is not appropriate, the principles of fairness in the ACAS Code of Practice apply (para 1). The *Burchell* approach of genuine belief (in lack of capability), reasonable grounds and reasonable investigation has been approved for capability dismissals (*Taylor* v *Alidair Ltd* (1978)). A reasonable employer will consider whether assistance or training would be appropriate.

Ill health

Ill health may be a reason for a capability dismissal, and such a dismissal may be fair, so long as the employer has followed a proper procedure, taking account of the nature of the illness, the length of absence, the need to get the job done, the possibility of transfer, medical advice and the views of the employee (*East Lindsey District Council* v *Daubney* (1977)). An employee who suffers from ill health may also be a disabled person and thus have the protection of the Disability Discrimination Act 1995 (which will be superseded by the Equality Act 2010). Unfair dismissal and disability discrimination are to be dealt with as separate issues, although a discriminatory dismissal is likely to be unfair. In *Rothwell* v *Pelikan Hardcopy Scotland Ltd* (2006) the EAT stated that it would be only in exceptional cases that an incapacity dismissal would not be unfair if there had not been consultation. That case was not one of those.

Retirement dismissals

An employee may be fairly dismissed because of retirement, so long as the retirement age is 65 or over (Employment Equality (Age) Regulations 2006 (EE(A)R 2006), reg 30; Equality Act 2010, Sch 9, para 9), or lower so long as the employer can justify it as a proportionate means of achieving a legitimate aim and thus not age discrimination. A challenge to the "default" retirement age of 65 as being contrary to EU Directive 2000/78 failed at the ECJ (*R (Age Concern)* v *Secretary of State for BERR* (2009)). It also failed when it returned to the High Court (2009), although, because the economic and political situation had changed since the EE(A)R 2006 were passed, this was stated to be a narrow decision and partly only unsuccessful because the 65-year age was currently under review.

The employer must also comply with the provisions of ss 98ZA–98ZF of ERA 1996, and the procedures in EE(A)R 2006, Sch 6, which place a duty on an employer to consider a request from an employee to work past retirement age and lay down a statutory procedure for making a request not to retire.

Redundancy dismissals

The ACAS Code of Practice does not apply to redundancy dismissals (para 1). Although a redundancy dismissal can be fair, it is subject to the same requirement of reasonableness as other dismissals. In the case of redundancy dismissals this will be most important in relation to the criteria by which the employee has been selected for redundancy and the procedures used in selection and handling the whole redundancy process, including consultation.

Selection of an employee for redundancy for an inadmissible reason will make the dismissal automatically unfair (ERA 1996, s 105). In other cases the question is whether or not the employer acted reasonably. The tribunal will not in general examine the economic reasons for the redundancy. In *James W Cook & Co (Wivenhoe) Ltd* v *Tipper* (1990) the Court of Appeal held that while a tribunal could investigate whether a decision to close down a business was genuine, it could not investigate the commercial or economic reasons which lay behind the closure.

The relevant issues are whether the employee was fairly selected by objective selection criteria, fairly applied; whether the employee (and any trade union) was adequately consulted and warned; and whether the possibility of alternative work was properly investigated (*Williams* v *Compair Maxam Ltd* (1982)).

Fair consultation means consultation when the proposal is still at a formative stage, giving adequate information and adequate time to respond (*King* v *Eaton Ltd* (1996)). There are also statutory procedures in the case of collective redundancies requiring the employer to consult with trade union or employee representatives, which will be considered in the following chapter.

Contravention of statute dismissals

If the employee's continued employment in his job would be contrary to legislation (such as if a driver was disqualified from driving), the dismissal is potentially fair. However, there is still the question of whether the employer has behaved reasonably in deciding to dismiss the employee. There may be a reasonable alternative which the employer should consider. In *Sutcliffe and Eaton Ltd* v *Pinney* (1977) a trainee hearing-aid dispenser was dismissed after failing to pass the necessary exams within the relevant time. Even although this made his employment illegal under the governing statute, the dismissal was found to be unfair. Continued employment being illegal is not conclusive: in this case the employer could have considered, and did not, applying for an extension to the training period for the employee.

Other relevant considerations could include the length of the likely illegality, the extent to which the employee is prevented from working and whether there is any alternative work.

The employment of the employee must be actually illegal. It is insufficient that the employer believed wrongly that it was illegal. In *Bouchaala* v *Trusthouse Forte Hotels Ltd* (1980) the employer dismissed the employee, a Tunisian national, whom the employer believed was not entitled to obtain a work permit, based on advice received from the Home Office. The advice was wrong. The EAT overturned the tribunal's decision that this dismissal came into the fair category: the wording of the statute is unambiguous and required that the employee must not be able to continue working without contravening the statute. However, the EAT went on to find that the genuine belief, based on advice from the Home Office, although it could not come under this category could come under the final fair category, some other substantial reason.

Some other substantial reason

The full statutory wording is "some other substantial reason of a kind such as to justify the dismissal of an employee holding the position which that employee held" (s 91(1)(b)). Some other substantial reason may include any reason which a reasonable employer would think necessary in the best interests of the business. As seen above in the case of *Bouchaala*, a genuine mistaken belief based on taking proper expert advice that it is unlawful to continue to employ an employee may be a substantial reason. A management style or personality which has led to a breakdown in relations may also amount to such a reason (*Perkin* v *St George's Healthcare NHS Trust* (2005)).

A much-criticised decision under this heading arose many years before the Employment Equality (Sexual Orientation) Regulations 2003 (EE(SO)R 2003) made discrimination because of homosexuality unlawful. In *Saunders* v *Scottish National Camps Association Ltd* (1981) the dismissal of an employee, who worked as a handyman, when it was discovered that he was homosexual was found to be within the band of reasonable responses, since the employer had a fear that parents of children would mistrust the company even although it was accepted by both ET and EAT that such fears were irrational. Such a dismissal would now be unlawful under EE(SO)R 2003 (Equality Act 2010), and in any event the EAT had commented in another unfair dismissal case shortly before the Regulations were introduced that the *Saunders* decision would probably not withstand interpretation to comply with the Human Rights Act 1998 (*X* v *Y* (2003)).

There have been a number of cases involving dismissal as a consequence of a business reorganisation. To determine whether such a dismissal is fair, the tribunal will consider whether the reorganisation was considered necessary for the business, whether the change relating to the employee was necessary to effect the reorganisation and whether there was adequate consultation in relation to the reorganisation and the consequences for the employee. A tribunal will look for a balance between the effect on the employee and the needs of the employer's business (*St John of God (Care Services) Ltd* v *Brooks* (1992)). However, fairness to the employee and the needs of the business may conflict, and so long as the employer has behaved reasonably it will be the needs of the business which will usually prevail.

DISMISSAL DURING INDUSTRIAL ACTION

The law distinguishes between three situations involving dismissal and industrial action. First of all there is protected industrial action, which is a form of official industrial action; second, there is other official industrial action; and, third, there is unofficial industrial action. A brief explanation will be given of the meaning of official, unofficial and protected industrial action before considering these three situations. The law is contained in TULR(C)A 1992.

Industrial action

A strike is one, but not the only, form of industrial action. Other forms could include a ban on overtime, a "work to rule" or non-co-operation in certain aspects of the job. There is no definition of either "strike" or "industrial action" in the Act. In *Power Packing Casemakers v Faust* (1983) the Court of Appeal held that it is not necessary for any breach of contract to be involved. The industrial action in that case was a ban on voluntary overtime (which by definition is non-contractual). It was held that this was industrial action as it was concerted action designed to put pressure on the employer. In that case the consequence was, in the light of the law as it then was, that there was no right to pursue an unfair dismissal claim.

It is a matter of objective fact whether or not an employee is taking industrial action. This could be difficult if, for example, an employee is absent from work on the day of the strike but claims not to have been striking; or where an employee does not co-operate with a programme at work but claims it was nothing to do with the industrial action taking place. The question is one of fact and not whether the employer either knew or reasonably believed that the employee was taking part in industrial action. In *Manifold Industries v Sims* (1991), where the industrial action was non-co-operation with a work study, an ET had wrongly held that it was the employer's actual knowledge of whether the employee was taking part that determined the question. In *Jenkins v P & O European Ferries (Dover) Ltd* (1991), where the industrial action took the form of a strike, an ET had wrongly decided the case on the basis that the employer reasonably believed the employees were on strike. In both cases the EAT held that the employer's knowledge was irrelevant: the question was a matter of fact for the ET as to whether the employee was taking industrial action.

Official and unofficial industrial action

Industrial action is official if it has been authorised or endorsed by the union organising the action. The employee or others involved in the action must be members of that union (s 237(2)). Authorisation or endorsement can come from the principal executive committee, the president, the general secretary, any committee or official of the union or any person employed by the union rules to authorise or endorse such acts (s 20). However, the industrial action may be repudiated by the executive, president or general secretary (and thus cease to be official) so long as it is repudiated as soon as reasonably practicable after it comes to their knowledge, and the statutory procedure is followed (s 21). On the other hand, if none of those involved in the strike are members of a union it is official. Any action which is not official is unofficial.

Protected industrial action

Protected industrial action is official action which has been called by the union and for which the union would have immunity from a delict action by the employer (s 238A(1)). At common law a union might be open to being sued by an employer for the delict of inducing breach of contract (such as inducing its members to breach their contracts of employment with the employer) or other applicable economic delicts. However, in order to permit industrial action to take place lawfully, TULR(C)A 1992 provides immunity from such delicts so long as the action complies with the provisions of the Act, including balloting procedures. The immunity has existed since the Trade Disputes Act 1906, but has been greatly restricted since the late 20th century.

Apart from the procedural requirements, the immunity exists when the industrial action is taken "in contemplation or furtherance of a trade dispute" (s 219). A trade dispute is defined by TULR(C)A 1992 as a dispute connected with particular matters: terms and conditions of employment, physical conditions of employment, engagement or termination or suspension of employment, employment duties, allocation of work, matters of discipline, membership or non-membership of trade unions, facilities for union officials, negotiation or consultation procedures or any other procedures relating to the matters covered (s 21).

Protected official industrial action

A dismissal is automatically unfair if the reason for the dismissal was that the employee took part in protected industrial action. For this to apply the date of dismissal must have occurred within the protected period, or in certain circumstances outside the period (s 238A). The period relates to how long the industrial action carries on for.

Protected period

The protected period is 12 weeks beginning with the first day of the protected industrial action ("the basic period"), plus additional days if, during the 12-week period, the workers were locked out by the employer (ie prevented from working by the employer) ("the extension period"). An individual employee is also protected if the dismissal takes place after the protected week period has elapsed but the employee had ceased to take part in the industrial action before the period had ended.

A dismissal outside the protected period is also automatically unfair if the action has carried on, but the employer had failed to take reasonable steps to end the dispute. In deciding whether an employer has failed in this respect, a number of factors should be taken into account: whether the employer or union complied with an agreed procedure; whether the employer or union offered or agreed to commence or reopen negotiations after the action started; whether the employer or union unreasonably refused to a request from the other to use conciliation or mediation services (such as through ACAS); or whether the employer or union, having agreed to conciliation or mediation, failed to comply with the arrangements (ss 238A and 238B).

Official action outside the protected period

Where the industrial action is official but not protected the general rule is that a tribunal has no jurisdiction to hear an unfair dismissal claim if the dismissal occurred while the employee was taking part in industrial action (or the employer conducting a lock-out) at the time of dismissal (s 238). This rule comes into play only after the protected period and is subject to two exceptions.

First, if the dismissal takes place during industrial action but the true or principal reason is one of the inadmissible ones (family, health and safety, working time, employee representative, flexible working, pension scheme membership, application for dependent leave), it is automatically unfair. This applies if the employee is selected for redundancy for one of those reasons during industrial action (s 238(2A)).

Second, where an employee is selectively dismissed there will be a right to raise an unfair dismissal action. This arises where an employee has been dismissed while taking industrial action but one or more "relevant employees" have not been dismissed, or alternatively one or more of these relevant employees have been offered re-engagement within 3 months of the employee's dismissal and the employee has not (s 238(2)). In this context, the term "relevant employees" refers to those employees at the establishment of the employer at which the employee works who were taking part in the action when the claimant was dismissed. In the case of a lock-out it would be all employees who were directly interested in the dispute regarding which the lock-out occurred. Thus the impunity from an unfair dismissal action that an employer otherwise has is lost if any striking employee is kept on or re-engaged within the 3-month period. In the case of re-engagement the employer must be aware, or should have been aware, that the re-engaged employee had been involved in the industrial action. In *Bigham and Keogh* v *GKN Kwikform Ltd* (1992), one of a number of employees dismissed from the employer's Middlesex site was re-employed within 3 months at the company's Luton office. He disclosed that he had worked for them before but did not disclose the dismissal (it was accepted he was not acting fraudulently). When it was discovered, he was dismissed immediately. When a dismissed striker from the Middlesex site raised an unfair dismissal action, basing his entitlement on this selective re-employment, the ET accepted the employer's defence that it had been a mistake. The EAT remitted it back because the ET had not considered whether the employer should have known of the earlier dismissal since the employee had revealed his previous employment. Advertising for recruits and accepting all dismissed strikers who apply will not operate as a defence against those who do not apply (*Crosville Wales Ltd* v *Tracey* (1993)). Once it has been established that the tribunal has jurisdiction to hear the unfair dismissal claim, it will go on to decide whether the dismissal was unfair.

Unofficial action

When an employee is dismissed while taking unofficial industrial action, the general rule is that there is no right to bring an action of unfair dismissal (s 237). Thus an employer may dismiss an employee who is taking unofficial industrial action with impunity: the selective dismissals exception does not apply in such a case.

However, as with a dismissal during official action, if the true principal reason for dismissal (or selection for redundancy) is one of a range of inadmissible reasons, the dismissal will be automatically unfair (s 237(1A)).

NATIONAL SECURITY

If the decision to dismiss was taken for the purposes of safeguarding national security, the tribunal must dismiss the claim (Employment Tribunals Act 1996 (ETA 1996), s 10). It was formerly the case that a certificate signed by or on behalf of a Government Minister was conclusive to that effect. This is now no longer the case, and the employer must prove that it is the case. In such actions, either after notice by the Minister concerned or by the ET itself, special procedures involving a specially constituted tribunal and the hearing of evidence in private may be followed (Employment Tribunals (Constitution and Rules of Procedure) Regulations 2004, regs 10–12).

The provisions may be relied on by any employer, not only a Crown employer. In *B* v *BAA plc* (2005) BAA were held to be entitled to rely on the provision in a case where an airport security guard had been dismissed when she had failed to obtain counter-terrorist clearance from the Department of Transport. However, although ETA 1996, s 10 provides that the tribunal must dismiss the claim once it has been proved, in the same case the EAT held that it was not sufficient simply to establish that the reason for dismissal had been to safeguard national security. The impact of the Human Rights Act 1998, s 3 (applying Art 6 of the ECHR) was to interpret this provision so that the fairness provisions of ERA 1996, s 98(4) were excluded no more than was necessary. This meant that the ET, having been satisfied that the dismissal was to safeguard national security, should have gone on to consider whether it was fair in all the circumstances (as an example of "some other substantial reason"). This would mean taking into account the extent to which redeployment of the employee would have been possible.

REMEDIES

A complaint of unfair dismissal must be presented to an ET within 3 months of the effective date of dismissal (ERA, s 111). If the action is successful and the dismissal is found to be unfair, the first remedy to be considered is that of re-employment (in the form of reinstatement or re-engagement). If this is not ordered the ET shall make an award of compensation. As noted in Chapter 4, both the common law and TULR(C)A 1992, s 236 render it incompetent for any court or tribunal to order an employer to employ an employee. Ultimately, compensation is the only remedy.

Re-employment

The ET will explain what orders for reinstatement and re-engagement mean and ask the successful employee if he wishes such an order to be made (ERA 1996, s 112). Reinstatement means that the employer must treat the employee as if he had not been dismissed: the order will specify the arrears and benefits and any seniority rights which must be given to the employee (s 114). Re-engagement means that the employee must be re-employed by the employer or an associate in comparable or other suitable employment: the order will specify the identity of the employer, the nature of the employer, the remuneration, any benefits payable for the period between dismissal and re-engagement and any rights to be restored (s 115).

The ET has a discretion as to which, if any, of these orders to make (s 113). It must first consider whether to order reinstatement, taking account of the wish of the claimant, whether it is practicable for the employer to comply with such an order and, where the employee contributed to the dismissal, whether it would be just to order reinstatement. If it does not order reinstatement it should then consider whether to order re-engagement, taking account of the same factors (s 116).

This remedy is not awarded very often, since the relationship between ex-employer and ex-employee has usually completely broken down on both sides by the time of the ET hearing. If an award is made but the employer does not comply, additional compensation can be awarded (s 117).

Compensation

The most common remedy is not the primary remedy of re-employment, but that of compensation. There are two elements to compensation: the basic award and the compensatory award (s 118). If re-employment has been ordered but not complied with, there is an additional award.

Basic award

This is calculated according to the formula: 1½ week's pay for every year the employee worked and was 41 or over; 1 week's pay for every year aged 22 or over; ½ week's pay for every year under 22. The maximum number of years' employment to be taken into account is 20 (s 119). There is a cap on the week's pay, fixed (usually) annually by ministerial order (currently £380, there having been no increase in February 2010) (s 227). There is a minimum basic award where the dismissal is for a trade union reason, or for acting as certain types of worker representative (currently £4,700).

The basic award can be reduced by any redundancy pay awarded, a just and equitable amount if the employee had unreasonably refused reinstatement and a just and equitable amount if the employee's conduct before dismissal warrants it (s 122).

Compensatory award

This is the amount which the tribunal thinks is "just and equitable in all the circumstances". It is to compensate for the loss suffered as a result of the dismissal (s 123).

Guidelines Guidelines for assessing the level of the compensatory award were given in an early case, *Norton Tool Co Ltd* v *Tewson* (1973), and these are still broadly applied. A tribunal will take into account immediate loss of earnings, the financial loss caused by the dismissal, future loss of wages, loss of statutory rights, loss of pension rights and expenses. The award compensates for financial loss, not distress, humiliation or damage to reputation. It had been suggested (*obiter*) by the House of Lords in *Johnson* v *Unisys* (2001) that unfair dismissal compensation could include compensation for distress, humiliation and damage to reputation. However, it subsequently reaffirmed that this is not the case, in *Dunnachie* v *Kingston upon Hull Council* (2004), holding that "loss" in the statutory provision referred to financial loss only.

Mitigation of loss The common law duty to mitigate loss applies, and an employee who does not do so should have their compensatory award reduced. This may apply, for example, where an ET finds that the employee has made no effort to find alternative work since dismissal. However, although, as was noted in Chapter 4, payment of notice is payment of damages for having been dismissed without notice, an ET does not have to apply the principle of mitigation of loss within the notice period if it does not think it is appropriate. Paying full notice even where the employee had obtained a job in the notice period was described by the EAT as "good industrial relations practice" in this context, in *Voith Turbo Ltd* v *Stowe* (2005).

Reduction of the award It is within the discretion of the ET to decide what amount it is just and equitable to award. In *W Devis & Sons Ltd* v *Atkins* (1977) the House of Lords distinguished between liability and compensation in a case where a company dismissed an employee for one reason, offering him an *ex gratia* payment, and subsequently discovering misconduct before the dismissal which they had not known about. They withdrew the payment on this discovery. The House of Lords held that the dismissal was unfair: the employer could not rely on a reason discovered after the dismissal. However, the ET could take account of misconduct before the dismissal in deciding what was just and equitable by way of compensation, even reducing the amount to a negligible or nil award if appropriate.

"Polkey *reduction*" This is a term given in situations where a dismissal has been held to be unfair because the employer had failed to follow a proper procedure, but it is argued that even if the procedure had been followed the employee would inevitably have lost their job. The ET will consider the likelihood that the employee would have retained the job if a proper procedure had been followed. They may find that it is 100 per cent likely that this would have happened (*Fisher* v *California Cake & Cookie Ltd* (1997)), or another percentage. In *Rao* v *Civil Aviation Authority* (1994) the ET found that there was a 20 per cent chance that the employee would have kept his job if a proper procedure had been followed and therefore reduced the compensatory award by 80 per cent.

Contributory fault   The award may be reduced by a just and equitable amount if the employee caused or contributed to the dismissal. In *Rao v Civil Aviation Authority* the Court of Appeal said that the ET should consider this aspect of the compensation after the issue of general just and equitable considerations, and take account of it in deciding what contribution, if any, to deduct.

Redundancy pay   The compensatory award may be reduced by the amount of any redundancy pay received.

Level of compensatory award   There is a cap on this award (currently £65,300, having been reduced (rather than increased) for the first time ever, in February 2010), except where the dismissal is for a health and safety reason or for a protected disclosure (s 124).

If there has been a failure to follow the ACAS Code of Practice on Disciplinary and Grievance Procedures the amount of compensation can be increased by up to 25 per cent in the case of failure by the employer, or decreased by up to 25 per cent in the case of failure by the employee (TULR(C)A 1992, s 207A).

Additional award of compensation

Where the employer has failed to comply with an order for reinstatement or re-engagement, the ET shall make an award of compensation including both basic and compensatory award, and an additional award of between 26 and 52 weeks' pay. The additional award shall not be made if the employer shows that it was not reasonably practicable to re-employ the employee. The fact of having employed a permanent replacement for the employee cannot be taken into account unless the employer can also satisfy the ET that he could only arrange for the work of the dismissed employee to be done by employing a permanent employee (ERA 1996, s 117).

It has been held that the additional award, when made, forms part of the compensatory award, so that the statutory maximum applies (*Parry v National Westminster Bank* (2005)). Thus, if the maximum award has already been made, any additional award cannot be given effect to, which makes the "primary" remedy even less meaningful.

Interim relief

Where an employee has been dismissed for a trade union reason or one of a number of the automatically unfair reasons, he may apply to a tribunal for an order of interim relief within 7 days (ERA 1996, ss 128–132; TULR(C)A 1992, ss 160–166). The effect of such an order is (if the employer is willing) reinstatement or re-engagement until the tribunal hearing or (if the employer is not willing) continuation of the contract of employment until the tribunal hearing, for payment of wages and benefits.

Essential Facts

• Provisions concerning unfair dismissal are set out in the Employment Rights Act 1996, Pt X.

• Unfair dismissal protection during industrial action is set out in the Trade Union and Labour Relations (Consolidation) Act 1992, ss 237–239.

Essential Cases

Western Excavations (ECC) Ltd v Sharp (1979): for the purposes of unfair dismissal law a resignation is treated as a dismissal ("constructive dismissal") only when the resignation is in response to a material breach of contract by the employer.

Polkey v A E Dayton Services Ltd (1987): the House of Lords disapproved the "no difference" rule some ETs had adopted. If an employer does not follow a proper procedure in deciding to dismiss an employee the dismissal will almost always be unfair, unless exceptional circumstances make it reasonable for the employer to have acted in that way.

HSBC Bank plc v Madden (2000): in an unfair dismissal action the employment tribunal decides the question of whether the employer has acted reasonably or unreasonably in dismissing the employee not by deciding whether in its view the employer acted reasonably, but by determining whether the employer's decision was within the "band of reasonable responses" of a reasonable employer.

British Home Stores v Burchell (1980): a very influential EAT decision. In deciding to dismiss, an employer does not require proof of misconduct or incompetence to the standard that would satisfy a court. The employer must have a genuine belief in the guilt or lack of competence, must have reasonable grounds for this belief and must have established these reasonable grounds after a reasonable investigation.

Williams v Compair Maxam Ltd (1982): in a decision that an ET had been perverse in deciding that redundancy dismissals were fair, the EAT gave guidelines as to a fair procedure in such cases, including fair warning and consultation; fair selection criteria and application; and consideration of alternative employment.

W Devis & Sons Ltd v Atkins (1977): the House of Lords held that misconduct by an employee committed before dismissal, but only discovered afterwards, could not be the basis for a finding of fair dismissal. However, it could be the basis for a reduction of the compensatory award on just and equitable grounds, even, in an appropriate case, to a nil award.

8 REDUNDANCY

When an employee is dismissed because of redundancy there are two major individual rights: the right to a statutory redundancy pay and the right not to be unfairly dismissed. This chapter will deal with the former right, the latter having been dealt with in the previous chapter. In addition, there are collective rights, requiring disclosure of information and consultation with trade unions or employee representatives in advance of any redundancies. This chapter will also outline these rights.

THE RIGHT TO REDUNDANCY PAY

The right to redundancy pay was introduced by the Redundancy Payments Act 1965 (now contained in ERA 1996, s 135). It was the first major employment protection measure, largely introduced to smooth the process of making redundancies. Statutory redundancy pay is a minimum provision, and many employees may be entitled to enhanced contractual rights, possibly as a result of a collective agreement. Any failure on the part of the employer to pay contractual redundancy pay would have to be enforced as a breach of contract. Unless otherwise stated, the following statutory references are to ERA 1996.

As with the right not to be unfairly dismissed, not all employees are eligible for statutory redundancy pay. An employee must have 2 years' continuous employment by the date of dismissal (s 155).

Dismissal

While it is common to refer to an employee as being "made redundant" or "taking redundancy" as if redundancy is something which happens without any dismissal taking place, it is necessary for the employee to have been dismissed by reason of redundancy for there to be a right to statutory redundancy pay. Dismissal is defined in the same way as for unfair dismissal: termination by the employer with or without notice; non-renewal of a fixed-term contract; and termination by the employee when justified (constructive dismissal) (s 136). The case law which applied to unfair dismissal applies here.

Requirement of dismissal

It is necessary that there is a dismissal, so, if there has only been a warning that redundancies might take place and no notice of dismissal has been given, the employee who leaves employment at that stage will have no entitlement to redundancy pay. This point was established early in redundancy case law. In *Morton Sundour Fabrics* v *Shaw* (1966), after an employee was informed that he would be dismissed for redundancy, he resigned when he found a new job. His claim for redundancy pay was rejected as he had not been given notice of dismissal. In that case not only had no notice of dismissal been given, but no date had been announced either. Subsequently, it has been held that it is the absence of formal notice of dismissal which is important. In *Doble* v *Firestone Tyre and Rubber Co Ltd* (1981) the date of closure of a factory had been decided and a notice handed to trade union officials incorporating a message to employees telling them that they would be receiving dismissal notice soon, which would be timed to expire on the date of closure. The employee resigned after receipt of this message but before receiving notice of dismissal. He was unsuccessful in his claim for statutory redundancy pay since he had not been dismissed.

Early termination by employee

There is, however, a provision by which an employee who has received notice of dismissal may resign before the actual date of termination in the notice and remain eligible for redundancy pay (ss 136 and 142). This right can only be exercised during the "obligatory period" of the notice. For this purpose, a notice period is divided up into obligatory and non-obligatory periods. The obligatory period of notice is the amount of notice the employer is obliged to give, by contract or statute, and that may well be the whole notice given. If the employer gives longer notice than is legally required, the latter part of the notice before the date of termination which amounts to the legal minimum is the obligatory period. If, for example, an employer gives all employees who are being made redundant 12 weeks' notice (the maximum statutory notice) regardless of length of service, for an employee with 3 years' service with no contractual notice provision the obligatory period would be the final 3 weeks before termination. For employees with service of 12 years or more, the obligatory period would be the whole period of the notice.

Within the obligatory period the employee may give the employer notice that he wishes to leave early. If the employer does not object, the employee may resign and be treated as if dismissed by reason of redundancy. In case of objection, the employer can issue a counter-notice requiring the employee to withdraw the notice and warning that it will contest the right to redundancy pay. If the employee leaves early having received this counter-notice, it will be up to a tribunal to decide if it is just and equitable for the employee to receive all or some of the redundancy pay.

This will depend on how reasonable the employer's attitude is in all the circumstances.

It is always possible for an employer and employee to agree that the employee can leave before the notice period ends and such an agreement could take place in the non-obligatory part of the notice. In *CPS Recruitment Ltd* v *Bowen* (1982) the employer agreed to allow an employee who was in the non-obligatory period of notice to swap with another employee and leave earlier, but then refused to pay redundancy pay. The EAT held that since he had left early by mutual agreement he was still entitled to his redundancy pay by virtue of the original dismissal.

"Volunteering" for redundancy

If the form that a termination takes is an agreement between the employer and employee, this does not stop the true nature being an employer termination. If an employer asks for volunteers from the workforce for dismissal, the volunteer is doing just that, volunteering to be dismissed by the employer. A tribunal will look to see who caused the termination, and whether there was a true agreement. In *Burton Alton and Johnston Ltd* v *Peck* (1975) an employee who had been off on long-term sick leave returned to work after an interview with his manager in which he was told that it would be in his interests to be made redundant, but that this could not happen while he was off sick. On his return he was given no work, no remuneration and no redundancy pay. The argument that his contract of employment had terminated by mutual agreement rather than unilateral act of the employer was rejected. The fact that the employee had agreed to the redundancy did not prevent it being a dismissal. Where there is a dispute about whether the employee was dismissed or not, the burden of proof is on the employee.

However, where there is a true agreement there cannot be a dismissal. In *Lornie* v *Renfrew District Council* (1996) the Inner House of the Court of Session held, contrary to the decisions of both ET and EAT, that there had been no dismissal in that case. The employee had agreed to take an early retirement package as part of a restructuring in which senior employees were asked if they wished to consider such a package. Having taken the package, he also claimed a redundancy pay. The Inner House found that it was the employee's agreement to retire which had terminated the contract and not the employer.

Redundancy

The right to statutory redundancy pay arises only when the reason for dismissal is redundancy as defined in the statute.

Presumption of redundancy

For the purposes of a claim for statutory redundancy pay, an employee who has been dismissed is presumed to have been dismissed by reason of redundancy (s 163). It is for the employer to prove otherwise. In *Willcox v Hastings* (1987) two employees had been dismissed to make way for one new employee. The ET had found that one of these dismissals must be for redundancy but it was impossible to tell which, and it refused to award redundancy pay to either. The Court of Appeal, however, held that, as the presumption that the dismissals were for redundancy had not been rebutted by the employer in respect of either dismissal, both must be presumed to have been dismissed by reason of redundancy and to be entitled to redundancy pay.

In an unfair dismissal action, however, there is no such presumption. The employer must satisfy the tribunal as to the reason for dismissal as discussed in the previous chapter.

Definition of "redundancy"

Redundancy is defined in s 139 as occurring where the dismissal is wholly or mainly attributable to one of four circumstances: first, where the employer has ceased or intends to cease to carry on the business for the purposes of which the employee was employed by him either altogether, or, second, in the place where the employee was employed: third, where the requirements of the business have ceased or diminished or are expected to cease or diminish for employees to carry out work of a particular kind either altogether, or, fourth, in the place where the employee is employed. Thus redundancy arises where there is total cessation of the employer's business; or cessation of the business at the particular workplace where the employee is employed; or diminished requirement of the employer's business for the sort of work the employee is employed to do; or diminished requirement of the business for that sort of work at the place where the employee is employed. Although redundancy often, or usually, occurs when there is economic decline in an employer's organisation, this does not have to be the case. A restructuring of an organisation might lead to certain jobs being no longer required, but the requirement for others might increase. Closing down one workplace might take place at the same time as another is opened. Reduction of numbers of employees in one workplace might be accompanied by an increase in numbers at another.

Total cessation of business   All of the forms of redundancy may be temporary or permanent situations. Even if the cessation of business is temporary, an employee is still entitled to a redundancy payment.

Cessation of business at a particular workplace Whether the employer closes down one workplace altogether, or closes the business down and relocates to another site, so far as the individual employee who is dismissed is concerned, this will be by reason of redundancy if he works in the workplace that is being closed. This is also the case where the form of redundancy is diminishing requirements for the sort of work the employee does at a particular workplace.

An employer might seek to move an employee from the workplace which is closing down to another workplace. Two questions arise in such a case: first, whether the employer has the right under an express or implied mobility clause in the contract of employment to require the employee to move; second, if there is a mobility clause by which the employee can be required to work at any place the employer chooses, whether in terms of s 139 it is the place where the employee worked, or anywhere that he could be required to work, which is the "particular workplace". The first of these questions is a matter for interpretation of the contract and in a case where an employer does not have the right to require an employee to move, or where the right is restricted and inapplicable in a particular case, an employee would be justified in resigning and would be considered to have been constructively dismissed. Both the first and second questions were considered in *Bass Leisure Ltd v Thomas* (1994). The employee had worked for 10 years from the employer's Coventry depot. Her contract of employment contained a mobility clause which gave the employer the right to require her to transfer to a suitable alternative place, subject to consideration of domestic circumstances and subject to the place being realistically accessible from her home. When the employer closed the Coventry depot, she was transferred to another depot 20 miles away, but after a trial period she found it did not suit and resigned. The employer refused to pay redundancy pay on the grounds both that she had not been dismissed, and that she was not redundant. It was held, first, that she had been entitled to resign: the transfer was not suitable and did not take account of her domestic circumstances; and second. it was held that the resulting dismissal was by reason of redundancy. The particular workplace means the workplace where the employee works, not any place she could be required to work. It is a matter of fact what the workplace of the employee is (*High Table Ltd v Horst* (1997)).

Diminished requirement for employees to carry out work of a particular kind   This form of redundancy may arise because there is a decline in the amount of work of a particular kind to be done, or it may arise because, although there is no decline, there is a reorganisation resulting in fewer employees being needed for the work. It is the requirement of the employer for employees to carry out the particular work and not the particular work itself which is relevant. In *McCrea* v *Cullen & Davison Ltd* (1988) the managing director of the company decided that he could do the employee manager's job as well as his own and dismissed him. Although the work of the manager still required to be done, the Northern Ireland Court of Appeal held that the requirement of the business for employees to carry out that work had diminished because of the reallocation of work. He had therefore been dismissed by reason of redundancy.

It is the kind of work that is relevant, not the time at which it is done. In *Johnson* v *Nottinghamshire Combined Police Authority* (1974) two clerks claimed redundancy pay when they were dismissed for refusing to work a new shift pattern. From working 5 days a week from 9.30 am to 5.30 pm, they were to work 6 days on one of two shifts (8 am to 3 pm or 1 pm to 8 pm). It was held that they had not been dismissed by reason of redundancy since the same work was being done. Stephenson LJ suggested that it could be a matter of degree whether a change in hours (or type of person employed, or status or responsibility or remuneration) amounted to a change in kind, but that did not apply in this case.

Work of a particular kind   The question for a tribunal is whether the dismissal of the employee was caused by the diminished requirements of the employer for employees to do the particular kind of work the employee does. Early cases tended to take one of two approaches in determining whether there was such a diminished requirement: either the contractual test (what kind of work the employee could be required to do in terms of his contract) or the function test (what kind of work the employee actually carried out). The House of Lords, however, decided in *Murray* v *Foyle Meats Ltd* (1999) that neither approach was correct on its own. In that case the employees were employed as meat plant operatives and worked in the employer's slaughter hall, although in terms of their contract they could be deployed anywhere in the factory. All the workers worked under the same contractual terms as meat plant operatives. After a reorganisation (caused by a decline in business) the employers found they had a requirement for fewer slaughterers and drew up selection criteria with the trade union for those who worked in the slaughter hall. When they were dismissed the employees argued that, since they were meat plant operatives and could be employed like any other employee anywhere in the factory, there was no diminished requirement for the kind of work they did. The House of Lords did not accept that argument, stating that "the definition of redundancy is simplicity itself". There are two questions to be asked: first, have the requirements to carry out work of a particular kind diminished?; and, second, was the dismissal wholly or mainly attributable to that? It is a factual causal test as to whether the dismissal of the employee was attributable to (caused by) the diminution of the employer's need for employees to do work of a particular kind "irrespective of the terms of the contract or the function which the applicant performed".

"Transferred redundancy" This is a description of a situation where there is a diminution in the employer's requirement for the kind of work done by one employee, but an employee doing a different kind of work in which there is no diminution in requirements is dismissed and the former takes over the latter's job. This is also referred to as "bumping". There had been conflicting EAT decisions as to whether such a redundancy met the statutory definition, but the decision in *Murray* v *Foyle Meats Ltd*, in approving a causal approach to this question, is taken to have approved transferred redundancy as a redundancy. The employer's requirement for a particular kind of work had diminished, and as a consequence an employee (who happened to be doing a different kind of work) was dismissed.

Lay-off or short time

In a decline an employer may not dismiss employees because of redundancy but may instead lay them off or place them on short time, with the intention of taking them back on or restoring full hours when business improves. An employee who is laid off or on short time may be able to claim statutory redundancy pay.

A lay-off occurs when the employee's remuneration depends on work being provided and no work is provided, short-time work where, because of a diminution in the work provided for the employee, his weekly remuneration is less than half a weeks' pay (s 147). If the employee has been laid off or placed on short time for 4 or more consecutive weeks or for 6 out of 13 weeks, he may serve written notice on the employer of intention to claim redundancy pay. The notice must be served within 4 weeks (s 148). The employer can serve a counter-notice within 7 days that the redundancy pay will be contested (s 150). In such a case it will be for a tribunal to decide whether redundancy pay should be paid, and it will not award it if, at the time the employee served the notice, it was reasonable to expect that within 4 weeks the employer would be able to provide 13 weeks of full employment (s 152). The employee is only entitled to redundancy pay if he resigns, giving the necessary contractual notice, or, if there is no contractual requirement, 1 week's notice (s 150).

Re-employment by the employer

If the employee is re-employed by the employer under a new contract starting immediately after or within 4 weeks of the termination of the previous one, he is not regarded as having been dismissed because of the ending of the previous one (s 138). If the new contract and the old are the same in respect of capacity and place and other terms and conditions of employment, that is a complete answer to a claim for redundancy pay in respect of dismissal from the previous post. However, if the employee accepts an offer of a new contract on different terms from the old one there is a statutory trial period from the end of the old one until 4 weeks after starting the new one, or a longer period agreed for retraining purposes. This is a period where both employer and employee can assess if the new arrangement is satisfactory. During the 4-week period the employee has a right to resign for any reason and to be entitled to redundancy pay for the dismissal from the original job. The employer also has a right to terminate the contract within the period with the same effect, so long as the reason relates to the difference between the old job and the new job.

If there has been a formal agreement between employer and employee to such re-employment, the employee's resignation must come within the 4-week period (unless the employer is prepared to agree otherwise). In *Optical Express Ltd* v *Williams* (2007) a manager who had reluctantly agreed to re-employment on a new contract which she considered inferior to the old contract did not resign until 2 weeks after the statutory trial period had ended. The EAT held that where there had been formal re-employment such as this, the formal statutory procedure had to be followed. She was therefore not entitled to redundancy pay in respect of the termination of her old contract.

This trial period is not to be confused with the period an employee might have to make up their mind whether or not to resign if the employer repudiates the contract and so be constructively dismissed. If the employer does not formally dismiss the employee but instead transfers him to a different job (not in terms of the contract), the employee will be entitled to resign and claim redundancy pay. An employee will have a reasonable time to decide whether or not to accept the employer's repudiation of the contract and resign. Any 4-week period should be in addition to this. In contrast to *Optical Express Ltd* v *Williams*, where there was a formal agreement for re-employment, in *Turvey* v *C W Cheney & Sons Ltd* (1979) four employees were transferred to another department which they were not contractually obliged to work in. Having worked for over 4 weeks, they decided they did not wish to continue and resigned. The ET found that they were not entitled to redundancy pay for the termination of the original job as they had worked beyond the 4-week trial period. However, the EAT held that the trial period was an improvement not a restriction of the common law position. Where employees are not dismissed but subjected to change, they have a reasonable period to make up their minds whether to accept the change or not, and following that are entitled to the statutory trial period.

Unreasonable refusal of suitable alternative employment

If the employee unreasonably refuses an offer of suitable alternative employment (or unreasonably resigns from suitable alternative employment during the trial period), the right to redundancy pay for the original dismissal is lost (s 141). To be suitable the new employment must either be the same as the old as to capacity, place of employment and other terms and conditions of employment, or differ but be suitable alternative employment. "Suitable" is not defined, but the elements of capacity, place and other terms and conditions of contract should have some equivalence. Although it may be difficult to separate the two elements of suitability of the offer of employment and unreasonableness of the refusal, they are separate and a different approach is adopted for each. The question of the reasonableness or otherwise of the refusal does not arise if the original offer was not suitable. In *Hindes* v *Supersine Ltd* (1979) there were a number of differences in the old job and the new job including a £10 drop in pay. The employee accepted the offer but resigned after 9 days. The ET found that the loss of money was not decisive since the employee had said that if he liked the new job it would not matter. The EAT held that the ET had confused suitability with reasonableness. The first stage is to assess objectively whether the new job is reasonably equivalent to the old job (and therefore suitable), and only to move on to the question of reasonableness once it has been decided that it is. In his case, as a result of the drop in wages, the employment was not suitable, so the issue of the reasonableness of the resignation did not arise.

While suitability of offer is decided objectively by assessing whether the new contract could reasonably be considered suitable for a person in the position of the employee, the approach to reasonableness of refusal is a subjective one, that is by considering the personal situation of the employee and assessing how reasonable the refusal is. In *Cambridge & District Co-operative Society Ltd* v *Ruse* (1993) the employee had been a manager with the employer for 23 years, first of all as manager of a mobile butchers and then of one of the butcher's shops. When the employee's shop closed, the employers no longer operated any independent butcher's shops and he was offered a job as a butchery department manager in a department store, under the jurisdiction of the store manager, without a key and without responsibility for banking. The employee believed this was an unacceptable loss of status and resigned. The offer was held to be objectively suitable, but the refusal, for the perceived loss of status, was held to be reasonable. It is therefore possible for the refusal of a suitable offer to be reasonable. Other examples could include an offer of employment at a workplace at a distance from home or for hours which would make it difficult for the employee to manage both work and family responsibilities.

Summary dismissal

If the employer is entitled to dismiss the employee without notice on account of misconduct, and does so, no redundancy pay will be due, even although the employee would otherwise qualify for redundancy. This would presumably arise only when the employer includes the employee amongst those who are redundant. If the employer gives notice to the employee, in order for the employer not to be obliged to pay redundancy pay the notice must be accompanied by a written statement that employment could have been terminated without notice because of the employee's misconduct (s 140). If the employee's misconduct occurs after he has been given notice of dismissal (during the obligatory period of the notice), he may still be entitled to some or all of the redundancy pay. It will be up to a tribunal to decide what amount of redundancy pay, if any, is appropriate.

If an employee takes strike action after having been given notice of dismissal (during the obligatory period), the right to redundancy pay is not lost. However, the employer may serve a notice of extension on the employee, requiring the days lost to be made up. Failure to do so could lead to losing the right to the redundancy pay (s 143).

Obtaining redundancy pay

If an employer does not pay statutory redundancy pay the employee can complain to an ET within 6 months of the dismissal (s 164).

The amount of redundancy pay

The relevant factors in calculating redundancy pay are length of service and age. It is calculated in the same way as the basic award for unfair dismissal. Thus a redundant employee is entitled to 1½ weeks' pay for each year in which he was aged over 41, 1 week's pay for every year between

22 and 41, and 1 week's pay for every year under 22. The maximum years to be counted (in reverse order) is 20 (s 162). There is a maximum week's pay (currently £380).

Written statement

The employer must give the employee a written statement showing how the redundancy payment is made up. Failure to do this without reasonable excuse is a criminal offence (s 165). This does not apply where the pay is awarded by a tribunal decision which specifies the amount to be paid.

COLLECTIVE RIGHTS ON REDUNDANCY

Employers are under a statutory obligation to consult trade union or other workers' representatives over larger scale redundancies. The ECJ found that UK law did not comply with the EC Collective Redundancies Directive 75/129 (since replaced by Directive 98/59) in *Commission of the EC v UK* (1994). The (amended) law is contained in TULR(C)A 1992, ss 188–198.

There are other more general provisions requiring consultation under the Information and Consultation of Employees Regulations 2004 (ICER 2004), passed to comply with the Information and Consultation Directive 2002/14. These include an obligation to consult about redundancies, but an employer can give written notice that redundancy consultation will take place under the rules in TULR(C)A 1992. The ICER 2004 provisions are beyond the scope of this book.

Duty to consult

The employer's basic duty is to consult the appropriate representatives when it is proposed to dismiss as redundant 20 or more employees at one establishment within a period of 90 days or less (s 188). Thus there is no statutory obligation to consult where fewer than 20 employees at one establishment are to be made redundant within 90 days. The requirements of the law of unfair dismissal apply to individual dismissals, part of which incorporates a reasonable requirement for consultation, both individual and collective.

Definition of redundancy

Redundancy is not defined in the same way for the purposes of statutory consultation as it is for the right to redundancy pay. This was one of the parts of the legislation which had to be amended to comply with the EC Directive. In this context a dismissal for redundancy is a dismissal "for a reason not related to the individual concerned" (s 195). As with the right to redundancy pay, a dismissal is presumed to be for redundancy unless the contrary is proved. The employer was found to have been in breach of the duty in *GMB* v *MAN Truck & Bus UK Ltd* (2000). After the merger of two companies, the employer decided to harmonise terms and conditions and did so by giving employees notice of dismissal from their existing jobs and an offer of re-employment under new terms and conditions. Although more than 20 employees were involved, the employer did not consult and argued that the duty did not arise since there were no job losses (assuming that employees accepted the new contracts). The EAT held that the duty to consult had arisen, since the employer had terminated the contracts of the employees on a group and not an individual basis. The ECJ had stated that a collective redundancy arose when there were dismissals because of new working arrangements even although there was no diminution in the business or demand for work.

At one establishment

The concept of establishment is derived from the Directive and is not defined there or in TULR(C)A 1992, and has no technical meaning. Under UK law it has been described as a matter of common sense for the tribunal. In *Barratt Developments (Bradford) Ltd* v *UCATT* (1978) the company had made 24 employees working on 8 of 14 building sites redundant. All 14 sites reported directly to the same headquarters. The EAT held that the tribunal had been entitled to find that this was one establishment, as ordinary people would understand it. The duty to consult therefore arose. The ECJ has also taken a broad view of its meaning. An establishment can be a distinct entity which has been assigned to perform one or more tasks, with a workforce and a certain organisational structure. It need not have legal, economic, financial, administrative or technological autonomy. Nor is it essential for it to have independent management or to be geographically separate from other parts of the organisation (*Athinaiki Chartopoiia AE* v *Panagiotidis* (2007)).

Start of consultation

The consultation must begin "in good time" but no less than 90 days before the first dismissal takes effect where the employer is proposing to dismiss 100 or more employees, or, where fewer than 100 are involved (but 20 or more), no less than 30 days before the first dismissal (s 188(1A)). This provision does not comply with Directive 98/59, which requires that an employer who is contemplating redundancies must consult with workers' representatives. To give notice of dismissal before or at the same time as commencing consultation is in breach of this obligation (*Junk* v

Kuhnel (2005)). The requirement of TULR(C)A 1992 could permit an employer to give or have given (sufficient) notice of dismissal before the duty to consult arose.

While TULR(C)A 1992 applies the duty to consult where the employer "proposes to dismiss", the duty under Directive 98/59 arises from when an employer is "contemplating" redundancies. The idea of contemplating redundancies is wider and implies an earlier stage than that of proposing redundancies, as the EAT in *Scotch Premier Meat Ltd* v *Burns* (2000) noted: contemplation involves a larger number of options than proposing, which involves a specific proposal. In this respect the UK duty does not comply with the Directive.

Appropriate representatives

If the employees are represented by an independent recognised trade union, the employer must consult with the union representatives. In any other case, the employer has a choice of representative: representatives specifically elected for the purpose of redundancy consultation, or representatives who have been elected for another purpose (either before or after the proposals) where it is appropriate to consult them about the proposed dismissals, taking account of why they were elected in the first place (s 188(1B)). The original provisions, which did not meet the Directive, applied only where there was an independent recognised trade union. TULR(C)A 1992 places obligations on the employer as regards the election of employee representatives, including numbers and conduct of the elections (s 188A)).

The employer must allow the appropriate representatives access to the employees affected by the proposals, and must provide them with accommodation and other facilities as is appropriate (s 188(5A)).

Consultation

The employer must disclose in writing to the representatives: the reasons for the proposals; the numbers and descriptions of employees whom it is proposed to dismiss as redundant; the total number of employees of that description at the establishment in question; the proposed method of selection; the proposed method of carrying out the dismissals; and the proposed method of calculating the amount of redundancy pay, where it is not going to be based on the statutory formula (s 188(4)).

Following the provisions of the Directive, it is specified that the consultation must include consultation about ways of avoiding the dismissals, reducing the numbers to be dismissed and mitigating the consequences of dismissal, and must be undertaken by the employer "with a view to reaching agreement" with the representatives (s 188(2)). The consultation must be meaningful, but does not oblige the employer to reach agreement. However, the ECJ in *Junk* v *Kuhnel* (2005) describes the Directive as appearing to impose an obligation to negotiate, which goes further than consultation.

An assessment of what amounts to fair consultation was given in *R* v *British Coal and Secretary of State for Trade and Industry, ex parte Price (No 3)* (1994). This case was not concerned with the statutory provisions but with the coal industry procedure. Nevertheless, the suggestion here gives an indication of what may be considered fair in this context in addition to the specific statutory requirements. Consultations should take place when proposals are still at a formative stage; there should be adequate information on which to respond and adequate time in which to respond; and a conscientious consideration by the employer of the response to consultation. Given the specific statutory requirements, an earlier view that the employer did not have to consult about the reasons for proposing or contemplating redundancies is no longer applicable, if it ever was (*UK Coal Mining Ltd* v *National Union of Mineworkers (Northumberland Region)* (2008)).

The obligation to consult can be qualified where there are special circumstances which render it not reasonably practicable for the employer to comply. However, in such a case the employer must take all such steps as are reasonably practicable in all the circumstances (s 188(7)).

Remedies for breach of duty to consult

Where an employer fails to comply with any of the collective redundancies provisions a complaint can be made to a tribunal. If it relates to the election of representatives, individual affected employees may claim; in the case of any other failure, such as failure to consult in good time or adequately, the trade union or employee representative may claim, or, if there is no trade union or representative, an individual employee (s 189). There are no criminal penalties for breach of the provisions, but, in addition to declaring that there has been a breach of duty, a tribunal can also make a protective award, which is viewed as a sanction and not simply as compensation.

Protective award

Although this award will usually be obtained by a trade union or employee representative, it is made in favour of each individual employee who has been dismissed. The award orders the employer to pay remuneration to the employees for the "protected period" (s 189). The protected period starts with the earlier date of the first dismissal or the award itself, and lasts for whatever period the tribunal thinks is just and equitable in the circumstances, taking into account the seriousness of the employer's failure to comply with the duty. It cannot, however, last for longer than 90 days. An application for a protective award can be made either before the last of the dismissals takes effect or within 3 months of that date. There is a cap on the remuneration (currently £380 per week).

The purpose of the protective award is to provide a sanction and thus to deter the employer from non-compliance with the consultation provisions. This was made clear by the Court of Appeal in *Susie Radin Ltd* v *GMB* (2004) where a protective award for the maximum period of 90 days was made by the tribunal because of a complete failure to follow the collective procedure. It also found that the dismissals were not unfair, because any individual consultation would have resulted in the same decision as was reached after the failed collective consultation. The Court of Appeal rejected the employer's argument regarding the level of the protective award that the tribunal should have taken account of its finding in relation to the unfair dismissal claim that consultation would have been futile. That was an irrelevant consideration. The focus of a protective award (unlike unfair dismissal compensation) is not on compensating the employee for loss, but is on the seriousness of the employer's failure to comply with the duty. The guidance given by the court to tribunals in cases where there has been no consultation was that, when calculating the extent of the protective award, they should start from the maximum (90 days) and reduce it only where there are mitigating circumstances justifying a reduction.

Essential Facts

- Statutory redundancy pay provisions are found in the Employment Rights Act 1996, Part XI.
- Consultation procedure for mass redundancies is set out in the Trade Union and Labour Relations (Consolidation) Act 1992, Pt IV, Chap II.

Essential Cases

Morton Sundour Fabrics Ltd v Shaw (1966): an employee who had been told that he would be redundant resigned to take up another job. His claim for statutory redundancy pay was unsuccessful as he had not been dismissed by the employer, but only warned that he was liable to be dismissed at some time in the future.

Lornie v Renfrew District Council (1996): employees were asked if they were interested in early retirement packages as part of a review of the local authority structure. The employee agreed a package with the employer and his employment terminated in accordance with the agreement. His claim for a statutory redundancy pay failed as his employment had been terminated by agreement and not dismissal.

Bass Leisure Ltd v Thomas (1994): the employer closed down the employee's workplace and required her to move to another. It did not take account of her circumstances, therefore it amounted to constructive dismissal. The dismissal was by reason of redundancy since the workplace at which she worked had been closed.

Johnson v Nottinghamshire Police Authority (1974): the shifts and hours of work of employees were changed, though they worked the same number of hours as before. They refused and were dismissed. This was held not to be a redundancy. It was a change in terms and conditions, but did not amount to diminished requirement for the particular work done by the employees.

Murray v Foyle Meats Ltd (1999): employees dismissed when the slaughterhouse they worked in closed down argued they were not redundant because under their contracts they could be required to work anywhere in the workplace. The House of Lords held that, since their dismissal had been caused by a diminished requirement for the work they did, it was a redundancy. The House of Lords rejected a function test and a contractual test in favour of a factual causal test.

Susie Radin Ltd v GMB (2004): the employer failed to comply with the statutory requirements to consult with the trade union over closure of the factory and mass redundancies. The ET made the maximum protective award, but at the same time found that individual unfair dismissal claims failed because the closure would have happened anyway. The Court of Appeal held that the purpose of the protective award is punitive, not compensatory, and in view of the seriousness of the failure to consult the maximum was appropriate. In such a case an ET should start from the maximum and reduce it if there were mitigating factors.

9 TRANSFER OF UNDERTAKINGS

An increasingly important aspect of employment protection is the set of rights which apply when businesses, or parts of businesses, are transferred from one individual or organisation to another. Until 1981, when a business was sold it was a matter for the incoming owner whether the existing employees of the business were offered employment after the transfer and on what terms. The EC Business Transfers Directive (BTD) 77/187 required Member States to pass legislation protecting workers' employment rights when businesses transferred. The first set of regulations passed to comply were the Transfer of Undertakings (Protection of Employment) Regulations 1981 (TUPE 1981). Since then, both EC and UK law has been amended. The current EC Directive, drafted to reflect the decisions of the ECJ interpreting the original, is Directive (BTD) 2001/23, and the relevant UK law, drafted to comply with the revised Directive, is the Transfer of Undertakings (Protection of Employment) Regulations 2006 (TUPE 2006). These Regulations contain provisions which are based on decisions interpreting the original regulations both by the ECJ and UK courts.

The aim of both the Directive and TUPE is to protect employees in the event of a change of employer (from a transferor to a transferee). The principal mechanism by which this is achieved is the automatic transfer of contracts of employment from the transferor to the transferee. In addition to individual rights, TUPE 2006 also provides for consultation, in a similar way to redundancy consultation. Unless otherwise stated, statutory references in this chapter are to TUPE 2006.

PROTECTION OF EMPLOYMENT

The protection given by TUPE 2006 is given to "employees". Although employee is given a wider definition than that in ERA 1996, it is not clear that this has any real practical effect. An employee is defined as any individual who works for another person, whether under a contract of service or apprenticeship or otherwise. It does not include someone who is employed under a contract for services (reg 2). Since at common law there is no intermediate concept between contract of service and contract for services, this will only extend the definition to include those who are employees by virtue of such concepts as implied contract (see Chapter 2).

A transfer may be made by more than one transaction (reg 3(6)). This could be more than one transaction between the transferor and transferee, or by a series of transactions. There does not have to be a contractual relationship between the transferor and transferee. In the case of service provision change, which will be explained below, where an organisation ends a contract for service provision with the transferor and enters into a contract to provide the service with the transferee, there is no direct relationship between transferor and transferee.

Any agreement to exclude the operation of TUPE or to preclude an employee from bringing proceedings under TUPE is void (reg 18; ERA 1996, s 203).

Relevant transfer

TUPE 2006 applies to "a relevant transfer". This may be a transfer of an undertaking or business (here called "business transfer"), or it may be a service provision transfer. In either case the transfer must be from one person to another person (reg 3). The parties to the transfer are the transferor and the transferee. If the identity of the employer remains the same, there is no relevant transfer. Thus TUPE does not apply to a change of control which is brought about by share purchase, since the identity of the employer remains the same and there is no transfer to another person. In *Brookes v Borough Care Services Ltd* (1998) the members of BCS Ltd, a company which ran care homes, resigned and were replaced by another company which ran care homes in a neighbouring area. BCS Ltd was a company whose members' liability was limited by guarantee; the second was an industrial and provident society. The members of the second company became directors of BCS Ltd. BCS Ltd then required its employees to agree to a change of terms and conditions of employment. In an action under TUPE 1981 to have the changes declared to be void (now reg 4(4) of TUPE 2006), the EAT held that there had not been a relevant transfer since the identity of the employer had not changed. TUPE therefore did not apply to make the changes void. However, in *Millam v The Print Factory (London) 1991 Ltd* (2007), where one company had taken control of another by share purchase, the Court of Appeal found that it was possible for there to be a relevant transfer since the second company had in fact, in its own name, taken responsibility for paying the wages of the employees of the first company. This is an exceptional case.

Business transfer

TUPE applies to the transfer of an undertaking or business (or part of either) which was situated in the UK immediately before the transfer: there must be a transfer of an economic entity which retains its identity after transfer (reg 3). TUPE applies to public and private undertakings engaged in economic activities whether or not they are operating for gain. The original provisions of TUPE 1981 applied to commercial undertakings only. However, decisions of the ECJ in references from other Member States had applied the BTD to non-commercial undertakings (eg *The Dr Sophie Redmond Stichting* v *Bartol* (1992)), and in *Commission of the EC* v *UK* (1994) it held that the UK was in breach of its obligations in not extending TUPE protection to employees of non-commercial organisations.

A relevant business transfer therefore involves two elements: the existence of an economic entity with its own identity at transfer, and the retention of that identity after transfer. This is not the identity of the owner, which, as seen above, must be another person. It is the identity of the entity as an economic unit. In *Cheesman* v *R Brewer Contracts Ltd* (2001) the EAT set out 5 principles for determining whether there is an undertaking, and 12 principles for determining whether there is a transfer.

An economic entity is an organised grouping of resources which has the objective of pursuing an economic activity, whether or not that activity is central or ancillary (reg 3(2)). TUPE 2006 applies to the transfer of a part of an undertaking, even where the part transferred is secondary to the main business. The part transferred must have its own economic identity. In *Rask* v *Iss Kantineservice A/S* (1993) the ECJ held that, where a company contracted out the running of its staff canteen, the BTD could apply. It was not necessary for the whole of a business to be transferred, or even for the element to be central to the business. What was necessary was that it had its own identity. Indeed, in *Schmidt* v *Spar- und Leihkasse der Früheren Amter Bordesholm, Kiel und Cronshagen* (1994) the ECJ held that it was possible for the BTD to apply in the case of the transfer of the cleaning functions of a bank to an outside agency, where the cleaning had been done by one employee of the bank at the time of transfer. The business must be "stable", that is not created for a one-off enterprise. The ECJ, in *Rygaard* v *Stro Mølle Akustik A/S* (1996), held that the BTD did not apply where all that was transferred, from one subcontractor to another, was one specific building contract.

The important thing is that the transferred entity retains its identity after transfer. Thus, sale of equipment or premises will not in itself amount to a relevant transfer (though it may be an indicator that a relevant transfer has taken place). Similarly, the fact that the new employer has employed all or a large number of the employees of the previous employer is not determinative on its own. In cases in the ECJ and in the UK courts, a wide range of situations has arisen, covering different types of business and forms of transfer. A distinction has been made in some of these cases between businesses which are "asset reliant", where ownership or control of particular equipment or premises is crucial, and businesses which are "labour intensive", where the principal resource for the business is the workforce (*Suzen* v *Zehnacker Gebaudereinigung GmbH Krankenhausservice* (1997); *Oy Liikenne AB* v *Liskojarvi* (2001); *Abler* v *Sodexho* (2004)).

Although the terms of some of these decisions have appeared to state that different principles apply in each particular type of case, creating, for example, in a labour-intensive enterprise a circular approach whereby if the workforce was not transferred this in itself would be evidence that there had not been a relevant transfer, the correct approach would appear to be to view such decisions as based on their own specific facts. Both the ECJ and the UK courts take a multi-factorial approach to the question.

In *Spijkers* v *Gebroeders Benedik Abattoir CV* (1986) the ECJ stated that the decisive question is whether the entity which has been sold retains its identity and continues with the same or similar economic activities. To decide whether this is the case, the following criteria should be taken into account: all the factual circumstances; the type of undertaking or business; the transfer or otherwise of tangible assets such as buildings and stocks; the value of intangible assets at transfer; whether the majority of staff are taken over by the new employer; transfer of customers; the degree of similarity between activities before and after transfer; the duration of any interruption of activities. No one element is decisive. In *Scottish Coal Co Ltd* v *McCormack* (2006) the Inner House of the Court of Session confirmed the *Spijkers* approach. The business concerned had the rights to extract coal from the Coal Authority. When this arrangement was terminated, a large number of workers were transferred to the new company, but none of the assets, which included valuable plant and buildings. The transferee argued that there could not be a relevant transfer since the business was asset-reliant and none of the assets had been transferred. The Inner House referred the case back to the ET with directions to consider all factors, including the non-transference of the plant. It was not necessary to characterise a business as being either asset-reliant or labour-intensive: there was a whole range of intermediate forms of business, and in any event it was a question of fact, in all the circumstances, whether the entity in question had retained its identity after transfer. Prior to that case, the EAT had confirmed a multi-factorial approach in *P&O Trans European Ltd* v *Initial Transport Services* (2003) where P&O had lost the contract to provide ferry services from the mainland to the Northern Isles to Northlink. Northlink had not taken over any of P&O's ships, but had employed the majority of the seafarer workers, used the same piers and buildings, provided a very similar service and serviced the same passengers as before. In an unsuccessful action for redundancy pay by the employees of P&O who had been employed by Northlink, it was held that, taking all the facts and circumstances into account, there had been a relevant transfer of a stable economic unit which retained its identity after transfer.

A tribunal is entitled to take account not only of the objective aspects of the business and the transfer, but also of the reason why a transferee has structured the transfer in a particular way. In *ECM (Delivery Systems) Ltd v Cox* (1999), a case involving the transfer of a service contract from one company to another (a "labour-intensive" business), the Court of Appeal held that a tribunal had been entitled to take account of the fact that the transferee had decided not to employ any of the transferor's employees because they had indicated that they would be raising claims under TUPE. This, together with the findings that the customers were the same and the activity carried on was the same, had entitled the ET to find that there had been a relevant transfer. Similarly, in *Lightways (Contractors) Ltd v Hood* (2000) the Inner House held that a tribunal had been entitled to take account of the fact that the transferee in this case had stated, when negotiating for the transfer of the relevant lighting maintenance contract to it, that TUPE would apply. There were objective factors in the case pointing both for and against the application of TUPE, and the ET had been entitled to treat this statement as decisive.

Service provision change transfer

Much of the case law under the original TUPE (and BTD) was concerned with the contracting out of service provision in both the private and public sectors. A service provision change is capable of amounting to a business transfer, as can be seen from many of the cases referred to in the previous section. However, TUPE 2006 contains a specific provision including a service provision change in the definition of a relevant transfer (reg 3).

A service provision change occurs in one of three ways: activities cease to be carried out by a client on its own behalf and are carried out by a contractor on the client's behalf (often referred to as "contracting out"); activities cease to be carried out by a contractor on a client's behalf and are carried out by a subsequent contractor; activities cease to be carried out by a contractor or subsequent contractor and are carried out instead by the client on its own behalf ("contracting in"). These could involve any service activity including the provision of cleaning or catering services.

This is subject to three conditions. First, immediately before the service provision change, there must be an organised grouping of employees situated in Great Britain whose principal purpose is carrying out the activities concerned on behalf of the client. As seen above in the case of *Schmidt* (1994), this need not be a large grouping, and may even amount to, as it did in that case, just one employee. The second condition is that the client must intend that the activities will be carried out by the transferee other than for a single specific event or short-term task. Therefore, buying in services for a one-off event will not be covered. The third condition excludes from the definition of transfer those situations where the activities consist wholly or mainly of the supply of goods for the client's use.

Administrative transfer

Although service provision change is included, and thus transfers of local authority services by contracting out, it is specifically provided that TUPE 2006 does not apply to an administrative reorganisation of public administrative authorities, or the transfer of administrative functions between public administrative authorities (reg 3). The ECJ held in *Henke* v *Gemeinde Schierke und Verwaltungsgemeinschaft Brocken* (1996) that the BTD did not apply to such transfers, since its aim was to protect workers against potentially unfavourable consequences of economic trends. Nevertheless, the Cabinet Office has issued a Statement and a Code of Practice which provides that TUPE will usually be complied with in relation to transfers within the public sector, even if this is not strictly required.

Effect of relevant transfer on the contract of employment

Transfer of contract of employment

The principal consequence of a relevant transfer is that the contracts of employment of the employees of the transferor do not terminate on the transfer of the business, but instead continue with the transferee (reg 4). The contract between employee and transferee is as it was originally made with the transferor. The employee's service with the transferor will count as continuous service with the transferee.

Employed immediately before the transfer The employees who are covered by this protection are those employed immediately before the transfer. In the early days of the original TUPE, in some cases this had been interpreted strictly to mean employed at the time of the transfer, thus leaving it possible to avoid its terms altogether by dismissing employees before the transfer took effect. However, in *Litster* v *Forth Dry Dock & Engineering Co Ltd* (1989) the House of Lords held that the provision had to be interpreted so as to comply with the intention of the Directive, and words were implied into TUPE which are express in TUPE 2006. This includes not only those employed immediately before the transfer but also those who would have been so employed if they had not been dismissed before then because of the transfer itself, or a reason connected with it (reg 4(3)). This provision, however, does not result in the employee in question being reinstated as an employee of the transferee. Instead it entitles the employee to raise an action of unfair dismissal against the transferee. The question of dismissal will be dealt with more fully below.

Assigned employees Where an entire business is transferred it is not difficult to identify which employees are transferred. If part only of a business is transferred, it is the employees who are assigned to the particular part (or "organised grouping of resources or employees") of the business (reg 4). Assigned means assigned other than on a temporary basis (reg 2). The ECJ in *Botzen v Rotterdamsche Droogdok Maatschappij BV* (1986) held that the Directive applied only in relation to those who were actually employed in the transferred departments.

Contract as originally made The contract of employment between the transferee and the employee is on the same terms as the contract between the transferor and the employee. It may be impossible for the transferee to provide the same benefits under the contract, as in *Mitie Management Services Ltd v French* (2002) where under the original contract the employees were entitled to take part in a profit-sharing scheme in the transferor's business. The EAT held that the ET had been wrong to declare that the employees were entitled to this identical term, since it was not within the control of the transferee. In such circumstances the transferee's obligation is to provide an equivalent scheme to that of the transferor.

The purpose of TUPE is to safeguard the existing rights of the employee on transfer, and its terms do not entitle the employee to enhanced rights, such as existing employees of the transferee might enjoy. In *Jackson v Computershare Investor Services plc* (2008) the transferee operated an enhanced redundancy scheme which the transferor had not. When Jackson was dismissed as redundant, she was treated on the basis that she had joined the scheme on the date of transfer, and not on the more generous basis that she was already entitled to it when the transfer took place. The Court of Appeal held that TUPE had no relevance to deciding this question since the term was not part of her original contract with the transferor.

Pensions Rights under occupational schemes are excluded from TUPE 2006. They are not transferred, and additionally a transferred employee is not entitled to bring a claim against the transferor for breach of contract or constructive dismissal based on loss of pension rights on transfer (reg 10). However, there is protection of pension rights under the Pensions Act 2004 and the Transfer of Employment (Pension Protection) Regulations 2005. The transferee under a transfer to which TUPE applies must ensure that an employee who had a pension entitlement with the transferor is provided with an equivalent entitlement by the transferee, either through a scheme which it operates or by paying into a stakeholder pension. There is a maximum limit to the employer's contribution of 6 per cent.

Collective agreements If the transferor was party to a collective agreement which is part of the contracts of employment of its employees, the agreement continues to have that effect after transfer (reg 5). This provision is in the same terms as the equivalent provision under the original TUPE. This had been interpreted by the EAT in *Whent* v *T Cartledge Ltd* (1997) as meaning that collective agreements would continue to have effect after the transfer, even although the transferee was not a party to them. Thus, if a contract of employment was stated to be subject to collective agreements agreed between X union and Y employer or group of employers (which the transferor would have been part of but the transferee is not), the employees would be entitled to the new terms negotiated between X and Y from time to time. In *Werhof* v *Freeway Traffic Systems GmbH & Co KG* (2006) the ECJ held that Art 3(1) of the Directive, on which the regulation is based, bound the transferee to the terms of any collective agreement in force at the date of transfer, but did not bind the transferee to any subsequent collective agreements. The Court of Appeal held in *Parkwood Leisure Ltd* v *Alemo-Herron* (2010) that this was the correct interpretation of the TUPE provision as well. It disapproved the EAT decision in *Whent*, and overturned the decision in the EAT below it that TUPE provided for an improvement on the EC law. The Court of Appeal found that there was nothing in reg 5 which expressly provided for the improved position adopted in *Whent*. That provision, in both TUPE 1981 and TUPE 2006, must always have had the meaning as stated by the ECJ. Thus, employees are not entitled to any pay increases negotiated under collective agreements after the date of transfer to which the transferee is not a party.

Variation of contract If the employee and employer (whether transferor or transferee) agree to vary the contract of employment because of the transfer, the variation is void (reg 4(4)). This applies where the reason or principal reason for the change is the transfer itself, or is a reason connected with the transfer, unless it is an "economic, technical or organisational reason entailing changes in the workforce" (ETO). The meaning of this phrase will be discussed more fully in relation to dismissal.

For the avoidance of doubt, the Regulations go on to state that this rule will not prevent employer and employee agreeing a variation which is for a reason unconnected with the transfer, or which is connected but is an ETO reason.

This provision may well apply to restrict the transferee but not the employee. In *Regent Security Services Ltd* v *Power* (2008) the Court of Appeal held that an agreement made between an employee and transferee employer at transfer to raise the employee's retirement age from 60 to 65 could be enforced by the employee (though it could not have been by the employer). Although this was decided under the prohibition on contracting out of the Regulations under TUPE 1981, which did not contain an equivalent provision to reg 4(4), the principle seems equally applicable to TUPE 2006. The Court of Appeal took the view that the aim of TUPE (and the Directive) is to safeguard the position of the employee: there is nothing to stop the employee enforcing an additional right granted by the transferee.

Transfer of liability

On the completion of the transfer it is not only the contract of employment which continues, but in addition all the transferor's "rights, powers, duties and liabilities" in connection with the contract of employment transfer to the transferee. Any act or omission by the transferor in relation to the contract of employment before the transfer will be deemed to be an act or omission of the transferee (reg 4(5)). This means that in addition to all contractual rights and duties, all statutory rights and duties are also transferred, and the liability for them. This would include unfair dismissal protection, maternity rights and other employment protection rights which are not contractual but which arise in connection with the contract of employment. In *Alamo Group (Europe) Ltd* v *Tucker* (2003) this extended to the transferee being held liable for the transferor's breach of the duty to consult under TUPE.

Criminal liability does not transfer (reg 4(6)).

Employee opt-out

An employee cannot be compelled to transfer to the employment of the transferee. An employee who does not wish to transfer must inform either the transferor or the transferee that he objects to becoming an employee of the transferee (reg 4(7)). The notice, which does not have to be in writing, must be given before the transfer. When the employee objects to the transfer, his contract of employment with the transferor is terminated by the transfer. The employee is not considered to have been dismissed by the transferor, unless the transfer would have involved a substantial change in working conditions to the material detriment of the employee, in which case he will be considered to have been dismissed by the transferor.

Dismissal

Where an employee is dismissed either before or after the transfer of a business, if the reason or principal reason for the dismissal is the transfer or a reason connected with the transfer, the dismissal is unfair (reg 7). However, if the reason for the dismissal was an ETO reason the dismissal will not be automatically unfair. However, it will be subject to the general law of unfair dismissal (see Chapter 7).

This provision applies not only to the employees of the transferor who are subject to the transfer, but also to other employees of the transferor, and to existing employees of the transferee. The object is to safeguard the position of all employees affected by the transfer (reg 7(4)).

Automatically unfair dismissal

If the principal reason for the dismissal is the transfer itself, it is automatically unfair. If it is for a reason connected to the transfer, the dismissal is automatically unfair, unless it is an ETO reason. Although it is automatically unfair, the normal qualification for a standard unfair dismissal applies. The employee must therefore have the necessary continuous service.

ETO reason

If the reason is connected to the transfer it is presumed to be unfair, and it will be for the employer to show that it was an ETO reason.

The ETO reason must be one which entails changes in the workforce of either transferor or transferee. Workforce means the workforce as a whole and not as individuals: otherwise the dismissal itself would involve such a change. The change must be in the workforce itself, and not in the terms and conditions of the workforce. In *Delabole Slate Ltd v Berriman* (1985) an employee resigned when his wages were reduced after a transfer in order to bring his wages into line with the level in the transferee's undertaking. The Court of Appeal held that his constructive dismissal was for a reason connected to the transfer and was not an ETO reason. The objective of the company must be to change the strength or establishment of the workforce, while in this case all that the company was seeking to do was to standardise terms and conditions. The dismissal was therefore automatically unfair. In *Crawford* v *Swinton Insurance Brokers Ltd* (1990) the EAT applied the reasoning in *Delabole Slate*, not only to a situation where there was a change in the numbers of the workforce but also where there was a change in the functions performed by the workforce.

If it is established that it is an ETO reason, the dismissal will then be regarded as having been for redundancy (if applicable) or for a substantial reason, both in terms of s 98 of ERA 1996. In *Gorictree Ltd* v *Jenkinson* (1984) the EAT said that one of the most common economic, organisational or technical reasons entailing changes in the workforce was in fact redundancy. In case of either redundancy or substantial reason the general provisions relating to an unfair dismissal claim would apply and the dismissal would have to be reasonable, both in terms of sufficiency of reason and procedure (see Chapter 7).

Remedy

The remedy open to an employee who is unfairly dismissed because of a transfer or for a reason connected with a transfer which is not ETO is a claim for unfair dismissal against the transferee, so long as he has the necessary qualifying service. Such a dismissal by either transferor or transferee is not "invalid". The House of Lords in *British Fuels Ltd* v *Baxendale* (1998) rejected the interpretation in the lower courts that an employee who had been dismissed contrary to the equivalent to reg 7 under the original TUPE had to be considered as having continued in employment with the transferee.

Insolvency

Where the transferor is insolvent, there are provisions which give total or partial exemption from the operation of TUPE 2006, depending partly on the nature of the insolvency proceedings. Where the proceedings are undertaken with a view to the liquidation of the assets of the transferor (ie not with a view to keeping the business going) and under the supervision of an insolvency practitioner, reg 4 (transfer of contract of employment) and reg 7 (dismissal) do not apply. Where the proceedings are undertaken under the supervision of an insolvency practitioner, but not with a view to the liquidation of the assets, while reg 4 and reg 7 do apply, certain debts owed to the transferor's employees do not transfer to the transferee, but are paid out of the National Insurance Fund under ERA 1996, Pt XII (reg 8). In the case of insolvency proceedings which are not under the supervision of an insolvency practitioner, there is no exception from the general application of TUPE.

In the second situation described above, where the insolvency proceedings are under official supervision but not with a view to the liquidation of assets, provision is made for agreement between transferor, transferee or insolvency practitioner on the one hand and employee representatives on the other hand to certain permitted variations to contracts of employment (reg 9).

Employee liability information

The transferor must provide the transferee with certain information concerning the individuals who are assigned to the entity which is being transferred not less than 14 days before the transfer, or, if there are special circumstances preventing this, as soon as possible after that (reg 11). If the transferor fails to comply with this duty, the transferee, on or after the transfer, may complain to a tribunal, which has the power to award compensation for each employee in respect of whom the transferor failed to give the required information.

DUTY TO CONSULT REGARDING TRANSFER

In advance of a relevant transfer, there is a duty on the part of an employer to consult with the representatives of the employees who are affected by the transfer. While the employees who are most immediately affected are the transferor's employees, and, where only part of the transferor's business is being transferred, the employees assigned to that part, this duty extends to all employees who may be affected by the transfer, whether employed by the transferor or transferee and whether or not assigned to the part in question (reg 13). Thus, obligations are imposed on both transferor and transferee, although the most significant will be the obligation imposed on the transferor.

Representatives

If there is a recognised independent trade union representing the affected employees, the employer must consult with its representatives. If not, in a similar provision to redundancy consultation, the employer can choose to consult with employee representatives appointed or elected by those employees for another purpose, or with employee representatives elected by those employees specifically for the purpose (reg 13(3)). The requirements for the latter elections are contained in reg 14.

Information

As a first step, long enough before the transfer to enable the employer to consult with the representatives, the employer must give certain information to the representatives. They must be informed of the fact that the transfer is to take place; when it is to take place; the reasons for the transfer; the legal, economic and social implications of the transfer for any affected employees; the measures which the employer envisages it will take in relation to the affected employees, or, if it envisages no measures, that fact. In the case of the transferor, in addition to the measures which it envisages taking itself, it must also inform the representatives of the measures which it envisages the transferee will take in relation to affected employees, or, if it envisages no measures, that fact. To enable the transferor to do this, the transferee must provide it with the relevant information in time for it to comply with this duty (reg 13).

If the employer fails to give accurate information, and the reason is that it genuinely believed that the information it was giving was accurate, it may not be in breach of its duty. In *Royal Mail* v *Communication Workers Union* (2009), where a number of Post Office branches were being transferred to a national retail chain, the transferor informed the union that no contracts of employment of employees would transfer, since all employees would either be relocated or accept voluntary redundancy. This was not the case and some employees did transfer automatically. The Court of Appeal held that the Post Office had not been in breach of its duty to inform, since it had genuinely believed that the information it had given (which related to the legal implications of the transfer) was accurate.

Duty to consult

The provision of this information may lead to voluntary consultations with the representatives. The employer may decide to initiate consultation, or the union or representatives may seek consultation. The only specific obligation on the employer to consult arises when it envisages that it will be taking measures in relation to an affected employee in connection with the transfer (reg 13(6)).

It is important therefore to be able to identify what is meant by "envisaging" "taking measures". This has been considered by the English High Court in *Institute of Professional Civil Servants* v *Secretary of State for Defence* (1987) and it was suggested that "measures" includes a specific "action, step or arrangement", while "envisage" means that the employer has it in mind to implement the measure, subject to consultation. Thus, the duty to consult would not arise until such a stage had been reached in the thinking of the employer.

Consultation about measures must take place with a view to seeking the agreement of the representatives to the measures: this does not oblige the employer to obtain such agreement. In the course of such consultations the employer must consider any representations made by the representatives, reply to them, and, if he rejects any of their representations, state the reasons.

Remedy for failure

In the case of failure to comply with the duties to inform and consult, the union, representatives and affected employees have the right to make complaints to a tribunal (reg 15). If a complaint against a transferee is upheld, the ET must make a declaration to that effect, and order it to pay appropriate compensation; if a complaint against a transferor is upheld, similarly it will be ordered to pay appropriate compensation, unless the failure was to inform about the measures envisaged by the transferee and the transferee's failure caused that, in which case the transferee will be ordered to pay appropriate compensation. Except in the last example, both transferor and transferee are jointly and severally liable for the compensation. Appropriate compensation means what is just and equitable to a maximum of 13 weeks' pay. As with the protective award in redundancy cases, this award is meant to act as a deterrent. Accordingly, in *Sweetin* v *Coral Racing* (2006) the EAT applied the same principle and held that, since there were no mitigating factors present, the failure to consult being gross, the maximum award should have been made.

Essential Facts

- Employment protection and consultation on transfer of undertakings is governed by the Transfer of Undertakings (Protection of Employment) Regulations 2006.
- The current EC Directive on acquired rights on transfer of business, reflected in TUPE 2006, is the Business Transfers Directive 2001/23.

Essential Cases

Brookes v Borough Care Services Ltd (1998): when a company became the sole shareholder in another company and its members the directors, it was held that this was a genuine share transfer agreement and therefore TUPE did not apply.

Spijkers v Geboeders Benedik Abattoir CV (1986): a decision by the ECJ under the Business Transfers Directive which stated that the key question was whether an economic entity had been sold which retained its identity and continued with the same or similar economic activities. It lists criteria which should be taken into account.

Scottish Coal Co v McCormack (2006): when the activities of a coal mining company were taken over, without any of its assets being taken over, it was argued that, since the business was "asset-reliant" there had been no relevant transfer. The Court of Session held that the key question was whether the entity retained its identity after transfer and that, although transfer of assets was one criterion, it was not decisive.

Werhof v Freeway Traffic Systems GmbH & Co KG (2006): the ECJ held that on a transfer contracts of employment, including terms incorporated from a collective agreement, were transferred. The transferee was bound by collective agreements in force at the time of the transfer, but would not be bound by any subsequent collective agreements to which it was not a party.

Delabole Slate Ltd v Berriman (1985): after a transfer the transferee reduced the wages of the employee, who had formerly been employed by the transferor, in order to bring his wages into line with the rest of the transferee's employees. The employee resigned in consequence. This was a constructive dismissal and the Court of Appeal held that it was not for an ETO reason. An ETO reason must involve change in the composition of the workforce, and not in terms and conditions.

Gorictree Ltd v Jenkinson (1984): when a garage was taken over employees were dismissed and offered contracts on a self-employed basis. This was an ETO reason, but also involved a redundancy. The employee was therefore entitled to a statutory redundancy payment.

10 DISCRIMINATION

Discrimination law has been thoroughly revised in the course of 2010. The Equality Act 2010 received Royal Assent in April, and the principal part is expected to come into force at the beginning of October 2010. The law stated here will be that in effect at May 2010, but the impact of the Equality Act will be described along with the current law.

The right not to be discriminated against is an important aspect of equality. There are currently six prohibited grounds of discrimination (to become nine protected characteristics under the Equality Act): sex, race, disability, religion or belief, sexual orientation and age. Each currently has its own separate legislation and each is also subject to EC law.

LEGISLATION

The principal statutes are the Equal Pay Act 1970 (EPA 1970), which deals with gender pay discrimination; the Sex Discrimination Act 1975 (SDA 1975); the Race Relations Act 1976 (RRA 1976); the Disability Discrimination Act 1995 (DDA 1995); the Employment Equality (Religion or Belief) Regulations 2003 (EE(RB)R 2003); the Employment Equality (Sexual Orientation) Regulations 2003 (EE(SO)R 2003); and the Employment Equality (Age) Regulations 2006 (EE(A)R 2006). All of these will be replaced by the Equality Act 2010 (EA 2010), when it comes into force.

Although EPA 1970 was passed before the UK joined the European Community and the SDA 1975 before the first EC Directive prohibiting sex discrimination in employment, EC law has been very influential on the development of UK sex discrimination law. For example, as seen in Chapter 6, the weekly hours requirement for qualifying continuous service was successfully challenged as being contrary to EC law in *R v Secretary of State for Employment, ex parte Equal Opportunities Commission* (1994). The RRA 1976 and DDA 1995 were passed before, in the case of the RRA 1976 long before, there was any EC competence to legislate in this area; but the other three grounds – religion and belief, sexual orientation and age were introduced to comply with EC law. The relevant EC Directives are the Equal Treatment Directive 2006/54 (originally Directive 76/207) on sex discrimination; the Race Directive 2000/43; and the Framework Equal Treatment Directive 2000/78 on disability, religion or belief, sexual orientation and age.

More recent challenges to UK discrimination law have included *Coleman* v *Attridge Law* (2008), referred to below, in which the ECJ held that DDA 1995 breached Directive 2000/78; and *R (Age Concern)* v *Secretary of State for BERR* (2009) in which the ECJ held that the provision of a default retirement age of 65 in EE(A)R 2006 was not necessarily contrary to Directive 2000/78. On the case returning to the English High Court, the default age was held not to have been in breach in 2006 when EE(A)R 2006 were passed, but the judge questioned their continuing validity. They were held not to be in breach, because the government had in the meanwhile established a review of the situation.

Equal pay

EPA 1970 applies only to gender inequality. It uses a different approach to establishing whether there has been sex discrimination in relation to pay or contractual terms to either SDA 1975, which governs sex discrimination more generally, or the legislation governing the other strands. It will be dealt with separately, at the end of this chapter.

PROTECTED CHARACTERISTICS

There is no general prohibition against discrimination. Currently there are the six grounds on which it is unlawful to discriminate, often referred to as the "six strands". Under the EA 2010, three grounds which were part of sex discrimination will become separate, and there will be nine "protected characteristics": age, disability, gender reassignment, marriage and civil partnership, pregnancy and maternity, race, religion or belief, sex, and sexual orientation (s 4).

Sex

It is unlawful to discriminate against a woman on ground of her sex (SDA 1975, s 1), and against a man on ground of his sex (s 2).

Marriage or civil partnership

It is unlawful to discriminate against a married person, or a civil partner, on ground of their marriage or partnership (s 3). Marriage or civil partnership will be a protected characteristic in its own right under EA 2010.

Gender reassignment

As a result of the ECJ decision in *P* v *S and Cornwall County Council* (1996) sex discrimination law was held to extend to transsexuals. As a result, SDA 1975 was amended to protect transsexuals, but only in employment, and only in relation to direct discrimination. Gender reassignment will be a protected characteristic in its own right under EA 2010.

Pregnancy and maternity

An early approach of the UK tribunals was to compare the treatment of a pregnant woman with a sick man in order to see if there had been gender discrimination (*Hayes* v *Malleable Working Men's Club* (1985)). As a result of ECJ decisions, since only women get pregnant, pregnancy discrimination was held to be sex discrimination without any need to make a comparison with a man (*Hertz* (1990), *Dekker* (1990)). Since 2005 there has been a specific provision in SDA 1975. The formulation was held to be contrary to EC law as it required a comparison to be made with someone who was not pregnant, which the ECJ cases did not (*Equal Opportunities Commission* v *Department for Trade and Industry* (2007)). The current provision is that it is discrimination if a woman is treated less favourably on grounds of pregnancy (at any time during the "protected period" – during pregnancy and statutory maternity leave) or on grounds of taking statutory maternity leave (s 3A). Pregnancy and maternity will be a protected characteristic in its own right under EA 2010.

Race

It is unlawful to discriminate against someone on racial grounds (RRA 1976, s 1; EA 2010, s 9). "Racial grounds" means colour, race, nationality or ethnic or national origins (RRA, s 3). Nationality includes citizenship.

Nationality

Nationality means being the citizen of a particular nation or state. Directive 2000/43 does not extend to nationality, and when RRA 1976 was amended in 2003 to bring it into line with the Directive the changes did not apply to nationality. The original provisions of RRA still apply so that there are different statutory provisions in relation to burden of proof, indirect discrimination, harassment and genuine occupational qualification. Under EA 2010 there will be no such difference.

Colour

Colour is not mentioned specifically in either Directive 2000/43 or the 2003 amendments to the RRA 1976. However, colour has been viewed as so closely related to race and ethnic origins as to be the "outward and visible manifestation" of them. The EAT therefore held that the amended provisions apply, in *Abbey National plc* v *Chagger* (2009). Colour is specified in EA 2010.

Ethnic origins

Ethnic origins refers to a group identity which may coincide with but is different from colour, race, nationality or national origins. This is not based on religion, although that might play a part in the ethnic identity. Since the introduction of religious discrimination legislation, many people who might have based a case on race discrimination will now rely on the newer legislation. A Rastafarian worker was unsuccessful in an action under RRA 1976 in *Dawkins* v *Department of the Environment* (1993) as it was held there was no common ethnic origin, but in *Harris* v *NKL Automotive Ltd* (2007) a successful claim was made under EE(RB)R 2003, as Rastafarians are a belief group.

The approach adopted by Lord Fraser in *Mandla* v *Lee* (1983) towards determining whether a group is an ethnic group has been very influential. A school refused to admit a Sikh boy unless he agreed to wear the school cap, and not the headgear which Sikhism required. In the lower courts the school had been successful in arguing that this was religious discrimination and therefore not covered by RRA 1976. The House of Lords, however, held that Sikhs were an ethnic group. Lord Fraser identified the characteristics which made up an ethnic group. The group must regard itself, and be regarded by others, as a distinct community by virtue of these characteristics. There are two essential characteristics: a long shared history of which the group is conscious as distinguishing it from other groups, and the memory of which it keeps alive; and a cultural tradition of its own, including family and social customs and manners, often but not necessarily associated with religious observance. It is this cultural element which is important. In addition there are other characteristics, not all of which need always be present. These are: either a common geographical origin, or descent from a small number of common ancestors; a common language, not necessarily peculiar to the group; a common literature, peculiar to the group; a common religion different from that of neighbouring groups or from the general community surrounding it; and being a minority or being an oppressed or a dominant group within a larger community.

As well as Sikhs, Jews, Gypsies (*CRE* v *Dutton* (1989)), Irish Travellers and Scottish Gipsy Travellers (*McLennan* v *Gipsy Traveller Education and Information Project* (2008)) have been held to be groups with a distinct ethnic origin based on these principles.

National origins

This can refer to the original nationality of a person who has adopted a new nationality. It can also refer to the heritage of a person in the sense of the national origins of their family. It can apply where a person's regional or national identification relates to an area which previously had statehood but does not currently. This applies to English, Welsh and Scottish identity (*Northern Joint Police Board v Power* (1997)). The Scots and the English have been held to be groups defined by national, but not ethnic origins.

Disability

A person has a disability where they have a physical or mental impairment which has a substantial and long-term adverse effect on their ability to carry out normal day-to-day activities (DDA 1995, s 1 and Sch 1; EA 2010, s 6 and Sch 1). This includes a person who has had a disability. One of the criticisms made of the legislation is that many cases involve a dispute about whether the employee is disabled or not, thus involving proof of a negative state of affairs.

Impairment

Under the original definition in DDA 1995, a mental impairment was relevant only where it resulted from mental illness which was a "clinically well-recognised illness". This restriction was removed in 2005.

Certain conditions are excluded from being treated as impairments by the Disability Discrimination (Meaning of Disability) Regulations 1996 (DD(MD)R 1996). This includes addiction to alcohol, nicotine or any other substance (unless the result of medical prescription/treatment). But physical or mental impairment caused by addiction can be relevant (*Power v Panasonic UK Ltd* (2003)). Other behaviours which are excluded are a tendency to steal; a tendency to physical or sexual abuse of others; exhibitionism; voyeurism.

Severe disfigurement   A severe disfigurement is to be treated as having a substantial adverse effect on the ability of the person concerned to carry out normal day-to-day activities (Sch 1). However, certain "deliberately acquired disfigurements" are excluded: tattooings which have not been removed; piercings for decorative or other non-medical purposes.

Normal day-to-day activities

The test of disability does not relate to the activities required for the job in question. The impairment must have a long-term substantial adverse effect on normal day-to-day activities. These are defined in an exclusive list as affecting one of the following: mobility, manual dexterity, physical coordination, continence, ability to lift, carry or otherwise move everyday objects, speech, hearing or eyesight, memory or ability to concentrate, learn or understand, perception of the risk of physical danger (DDA 1995, Sch 1). This statutory list of what comprises normal day-to-day activities has been heavily criticised as restrictive, and in EA 2010 there is no such list. The fact that a person can carry out such activities does not mean that their ability to do so is unimpaired. The focus of the Act is on what the applicant either cannot do or can only do with difficulty, rather than on what they can do. It is an error for a tribunal to balance what a person can do against those things which he cannot do or can only do with difficulty (*Goodwin* v *Patent Office* (1999)).

Although the emphasis is on day-to-day activities, those carried out at work may still be relevant. Where the effects of an impairment fluctuate and are exacerbated by work conditions, a tribunal should consider the employee's ability to carry out normal day-to-day activities both outside and at work (*Cruikshank* v *VAW Motorcast Ltd* (2002)).

The decision of the ECJ in *Chacon Navas* v *Eurest Colectividades SA* (2006) noted that Directive 2000/78 aims to combat discrimination which "hinders the participation of the person concerned in professional life". This places the emphasis more directly on work activities. In *Chief Constable of Dumfries and Galloway* v *Adams* (2009) the EAT held that normal day-to-day activities included activities found across a range of jobs (rather than highly specialised activities). In that case, a police officer who suffered from a condition which made working at nights difficult was held to be disabled, since working night shift was common, and therefore a normal day-to-day activity.

Substantial adverse effect

While the Act does not define "substantial", it is accepted as meaning "more than minor or trivial", and not "very large" (*Goodwin* v *Patent Office*).

If an impairment would have a substantial adverse effect, but for the fact that measures such as medical treatment or an aid are being used to treat or correct it, it is to be treated as if it had that effect. This does not apply where a sight impairment is being treated by spectacles or contact lenses.

"Deemed" disability   As a result of amendments made in 2005, a person who has cancer, HIV infection or multiple sclerosis is deemed to be disabled (without having to meet the four-part definition of disability).

Regulations may be introduced to restrict this in the case of certain cancers.

Progressive conditions In the case of other conditions which are progressive, if the condition results in an impairment which has an effect (but not a substantial adverse effect) on a person's ability to carry out normal day-to-day activities, they shall be taken to have an impairment with a substantial adverse effect if that is likely to result. This applies from the development of minor symptoms.

Long-term effects

The effect of an impairment is long-term if it has lasted at least 12 months, or is likely to last at least 12 months or for the rest of the person's life. Where it ceases to have a substantial adverse effect but is likely to recur it is to be treated as continuing.

Religion or belief

It is unlawful to discriminate against a person on ground of their religion or belief (EE(RB)R 2003, reg 2; EA 2010, s 10). Religion means any religion. Belief means any religious or philosophical belief. This includes lack of religion or belief. In *McNab* v *Glasgow District Council* (2007) an atheist teacher who had been refused a guidance post in a Catholic school was successful in his tribunal action. Religious discrimination is discrimination because of the religion of the victim of the discrimination or of a third party but not that of the discriminator.

Not all beliefs can qualify as a belief for the protection of EE(RB)R 2003. In *Grainger plc* v *Nicholson* (2010) the EAT held that it was possible for belief in climate change to be such a belief. Taking account of ECHR case law, it stated that for a philosophical belief to qualify five conditions must be satisfied: the belief must be genuinely held; it must be a belief and not an opinion or viewpoint based on the present state of information available; it must be a belief as to a weighty and substantial aspect of human life and behaviour; it must attain a certain level of cogency, seriousness, cohesion and importance; and it must be worthy of respect in a democratic society, be not incompatible with human dignity and not conflict with the fundamental rights of others. Thus, racist beliefs, for example, could not qualify for this protection as they could not fulfil the last two criteria.

Sexual orientation

It is unlawful to discriminate against a person on grounds of sexual orientation. This is defined as a sexual orientation towards those of the same sex; towards those of the opposite sex; towards those of the same sex and of the opposite sex (EE(SO)R 2003, reg 3; EA 2010, s 12).

Age

It is unlawful to discriminate against a person on ground of their age (EE(A)R 2003, reg 3; EA 2010, s 5). This applies to all ages and age groups. This includes the person's apparent age. An "age group" is a group defined by reference to a particular age or a range of ages.

Combined discrimination

Currently, if there has been discrimination on more than one ground, say (for example) because the victim was a black woman, action has to be raised on two separate grounds and proved separately (*Bahl* v *Law Society* (2004)). When this part of EA 2010 comes into force (expected to be April 2011) it will be possible to allege combined discrimination: that is, direct discrimination because of a combination of two protected characteristics, but no more than two (s 14). It will not be necessary to prove that there has been direct discrimination on each ground separately.

AN ACTION OF DISCRIMINATION

An action of discrimination must allege two things: that there has been an unlawful act of discrimination; and that there has been a breach of duty under the legislation, for these purposes a breach of a statutory duty owed by an employer.

DISCRIMINATION

There are three forms of unlawful acts which are common across all the grounds. These are direct discrimination, victimisation and harassment. A fourth, indirect discrimination, applies in all the strands except disability; while in the case of disability there are two specific forms of discrimination, disability-related discrimination and breach of the duty to make adjustments. When EA 2010 comes into effect indirect discrimination will apply to disability as well.

Direct discrimination

Direct discrimination occurs when one person treats another less favourably, on the prohibited ground, than they have treated or would treat someone to whom that ground did not apply (SDA 1975, s 1/1A; RRA 1976, s 1/1A; DDA 1995, s 3A(5); EE(SO)R 2003, reg 3; EE(RB)R 2003, reg 3; EE(A)R 2006, reg 3). It is not sufficient to show that a person has been treated less favourably and that the prohibited ground (protected characteristic) applies: for example, that she is woman. It is necessary to show that the less favourable treatment was because of the protected characteristic.

Under EA 2010 there is one definition of direct discrimination applicable to all the strands. Direct discrimination is where A treats B less favourably than A treats or would treat others, because of a protected characteristic (s 13). This is intended to have the same meaning as the existing definitions, "on ground of" having been interpreted as "because of" in case law.

Less favourable treatment

The usual first stage is to prove that there has been less favourable treatment. Unlike unfair dismissal where it is unfair treatment which is unlawful, in direct discrimination it is not unfairness but less favourable treatment. In theory, if everyone is treated equally unfairly, there is no direct discrimination. A comparison must be made between the treatment of the claimant and the treatment of a comparable person without the protected characteristic. The relevant circumstances of those being compared must be the same or not materially different (SDA 1975, s 5; RRA 1976, s 3; EE(RB)R 2003, reg 3; EE(SO)R 2003, reg 3; EE(A)R 2006, reg 3; EA 2010, s 23). The relevant circumstances would be whatever in the particular case was relevant to the employer's action complained of, apart from the protected characteristic: for example, in the case of a complaint that a promotion had been refused, the comparison would be with someone without the characteristic who had the same or similar level of qualification for the post.

The comparison does not have to be made with an actual person who was treated more favourably, but can be with a hypothetical person with the same relevant circumstances except the characteristic. In *Hurley v Mustoe* (1981) an employer dismissed a woman employed as a waitress the day after she was recruited when he discovered that she was a mother of under school-age children. As he told the local press, he found such employees to be unreliable and in any event believed they should be with their children. There was no actual male waiter with under school-age children to compare her treatment with. However, it was held that, since he would not have treated such a male in the same way, he had treated her less favourably on the ground of her sex.

Because of a protected characteristic

The second stage is to prove that the less favourable treatment was on ground of the protected characteristic. This does not mean that the treatment was motivated by the protected characteristic, for example by racism or homophobia, but that it was because of the protected characteristic. This has been described in the House of Lords as meaning that the claimant must show that she would have received the same treatment as the other person received or would have received "but for" her sex (or other protected characteristic) (*James v Eastleigh Borough Council* (1990)). Thus the protected characteristic must be the cause, but not necessarily the motive for the treatment. The discrimination may be unconscious as well as conscious (*Nagarajan v London Regional Transport* (1999)). The House of Lords has also approached this by saying that the courts can focus on "the reason why" the less favourable treatment took place (*Shamoon v Chief Constable of the RUC* (2003)). This would be the reason why the employer had acted in the particular way. If the issue was failure to obtain promotion, this would be the reason why the employee was unsuccessful.

The protected characteristic need not be the sole cause of the less favourable treatment, so long as it is an important factor. In *Owen and Briggs v James* (1982) the Court of Appeal held that it was sufficient that the applicant's colour was a significant factor in the decision not to employ her, as well as her level of expertise.

"Associative discrimination"

This arises where a person is directly discriminated against because of someone else's protected characteristic. It might be because of a partner's characteristic, or a mistaken belief that a person possessed a protected characteristic (such as a mistaken belief in a person's religion), or it might arise where an employee has refused to follow an instruction to discriminate against a third party. Under the current law, the position is not uniform. It is dependent on the precise wording of direct discrimination in each statute whether this amounts to unlawful direct discrimination.

RRA 1976 defines direct discrimination as less favourable treatment "on racial grounds", EE(RB)R 2003 as less favourable treatment "on the grounds of the religion or belief of B (the victim) or any other person except A (the discriminator)" and EE(SO)R 2003 as less favourable treatment "on grounds of sexual orientation". In each of these cases, it does not have to be the claimant's race, religion or sexual orientation which is the cause of the treatment. In *Weathersfield Ltd v Sargent* (1999) the Court of Appeal held that a white woman who had been told in her induction training to refuse service to coloured people and Asians and who had resigned as a result, had been constructively dismissed on racial grounds and thus suffered direct race discrimination.

By contrast, SDA 1975 defines direct discrimination as less favourable treatment of a woman "on ground of her sex", DDA 1995 as less favourable treatment on the ground of the disabled person's disability. In *Coleman* v *Attridge Law* (2008) a woman whose son was disabled complained of direct discrimination and harassment by her employers, because of time taken to look after her son. The ET referred the case to the ECJ, which held that the restriction in DDA 1995 to the disabled person was in breach of the Directive. Subsequently, the EAT (2010) read words into DDA 1995 to extend its coverage to direct discrimination and harassment against persons associated with a disabled person.

EE(A)R 2006, like SDA 1975, prohibit discrimination on grounds of the victim's age. However, there is a provision which makes it unlawful to treat someone less favourably because they have not carried out, or have complained about, an instruction which was itself discriminatory. Thus associative discrimination would be caught to that specific extent (reg 5).

Under EA 2010, as direct discrimination is defined in all cases as less favourable treatment "because of a protected characteristic", associative discrimination will be covered for them all.

Burden of proof

The burden is on the claimant to prove that the respondent has discriminated against him. As a result of difficulties of obtaining direct proof, once the claimant has proved facts from which the tribunal could conclude, in the absence of an adequate explanation, that there has been discrimination, the burden shifts to the respondent to prove that it did not discriminate (SDA 1975, s 63A; RRA 1976, s 54A; EE(RB)R 2003, reg 29; EE(SO)R 2003, reg 29; EE(A)R 2006, reg 37). In the case of nationality discrimination the burden does not formally shift to the respondent, but once the claimant has proved a prima facie case of direct discrimination, the evidential burden will shift to the respondent to give a non-discriminatory explanation of the treatment. In the absence of a satisfactory explanation the tribunal may, not must, draw an inference of unlawful discrimination (*King* v *The Great Britain China Centre* (1991)).

Guidance on how to approach the shifting burden of proof was given by the Court of Appeal in *Igen Ltd* v *Wong* (2005).

Under EA 2010, in all cases, once there are facts from which a court could decide, in the absence of another explanation, that a person had discriminated unlawfully, it must hold that this occurred, unless the respondent shows it did not (s 136).

Inferences may also be drawn from more general evidence. Evidence of a respondent's record in dealing with women, or members of racial groups, for example, may be relevant to establishing an inference of unlawful discrimination (*Singh* v *West Midlands Passenger Transport Executive* (1988)).

There is a statutory questionnaire which, either before or after initiating action, an employee may send to the employer or other alleged discriminator, containing some standard questions and allowing the claimant to ask other relevant questions. It is not compulsory for the respondent to answer, but the questionnaire and any answers are admissible as evidence at any hearing, and if the respondent has failed to reply within a reasonable time without cause, or the answers are evasive or equivocal, the tribunal may draw an inference from that, including an inference of discrimination. This applies to both direct and indirect discrimination (SDA 1975, s 74; RRA 1976, s 65; EE(RB)R 2003, reg 33; EE(SO)R 2003, reg 33; EE(A)R 2006, reg 41; EA 2010, s 138).

Justification of direct age discrimination

The general rule is that direct discrimination cannot be justified. The exception to this is age discrimination where the discriminator may put forward a defence that the treatment is "a proportionate means of achieving a legitimate aim" (EE(A)R 2006, reg 3; EA 2010, s 13(2)). The alleged discriminator must establish the defence. This is the same defence that is available in the case of indirect discrimination and will be considered below.

Neutral application

Although the protection for each characteristic has been introduced because of discrimination suffered by particular groups (for example, racial or religious minorities, homosexuals or women), the legislation is neutral in effect. Thus, a member of a racial or religious majority, a heterosexual or a man who feels directly discriminated against on a protected ground may rely on the legislation. This is not the case, however, in the case of disability. Having a disability is a protected characteristic, and a person who is not disabled may not rely on the legislation if they feel that they have been treated less favourably than a disabled person.

Indirect discrimination

Direct discrimination prohibits treating someone less favourably because of a protected characteristic. It therefore requires that people are treated the same. This form of equal treatment is usually described as "formal equality": it is not concerned with whether there are equal outcomes or with what is often called substantive equality, but with ensuring that there is procedural equality. Sometimes, however, in order to achieve equality, or not to discriminate, it is necessary to treat people differently. Indirect discrimination arises where, instead of applying an inflexible policy or practice, an employer ought to make an exception because of the impact on someone with a particular protected characteristic.

The general idea of indirect discrimination is sometimes summed up as "disparate impact". It introduces a group dimension to the concept of unlawful discrimination. It arises where, with or without intention to discriminate, a condition is applied or a practice established which it is in practical terms more difficult for a particular group to fulfil than others who do not belong to the group. The group here is defined by reference to the protected characteristics. Unlike direct discrimination, where the impact of the practice or condition is unintentional, it is possible to justify it so long as the justification is objective and not linked to the protected characteristic.

There have been different definitions and currently in employment there are two: one applying to nationality and the other applying to all other grounds. Currently, indirect discrimination does not apply in the case of disability discrimination. The original UK definition of indirect discrimination still applies to nationality discrimination and is more restrictive than the definitions currently applying elsewhere and which were introduced to comply with EC law. Indirect discrimination under EA 2010 reflects the current general definition, and applies to all the protected characteristics, including nationality and disability (s 19).

Definition

Indirect discrimination occurs where a provision, criterion or practice (PCP) is applied which puts people who belong to the same group as the claimant (defined by reference to a protected characteristic) at a particular disadvantage compared to others not in that group, which puts the claimant at that disadvantage and which cannot be shown to be a proportionate means of achieving a legitimate aim (SDA 1975, s 1A; RRA 1976, s 1A; EE(RB)R 2003, reg 3; EE(SO)R 2003, reg 3; EE(A)R 2006, reg 3; EA 2010, s 19).

In other words, it arises where an individual is being treated the same as others in circumstances where this treatment has an adverse impact on a group the individual belongs to, defined by one of the protected characteristics, where this cannot be justified in the circumstances.

The claimant must prove that a PCP was applied to him; that the PCP places people with the particular protected characteristic which they share at a particular disadvantage compared to others without that characteristic; and that he is placed at that disadvantage. The respondent must prove that the PCP is justifiable as a proportionate means of achieving a legitimate aim.

An example of indirect discrimination is one of the earliest cases under SDA 1975. In *Price* v *Civil Service Commission* (1977), the employee, a 36-year-old woman, claimed that she had been indirectly discriminated against by the imposition of an age restriction of 17½–28 for the post of executive officer. Her claim was successful: at that age women were more likely than men to be absent from work because of childbirth and child-rearing responsibilities, and the Civil Service Commission was unable to provide a justification for this rule. As a result of this case the age bar was removed. Such a case would probably now be dealt with under EE(A)R 2006. A more recent example, which will be referred to below, is *Azmi* v *Kirklees Metropolitan Borough Council* (2007) in which a Muslim bilingual support worker in a school claimed that she had been indirectly discriminated against by being required to remove her veil when teaching, since this would disadvantage Muslims compared to non-Muslims.

Provision, criterion or practice (PCP)

If the PCP is in itself discriminatory it will amount to direct discrimination. The PCP must appear to be neutral: on the face of it, it must not appear to discriminate. Many sex discrimination cases have been concerned with less favourable treatment of part-time workers compared with full-time workers. In *Bilka-Kaufhaus GmbH* v *Von Hartz* (1986) the ECJ held that a pension scheme which refused access to part-time employees unless they had worked for 15 out of 20 years discriminated indirectly against women contrary to Art 119 (now 157) of the Treaty of Rome, unless it could be shown that it was objectively justified. More women than men tend to work part-time, again because of family responsibilities.

The early definition of indirect discrimination under RRA 1976 still applies to nationality discrimination and, instead of a PCP, the respondent must apply a requirement or condition. A requirement or condition involves placing an obligation and therefore cannot include something which operates as a guideline (which a PCP can).

Group disadvantage

It is not necessary to prove that the members of the group or the claimant cannot physically comply with the PCP, so long as it can be shown that in terms of social and cultural factors it will place them at a particular disadvantage. For example, Ms Azmi could physically remove her veil, but that does not determine whether she and other Muslims are placed at a disadvantage by a requirement not to wear one.

It is necessary to prove that there is a group disadvantage, not simply an individual disadvantage. In *Eweida* v *British Airways plc* (2009) the employee argued that a requirement that uniformed staff must wear any jewellery underneath the uniform, unless it was a requirement of faith and agreed with the employer, disadvantaged her as a Christian. She did not argue that she believed it was a requirement of her faith that she wear her cross, but saw it as an expression of her personal faith. The Court of Appeal held that the claimant must show that there was an identifiable religious group which was disadvantaged, which the claimant had failed to do.

It is not necessary that the belief or practice be mandatory, so long as it could be shown that it was reasonably believed to be of exceptional importance (*R (Watkins-Singh)* v *Governing Body of Aberdare Girls School* (2008)).

In some cases it may be necessary to establish the group disadvantage by statistical analysis of advantage and disadvantage comparatively between members of the group and those not of the group. This statistical approach has been most common in cases of sex discrimination. It is necessary to choose a relevant pool of people in order to see whether the impact of the PCP is substantially greater on, for example, women than men. It is up to the tribunal to decide in the circumstances of any case what the appropriate pool for comparison is. For example, the relevant pool might be "all people", or "all people in X locality", or "all people qualified for Y job" or "all people qualified for Y job in X locality". The tribunal decides what is the appropriate pool and it must be one which is able to demonstrate whether there is disadvantage or not. There may be more than one pool possible, but in some cases there may be only one logical one (*Somerset County Council* v *Pike* (2009)).

Puts the individual at that disadvantage

Only an individual who is placed at the disadvantage at which the group they belong to is placed by the PCP may raise an action.

Proportionate means of achieving a legitimate aim

While direct discrimination cannot be justified, it is possible for a respondent to justify adopting a PCP which places a group at a particular disadvantage. The respondent must prove: that the PCP furthers a legitimate aim; and that it is a proportionate means of furthering the aim. Although this defence is based on the relevant provision in the EC Directives, it does not exactly replicate them. The Directives state that the

PCP must be objectively justified by a legitimate aim, and the means of achieving that aim must be appropriate and necessary.

It is not enough for the respondent to show that the PCP furthered a legitimate aim: it must also prove that it is a proportionate means of furthering that aim. In *Azmi* v *Kirklees Metropolitan Borough Council* the Council established to the satisfaction of the ET and EAT that their aim in requiring her to remove her veil was legitimate, in that it was to enable her to communicate effectively with the children whom she was supporting, and also that the requirement was a proportionate means of attaining that aim. It had been introduced after consultation with her, it had not been introduced immediately and did not extend any more than was necessary, since she could wear her veil when not engaged with the children.

In the business context it has been held that the question is whether, on a fair and detailed analysis of the working practices and business considerations involved, the PCP was reasonably necessary (*Hardy and Hansons plc* v *Lax* (2005)).

Disability-related discrimination/Discrimination arising from disability

Direct discrimination because of disability has the same definition as for the other protected characteristics and cannot be justified. This separate form of discrimination applies only to disability and can be justified. As the result of a decision by the House of Lords in *London Borough of Lewisham* v *Malcolm* (2008), EA 2010 provides a different definition which is intended to reverse part of the effect of that case.

Currently, disability-related discrimination occurs when an employer, for a reason which relates to the disabled person's disability, treats that person less favourably than he treats or would treat others to whom that reason does not or would not apply, and cannot show that the treatment is justified (DDA 1995, s 3A). What makes this different from direct discrimination is that the treatment is not because of the protected characteristic (disability) but "for a reason which relates to the disabled person's disability". This is wider and may include things which are caused by the person's disability such as absences due to ill health.

In a case of direct discrimination the appropriate comparator is someone without the claimant's disability. In disability-related discrimination it is someone to whom the reason for the treatment does not apply. From 1999 until 2008 the decision of the Court of Appeal in *Clark* v *TDG Ltd t/a Novacold* (1999) was accepted as the correct approach to this. It rejected the idea that the comparator should be someone to whom the reason applied but who was not disabled: in a case involving absence from work caused by disability, that would have meant someone who was absent from work but who was not disabled. Instead, the proper comparison was with someone who had not been absent from work (i.e someone to whom the reason did not apply), whether or not they were disabled. This did not mean that an employer could not take any action, since there was a justification defence, but it would mean that an employer had to factor the issue of the employee's disability into decision-making. The consensus around this interpretation was ended when the House of Lords held that *Clark* v *Novacold* had been wrongly decided, and that the correct comparator is someone to whom the reason applies without the disability (in our example, people absent from work without a disability). *Malcolm* was a housing and not an employment case, but it applies in employment cases (*Child Support Agency* v *Truman* (2009)).

This interpretation was greeted with some dismay, and the equivalent definition in EA 2010 is significantly different. Discrimination occurs when a disabled person is treated unfavourably because of something arising in consequence of the disability, and this cannot be shown to be a proportionate means of achieving a legitimate aim (EA 2010, s 15). The comparison has gone entirely: the question is whether the disabled person has been treated unfavourably (not less favourably than someone else) because of something arising as a consequence of the disability.

One aspect of the House of Lords' judgement in *Malcolm* has been retained in the new definition. Previous case law had held that it was not necessary for the employer to be aware that the person is disabled in order to be liable for disability-related discrimination (*H J Heinz Co Ltd* v *Kenrick* (2000)). The House of Lords held that this was also in error. EA 2010 confirms that it is not this form of discrimination if the alleged discriminator does not know, and could not reasonably have been expected to know, that the victim had the disability.

Justification

The employer must prove that the treatment is justified. Under DDA 1995 justification has a fairly wide definition. Treatment is justified if the reason for it is both material to the circumstances of the particular case and substantial (s 3A(3)). "Material" means relevant and important: there must be a reasonably strong connection between the employer's reason and the facts of the case. "Substantial" means not just trivial or minor. However, the threshold for DDA justification has been described as "low" and it is suggested that tribunals should take the same "band of reasonable responses" approach in relation to this as is taken for unfair dismissal (*Jones v Post Office* (2001)).

The new definition in EA 2010, however, adopts the same, stricter, standard of justification as is required for indirect discrimination or direct age discrimination: the treatment must be a proportionate means of achieving a legitimate aim.

Duty to make reasonable adjustments

An employer has a duty to make reasonable adjustments (DDA 1995, s 4A; EA 2010, ss 20 and 39). Failure to comply with this duty amounts to discrimination (DDA 1995, s 3A; EA 2010, s 21). There is no free-standing right to enforce the duty to make adjustments.

When the duty arises

The current duty arises where a PCP applied by an employer or any physical feature of the employer's premises places the disabled employee at a substantial disadvantage in comparison with those who are not disabled.

The duty under EA 2010 arises in these two circumstances and in addition where a disabled person would, but for the provision of an auxiliary aid, be put at a substantial disadvantage in comparison with those who are not disabled.

The duty does not arise if the employer does not know or could not reasonably be expected to know that the employee is disabled and likely to be placed at the disadvantage. In the case of an applicant for a job, this includes knowledge that the disabled person is or may be an applicant (DDA 1995, s 4A; EA 2010, Sch 8, para 20).

Compliance with the duty

When the duty arises, the employer must take such steps as it is reasonable to take in all the circumstances of the case to prevent the PCP, or the physical feature of premises placing the disabled person at a substantial disadvantage compared to those who are not disabled (DDA 1995, s 4A).

Under EA 2010, the employer must take such steps as it is reasonable to take to avoid the disadvantage in each of the three circumstances (s 20).

In deciding whether it is reasonable for an employer to take a particular step to comply with the duty to make reasonable adjustments, currently the legislation itself contains a list of factors, including practicability, financial resources and the size of the undertaking (DDA 1995, s 18B(1)). It also gives some examples of steps which an employer may have to take in order to comply with this duty, including making adjustments to premises, reallocating duties, transferring the employee, altering hours or place of work, modifying equipment and providing support (s 18B(2)).

There are no such lists in EA 2010, and equivalent guidance is likely to be found in Regulations or a Code of Practice which should come into effect at the same time as the Act itself. In situations where it is a physical feature of the employer's premises which has put the disabled employee at a substantial disadvantage, avoiding the disadvantage includes removing the feature, or altering it or providing a reasonable means of avoiding it (s 20(9)).

The effect of the duty is that an employer must take positive steps. In *Archibald v Fife Council* (2004) the House of Lords said that the duty "necessarily entails an element of more favourable treatment". In that case an employee with a manual job was unable to continue with it after an accident damaged her back. She applied for over a hundred jobs internally, which she was qualified for, but was unsuccessful and eventually dismissed. The House of Lords held that in such circumstances offering a job for which the employee was qualified without competitive interview could be a reasonable adjustment.

It may involve having to pay additional sick pay in appropriate circumstances, such as where the cause of the sickness was the fault of the employer (*Meikle v Nottinghamshire County Council* (2004)). However, this is not a general rule (*O'Hanlon v Revenue and Customs Commissioners* (2006)). In appropriate circumstances an employer might be expected to consider designing a job specifically for the disabled person (*Southampton City College v Randall* (2006)). In others it may not be reasonable to expect the employer to do this (*Tarbuck v Sainsbury's Supermarkets Ltd* (2006)).

Victimisation

Victimisation is designed to protect those who are treated less favourably because they seek to use the legislation. Victimisation occurs when someone is treated less favourably "by reason that" they have carried out one of the specified "protected acts": brought proceedings under the relevant legislation; or gave evidence or information in connection with proceedings brought under the relevant legislation; or did anything under or by reference to the legislation, or alleged that someone was in breach of the legislation (SDA 1975, s 4; RRA 1976, s 2; DDA 1995, s 55; EE(SO)R 2003, reg 4; EE(RB)R 2003, reg 4; EE(A)R 2006, reg 4; EA 2010, s 27). Making a false allegation in bad faith is not protected.

An employee who, for example, makes a complaint of race discrimination at work and who is then treated less favourably because of the complaint, may be successful in the victimisation action even if the race discrimination complaint is unsuccessful. It is not necessary to prove that the victimisation itself was carried out on one of the prohibited grounds.

The House of Lords has held that victimisation is different from direct discrimination in that for victimisation it is necessary to look at the subjective reasoning of the alleged discriminator to determine whether the treatment was "by reason of" the protected act, unlike the objective causative approach to direct discrimination. If the less favourable treatment is "honestly and reasonably" not because of the bringing of the action but for another substantial reason it will not be unlawful victimisation. In *Chief Constable of West Yorkshire Police* v *Khan* (2001) a refusal to give a reference for a police officer who had raised a race discrimination case against the force was held to have been in order to preserve the Chief Constable's position in the race case, rather than because the claimant had raised the action. The House of Lords has questioned its own reasoning in *Khan* as concentrating on the perspective of the discriminator rather than that of the victim. Its conclusion in the subsequent case, however, is difficult to apply to the *Khan* facts, without deciding that it was wrongly decided, which the House of Lords declined to do (*St Helens Metropolitan Borough Council* v *Derbyshire* (2007)).

Harassment

The earliest legislation did not include a specific prohibition against harassment. Nevertheless, the courts constructed harassment as a form of direct discrimination under SDA 1975 and RRA 1976 (*Porcelli* v *Strathclyde Regional Council* (1984), but see *Macdonald* v *Advocate General for Scotland*; *Pearce* v *Governing Body of Mayfield School* (2003)). The EAT has suggested that this older case law will not be helpful in interpreting the current harassment provisions (*Richmond Pharmacology Ltd* v *Dhaliwal* (2009)).

The current statutory definition of harassment is common to all strands and derived from the relevant EC Directives. In *EOC* v *DTI* (2007) the provision in the updated SDA 1975 was held to be in breach of Directive and as a result was amended. Although the same argument applied to the other strands, they were not amended.

The current definition for race, disability, religion or belief, sexual orientation and age is that harassment occurs when one person (A) treats another (B), on a prohibited ground in the following manner: A engages in unwanted (by B) conduct which has the purpose or effect of violating B's dignity or creating an intimidating, hostile, degrading, humiliating or offensive environment for B (SDA 1975, s 4A(3) (gender reassignment); RRA 1976, s 3A; DDA 1995, s 3B; EE(RB)R 2003, reg 5; EE(SO)R 2003, reg 5; EE(A)R 2006, reg 6). This was also the definition in SDA

1975: the successful challenge in *EOC* v *DTI* (2007) was to the requirement that the harassment had to be on the ground of sex. The Directive did not require a comparison to be made between how a man or woman would have been treated, but required the prohibition of harassment related to sex. As a result SDA 1975, s 3A (but not the other legislation) was amended so that harassment occurs when a person engages in unwanted conduct "that is related to (the woman's) sex". For harassment to relate to the protected characteristic, rather than be on the ground of it, is a wider concept.

Under EA 2010, harassment is unwanted conduct related to a protected characteristic, across all the protected characteristics which, like the current provision, has the purpose or effect of violating the victim's dignity or creating an intimidating, hostile, degrading, humiliating or offensive environment for him (s 26). The harassment provisions will not apply to the protected characteristics of marriage or civil partnership, or pregnancy or maternity (s 26).

The definition of harassment goes further than is required by EC law in that it applies to conduct which has either a prohibited purpose or effect while the EC Directives propose that both must be present.

Thus the conduct must be unwanted by the victim. It may be intended either to violate the victim's dignity or to create a hostile etc environment for him. Although the EAT in *Richmond Pharmacology Ltd* v *Dhaliwal* suggested that the intention of the perpetrator was relevant in deciding the reasonableness of the effect, this does not appear to be what the provision says: intention and effect are alternatives. Similarly, if the conduct has one of the specified effects, whether it is intended to or not, it amounts to harassment. Thus the person who makes a racist joke intending to humiliate the victim will be harassing him, even if the victim does not feel humiliated by it; while the person who makes a racist joke, imagining that it will be taken in a spirit of "banter", may be harassing the victim if he feels his dignity is violated or that a hostile environment has been created.

In the second situation, where the complaint is that the harassment had the relevant effect (as opposed to purpose), it is not sufficient that the victim believed his dignity had been violated, or a hostile etc environment created, although this is relevant. It must be reasonable in all the circumstances that the conduct had the effect. In particular, the perception of the victim must be taken into account.

There is no requirement that there be a series of incidents to amount to harassment. Under the discrimination approach to harassment, before the statutory definition, it had been held that one incident of sufficient seriousness could amount to harassment (*Insitu Cleaning Co Ltd* v *Heads* (1995)), and that a series of less serious incidents may also amount to harassment (*Reed and Bull*

Information Systems v *Stedman* (1999)). In the latter case, the importance of the subjective perception of the victim was emphasised.

Sexual harassment

There are two additional forms of harassment under SDA 1975, s 4A, which are replicated in EA 2010, s 26. The first occurs where the perpetrator engages in any form of unwanted verbal, non-verbal or physical conduct of a sexual nature which has the purpose or effect of violating the victim's dignity or of creating an intimidating, hostile, degrading, humiliating or offensive environment for the victim.

The second occurs where, on the ground of the victim's rejection of or submission to sexual harassment or harassment related to sex, the perpetrator treats the victim less favourably than he would have treated her had she not rejected or submitted to the harassment.

Employer's duty

An employer owes duties to those who are in its employment, that is those who are employed under a contract of service or apprenticeship and also under a contract personally to execute work or labour (SDA 1975 s 82; RRA 1976, s 78; DDA 1995, s 68; EE(RB)R 2003, reg 2; EE(SO)R 2003, reg 2; EE(A)R 2006, reg 2; EA 2010, s 212). Although the concept is wider than the common law meaning, the term "employee" is used in the legislation.

It is an employer's duty not to discriminate against, victimise or harass employees and applicants for employment (SDA 1975, s 6; RRA 1976, s 4; DDA 1995, s 4; EE(RB)R 2003, reg 6; EE(SO)R 2003, reg 6; EE(A)R 2006, reg 6; EA 2010, ss 39 and 40).

Applicants

The employer's duty not to discriminate applies in relation to the arrangements for determining who should be offered employment; the terms on which employment is offered; or refusing to offer employment. The arrangements can include advertising, short-listing and interview (*City of Bradford Metropolitan County* v *Arora* (1989)).

Employees

The duty applies in relation to terms of employment; access to opportunities for promotion, transfer or training, or to any other benefits, facilities or services; dismissal, including constructive dismissal; or subjecting an employee to any other detriment.

Detriment   Detriment means putting at a disadvantage. The test is whether a reasonable worker might take the view that the treatment was in all the circumstances to his detriment. It must be applied from the victim's point of view. An unjustified sense of grievance cannot be a detriment, but a justified and reasonable sense of grievance may well be so (*Shamoon* v *Chief Constable of the Royal Ulster Constabulary* (2003)).

Clothing requirements   Imposing clothing requirements may amount to direct or indirect discrimination. Different clothing requirements for men and women may amount to direct sex discrimination, but not if the requirements though different are comparable: for example, equally smart. In *Department for Work and Pensions* v *Thompson* (2004) the EAT held that a requirement for all employees to dress in a businesslike manner, which required male employees to wear a collar and tie, while female employees were only required to dress appropriately and to a similar standard, was not direct sex discrimination as they were comparable. It is not enough to show that the requirements are different: it must be shown that the requirements for one are less favourable.

A uniform clothing requirement may amount to indirect race or religious discrimination if it would disadvantage a racial or religious group. In *Azmi* v *Kirklees Metropolitan Borough Council* (2007) the requirement that the claimant not wear a veil while teaching did disadvantage the religious group to which she belonged and her but did not amount to indirect discrimination in that case because the employer was able to justify it.

Ex-employees

An employer must not discriminate against or harass an ex-employee where the discrimination or harassment arises out of and is closely connected to the employment relationship (SDA 1975, s 20A; RRA 1976, s 27A; DDA 1995, s 16A; EE(RB)R 2003, reg 21; EE(SO)R 2003, reg 21; EE(A)R 2006, reg 24; EA 2010, s 108).

Occupational requirements

There are exceptional cases where a protected characteristic may be a relevant criterion for determining who is appointed to a job. Under the SDA 1975, and in relation to nationality under RRA 1976, there are specific lists of "genuine occupational qualifications". Under RRA 1976, generally, EE(RB)R 2003, EE(SO)R 2003 and EE(A)R 2006 there are more general provisions permitting a "genuine occupational requirement".

EA 2010 will introduce an equivalent "occupational requirement" to all protected characteristics.

Genuine occupational qualification (GOQ)

In SDA 1975 there is a list of situations in which gender will be a GOQ. These include: where authenticity is required, such as in a dramatic performance; where decency or privacy is concerned because the situation might involve undressing or intimate contact; where there are close living arrangements; or where the job involves providing personal services promoting welfare or education or similar and can only effectively be provided by a man or woman (SDA 1975, s 7).

Excluded from the operation of SDA 1975 are the appointment of police and prison officers (regarding height) (s 17), and of ministers of religion (regarding gender and religious doctrine) (s 19).

In relation to undergoing gender reassignment, being a man or woman may be a GOQ so long as the employer can show it is reasonable in relation to the sex GOQs (s 7A). There are also supplementary GOQs which effectively permit the exclusion of transsexuals in certain cases, including where statutory physical searches are required, or the job or accommodation involves intimate contact with others who might reasonably object, or where the holder of the job provides vulnerable individuals with personal services promoting welfare or similar, and in the reasonable view of the employer these cannot be effectively provided by a person while undergoing gender reassignment (s 7B). This does not apply to someone who has completed transition.

There is a list of GOQs in relation to nationality which include authenticity: for example, in a dramatic performance and the provision of personal services promoting welfare to a particular racial group, where these can be done most effectively by a member of that group (RRA 1976, s 5).

(Genuine) occupational requirement ((G)OR)

Currently, in relation to the other grounds with the exception of disability, there is a similar, general GOR. They state that it is not discrimination to require a protected characteristic for work where, having regard to the nature and context of the employment, being of a particular race, religion or belief, sexual orientation or age is a genuine and determining occupational requirement, and it is proportionate to apply it in the particular case, and the person turned down as a result does not meet it (RRA 1976, s 4A; EE(RB)R 2003, reg 7; EE(SO)R 2003, reg 7; EE(A)R 2006, reg 8).

The equivalent provision in EA 2010, which covers all protected characteristics, applies where, having regard to the nature and context of the employment, a protected characteristic is an occupational requirement, its application is a proportionate means of achieving a legitimate aim, and the person affected does not meet it (Sch 9, para 1). The word "genuine" is unnecessary as it is implicit.

There are currently additional GORs for religion or belief and sexual orientation. Where the employer has an ethos based on religion or belief, having regard to the ethos and nature of the employment, being of that religion or belief may be a GOR so long as it is proportionate to apply it in a particular case (EE(RB)R 2003, reg 7(3)). In *McNab* v *Glasgow City Council* (2007), where an atheist teacher was not interviewed for a guidance post in a Catholic school, the EAT held that the GOR could not apply as the Council did not have an ethos based on religion or belief.

More controversially, where the employment is for the purposes of an organised religion, the application of a requirement related to sexual orientation may be a GOR, either so as to comply with the doctrines of the religion, or because of the nature of the employment and the context in which it is carried out, so as to avoid conflicting with the strongly held religious convictions of a significant number of the religion's followers (EE(SO)R 2003, reg 7(3)). This is equivalent to the exclusion of the appointment of ministers from SDA 1975. A challenge to this additional GOR, as being incompatible with EC Directive 2000/78, was unsuccessful. Employment for the purposes of an organised religion will be interpreted narrowly. Where the GOR is based on conflict with strongly held religious convictions, an "objective" approach must be taken, rather than the particular views of the alleged discriminator (*R (Amicus)* v *Secretary of State for Trade and Industry* (2004)). Thus current law permits the exclusion of female or homosexual ministers of religion.

EA 2010 provides similar additional ORs. In the case of an organisation with an ethos based on religion or belief, being required to be of that religion or belief may be an OR having regard to the ethos and nature or context of the work, so long as its application is a proportionate means of achieving a legitimate aim (EA 2010, Sch 9, para 3). So far as employment for the purposes of an organised religion is concerned, ORs may require a person not to be of a particular sex, not to be a transsexual, not to be married or a civil partner, not to be married to or the civil partner of someone with a living former spouse or civil partner, or may relate to how the marriage or civil partnership came to an end, or relate to sexual orientation, so long as they meet the "compliance" or "non-conflict" principles. These are the equivalent of the current provisions. The compliance principle is the requirement to comply with the doctrines of the religion. The non-conflict principle is the requirement to avoid conflicting with the strongly held religious convictions of a significant number of followers (Sch 9, para 2).

Other employment relationships

Discrimination law imposes duties on a wide range of relationships in the employment context. This includes: the duty of a principal not to discriminate against or harass a contract worker (SDA 1975, s 9; RRA 1976, s 7; DDA 1995, s 4B; EE(RB)R 2003, reg 8; EE(SO)R 2003, reg 8; EE(A)R 2006, reg 9; EA 2010, s 41); the duty of a partnership not to discriminate against or harass a partner or an applicant for partner (SDA 1975, s 11; RRA 1976, s 10; DDA 1995, ss 6A–6C; EE(RB)R 2003, reg 14; EE(SO)R 2003, reg 14; EE(A)R 2006, reg 17; EA 2010, s 44); the duty of a trade organisation, including trade union or employer's organisation, not to discriminate against or harass a member or applicant for membership (SDA 1975, s 12; RRA 1976, s 11; DDA 1995, ss 13–14; EE(RB)R 2003, reg 15; EE(SO)R 2003, reg 15; EE(A)R 2006, reg 18; EA 2010, s 57); the duty of qualifying bodies, which confer qualifications or authorisation for a trade or profession, not to discriminate against applicants (SDA 1975, s 13; RRA 1976, s 12; DDA 1995, ss 14A–14B; EE(RB)R 2003, reg 16; EE(SO)R 2003, reg 16; EE(A)R 2006, reg 19; EA 2010, s 53); the duty of an employment agency, or employment service-provider not to discriminate against or harass anyone in relation to the provision of the body's services (SDA 1975, s 15; RRA 1976, s 14; EE(RB)R 2003, reg 18; EE(SO)R 2003, reg 18; EE(A)R 2006, reg 21; EA 2010, s 55).

Responsibility for discrimination

The primary duty not to discriminate under the employment provisions of the legislation is owed by the employer. Individual acts of discrimination will be carried out by individual people (who may not be those with the primary duty not to discriminate), and the legislation provides for allocation of responsibility.

Vicarious liability

Anything done by a person in the course of his employment is to be treated as done by the employer as well as by the employee, whether or not it was done with the employer's knowledge and approval (SDA 1975, s 41; RRA 1976, s 32; DDA 1995, s 58; EE(RB)R 2003, reg 22; EE(SO)R 2003, reg 22; EE(A)R 2006, reg 25; EA 2010, s 109). This is not precisely the same concept as "in the course of employment" at common law. In *Tower Boot Co Ltd v Jones* (1997) the Court of Appeal held that a wide concept was required in order to give effect to the purpose of the legislation and protect employees from racial discrimination. In that case an employee had been subjected to racist verbal and physical assault and the ET and EAT had held that this was not in the perpetrator's course of employment. The Court of Appeal noted that, unlike common law, the primary duty was on the employer and there was a defence available to an employer. In the course of employment means arising out of employment. At the time of this decision the common law concept was very restricted, but even the current doctrine of "close connection" is narrower. Anything that is an extension of employment also arises out of it, including a social event arranged from work (*Chief Constable of Lincolnshire Police v Stubbs* (1999)).

Employer's defence   The employer has a defence to vicarious liability if it proves that it took such steps as were reasonably practicable to prevent the employee from doing the particular act or acts like it. Under the EA 2010, the defence is to take all reasonable steps. In *Canniffe v East Riding of Yorkshire Council* (2000) the EAT held that it was not a defence that no steps would have prevented the act taking place. A tribunal must first see what steps the employer took to prevent such acts, and then go on to see if there were any other reasonably practicable steps it could have taken. It is not relevant whether these would in fact have prevented the discriminatory acts.

Harassment by a third party

An employer cannot be vicariously liable for the behaviour of anyone other than an employee. A decision by the EAT in *Burton v De Vere Hotels* (1996) that an employer who should have foreseen that racial harassment of waiting staff by hotel guests might take place could be liable for breach of duty for failing to protect employees, was overruled by the House of Lords in *Macdonald v Advocate General for Scotland*; *Pearce v Governing Body of Mayfield School* (2003). It was held that it was necessary to prove that the employer's failure to protect was because of the link with the protected characteristic. The interpretation and validity of this decision was questioned in *EOC v DTI* (2007). As a result, SDA 1975 was amended to make an employer liable for harassing an employee when a third party harasses them in the course of their employment, and the employer has failed to take reasonably practicable steps to prevent the third party doing this (s 6(2B)). This arises only where the employer knows that the employee has been harassed on at least two previous occasions (not necessarily by the same person each time). Currently this provision applies to sex discrimination only; but it will extend to all protected characteristics under EA 2010 (s 40).

Aiding discrimination

A person who knowingly aids another to discriminate unlawfully is to be treated as doing an unlawful act himself (SDA 1975, s 42; RRA 1976, s 33; DDA 1995, s 47; EE(RB)R 2003, reg 23; EE(SO)R 2003, reg 23; EE(A)R 2006, reg 26; EA 2010, s 112).

Employee liability Under the current law, this is the provision under which an employee who has committed an act of discrimination might have an action taken against them personally, alongside the employer. Where an employer escapes primary liability, because of the employer's defence, the individual who aided the discrimination may still be liable (*Gilbank* v *Miles* (2006)). EA 2010 introduces an additional specific provision under which the employee who committed a discriminatory act for which the employer is liable, is personally liable whether or not the employer has a defence (s 110).

Instructing, causing or inducing discrimination

Currently it is unlawful for a person to instruct or induce someone to discriminate unlawfully but only under SDA 1975 (ss 39 and 40), RRA 1976 (ss 30 and 31), and DDA 1995 (s 16C).

Under EA 2010 it will be unlawful to instruct, cause or induce contraventions of the Act in relation to all protected characteristics (s 111).

REMEDY

Complaints must be presented to an employment tribunal within 3 months of the act of discrimination taking place; or the tribunal may accept a late claim if it considers it just and equitable to do so (SDA 1975, s 76; RRA 1976, s 68; EE(RB)R 2003, reg 34; EE(SO)R 2003, reg 34; EE(A)R 2006, reg 42; EA 2010, s 123).

The tribunal may make an order declaring the rights of the claimant and the discriminator; an order of compensation; or a recommendation that the employer should take steps in a certain time to obviate or reduce the adverse affect on the claimant of the discrimination. If the employer does not comply with the recommendations without reasonable justification, the tribunal can order or increase compensation (within the maximum) if it could have awarded compensation in the first place (SDA 1975, s 65; RRA 1976, s 56; EE(RB)R 2003 reg 29; EE(SO)R 2003, reg 29; EE(A)R 2006, reg 38; EA 2010, s 124). Under EA 2010 a recommendation may relate to a third party, not solely the successful claimant as currently. Unlike unfair dismissal, compensation can take account of hurt feelings. There is no maximum limit on the award which can be made, but there are guidelines from the Court of Appeal (*Vento* v *Chief Constable of West Yorkshire Police* (2003), updated by *Da'Bell* v *NSPCC* (2010)).

POSITIVE ACTION

Given the neutral application of discrimination law, apart from disability discrimination, taking positive steps to end disadvantage or to promote equality in a particular case has the danger of amounting to direct discrimination against someone from an advantaged group. Article 157 and the EU Directives permit measures to prevent or compensate for disadvantage and, in the case of Art 157, to provide specific advantages to make it easier for the under-represented sex to take part in work. Cases under Art 157 and Directive 2006/54 (and predecessors) have permitted measures giving preference to women where there is under-representation, such as reserving workplace nursery places for women, with men having access in an emergency (*Lommers* v *Minister van Landbouw, Natuurbeheer en Visserij* (2002)). However, such measures must not go so far as to permit automatic selection because of gender and leave out of account altogether the individual merit of male applicants (*EFTA Surveillance Authority* v *Kingdom of Norway* (2003)).

Currently, UK law permits limited forms of positive action in employment. Under DDA 1995, positive action is permissible because the Act only applies to workers with disabilities and in appropriate circumstances there is a duty to take action (under the duty to make adjustments). Under the other legislation, in the case of under-representation in the case of race and sex, and disadvantage in the case of religion and sexual orientation, training bodies and employers are permitted to take some positive measures involving training and encouragement to apply for particular work or posts (SDA 1975, ss 47–48; RRA 1976, ss 37–38; EE(RB)R 2002, reg 25; EE(SO)R 2003, reg 26; EE(A)R 2006, reg 29). This does not permit preferential hiring.

EA 2010 contains a more general provision regarding positive action permitting employers to enable and encourage people with protected characteristics to overcome disadvantage, associated with the characteristic, or to meet particular needs not shared with others, or to encourage participation where it is disproportionately low (s 158). It also provides for a possible "tie-break" provision. In cases of disadvantage or disproportionately low participation, an employer may recruit on the basis of the protected characteristic, so long as the applicant is as qualified as someone without the protected characteristic who was rejected, and there is no general policy of treating people with the characteristic more favourably (in other words, it is a genuine positive action measure and not a preference for persons with the characteristic). Taking this decision must be a proportionate means of enabling and encouraging people with the characteristic to minimise the disadvantage, or participate in the work (s 159). It is not clear if this provision will be implemented at the same time as the main body of the Act.

EQUAL PAY

Discrimination in pay, or other contractual terms, on any other ground than sex is dealt with in the same way as other workplace discrimination. Sex discrimination in pay was more institutionalised in the UK, with women's rates, lower than all other rates, being common. EPA 1970 was passed specifically to deal with unequal pay for women. It was phased in over 5 years, coming fully into effect at the same time as SDA 1975. On the UK's accession to the EC in 1972, the law of the EC became relevant: in particular, Art 141 (formerly 119) of the Treaty of Rome, which requires equal pay. Because it is part of the constitution of the EC, it has horizontal direct effect, and has been relied on, not just for interpretation of EPA 1970, but also as the legal basis for a number of claims. EPA 1970 had to be amended to introduce a work of equal value provision in 1983 after the ECJ in *Commission of the EC v UK* (1982) held that the UK was in breach of Art 119 in not having such a provision in its law.

Equal pay and sex discrimination

EPA 1970 and EA 2010, ss 127–135 (which will replace it and refer to "equality of terms" rather than equal pay) take precedence over SDA 1975. Currently, no actions concerning pay can be raised except under EPA 1970 (SDA 1975, s 6(5)); under EA 2010 it will be competent to raise an action relating to pay under the general anti-discrimination provisions if it not possible to do so under the equality of terms provisions (EA 2010, s 71). So far as contractual terms other than pay are concerned, if they can be raised under the equal pay/equality of terms provisions they must be (EPA 1970, s 8; EA 2010, s 70). Non-contractual matters, benefits and treatment are covered solely by SDA 1975 and the general discrimination provisions of EA 2010. An important difference between equal pay and sex discrimination claims is that in the latter, but not the former, a hypothetical comparator may be used. In non-pay contractual terms, and under EA 2010 pay claims as well, if there is a comparator the equal pay provisions must be used; if there is not, the general provisions may be.

Equality clause

The equal pay system operates by implying into a woman's contract an equality clause (a sex equality clause under EA 2010) which has the effect of equalising individual terms of the woman's contract with the more favourable terms in her comparator man's contract, or by including in her contract a term which is in his contract but missing in hers (EPA 1970, s 1(1); EA 2010, s 66). The equality principle applies to each individual term, so that if one term is less good than the equivalent in the comparator's contract but another is better, the worker is still entitled to the benefit of the equality clause for the less good term. In *Hayward* v *Cammell Laird* (1986) the House of Lords held that a cook who had been successful in her claim that she did work of equal value with a painter, a joiner and a heating engineer and who received less pay but better sick pay and holidays was entitled to have the pay term equalised.

An individual term has been held by the Court of Appeal to mean the total of an individual element, so that in *Degnan* v *Redcar and Cleveland* (2005) the total remuneration of the woman claiming equal pay had to be compared with the total remuneration of each of her comparators. She could not pick different parts, such as bonus or attendance allowance, from different comparators.

An equality clause can only give the woman equal pay with her comparator: it cannot give her higher pay. In *Evesham* v *North Hertfordshire Health Authority* (2000) a successful claimant who had been employed for a number of years while her comparator was in his first year of employment was entitled only to the same pay as the comparator and a placing on the salary scale commensurate with her years of experience.

Pay and contractual terms

EPA 1970 and EA 2010 apply in relation to all contractual terms. The impact of Art 157 of the Treaty of Rome has been to extend application to any payment "in respect of employment" from the employer whether directly or indirectly. This has had the important effect of applying equal pay law to pensions. In *Barber* v *Guardian Royal Exchange Assurance Group* (1990) the ECJ held that unequal access to occupational pensions, in this case affecting men, was in breach of Art 141 (now 157). As a result of the potential European-wide impact of the decision, a *"Barber* protocol" was adopted, which provides that service before the date of decision in 1990 could not be relied on.

There has been much litigation on the subject of pension entitlement involving direct and indirect sex discrimination in access and conditions. Specific provisions are contained in the Pensions Act 1995 (EA 2010, ss 67–68). It is beyond the scope of this book to deal with this.

A claim for equal pay

The right to claim equal pay or equality of terms applies to workers. Like all sex discrimination law it may be used by men as well as women. The claimant must prove that she qualifies for equal pay by doing either like work, or work rated as equivalent, or work of equal value to her chosen comparator, who must be employed by her employer. Although EPA 1970 places the burden of proving this on the claimant, the ECJ in *Danfoss* (1989) held that when a pay system is opaque (that is, it is not clear how it operates), and it operates to the disadvantage of women, the burden must be on the employer to prove that the system is free from discrimination. Once the claimant has established this first stage, it is open to the employer to prove that the difference in pay is due to a "genuine material factor" (to be called simply "material factor" under EA 2010) which does not amount to sex discrimination. Equal pay claims can involve large numbers of claimants and, particularly where equal value claims are involved, can be very complex and lengthy.

The comparator

A claimant must compare her work with that of an actual comparator of the opposite sex. Under EA 2010, however, where there is no actual comparator, the claimant will be able to compare herself with a hypothetical comparator under the direct discrimination provisions (s 71). The claimant chooses her comparator, and she may choose more than one comparator (*Ainsworth* v *Glass Tubes and Components Ltd* (1977)).

The comparator must be in the same employment as the claimant, that is employed by the same employer and either employed at the same establishment or, if not, both must be at establishments at which common terms and conditions apply (EPA 1970, s 1(2) and (6); EA 2010, s 79).

The ECJ held that a comparison could be made with someone who was previously employed in the job in question (*MacCarthys Ltd* v *Smith* (1980)). EA 2010 provides that the comparison is not restricted to work done contemporaneously (s 64), thus permitting comparison with both a predecessor and successor.

Same employer   EPA 1970 and EA 2010 require the claimant and her comparator to be employed by the same or an associated employer. Employers are associated if one is a company of which the other has control, or both are companies of which a third person has control. There is no such rule in Art 157, but the ECJ has held that the employer must be "responsible for the inequality and able to restore equal treatment" (*Lawrence* v *Regent Office Care Ltd* (2002)). This has been interpreted as meaning a "single source" of terms being necessary. This worked to the advantage of a headteacher in *South Ayrshire Council* v *Morton* (2002) who was able to compare herself with a headteacher employed by another Council as their salary scales were set by the same statutory body. It worked to the disadvantage of civil servants in *Robertson* v *DEFRA* (2005) who were not permitted to compare themselves with civil servants working in another government department since, though both were employed by the Crown, salaries were negotiated separately in each department.

Common terms and conditions   If both claimant and comparator work at the same establishment, that is sufficient. If they do not, common terms and conditions (under EA 2010, simply common terms) must apply at the establishments at which they are employed. This does not mean identical, but substantially comparable on a broad basis. The House of Lords in *British Coal Corporation* v *Smith* (1996) said that the woman must show that the terms and conditions of her comparator were broadly similar to the terms which would apply to someone in a similar job at her establishment. The EAT in Scotland seems to have gone much further in *Dumfries and Galloway Council* v *North* (2009) by saying that the woman would also have to show there was a real possibility of the comparator's class of worker being employed at her establishment.

Like work

A woman is regarded as being employed on like work with her comparator where her work and his is the same or broadly similar (EPA 1970, s 1; EA 2010, s 65). Any differences between their work should not be of practical importance. Early appeals established that tribunals were to take a broad view of this, and not look for reasons to find lack of similarity (*Capper Pass* v *Lawton* (1976)). They were to be guided by what happened in practice, not what it said in the contract, where perhaps extra duties might be mentioned which were never carried out. The Court of Appeal reviewed the case law thoroughly in *Shields* v *Coombe Holdings Ltd* (1978). They found that the extra security duties which a male counter hand in a betting shop was contractually obliged to perform rarely happened in practice, and that the only reason he had been given the additional duties and the claimant had not was because of his gender.

Work rated as equivalent

If a job evaluation study has rated the woman's and her comparator's jobs as equivalent, she is entitled to equal pay. ACAS describes job evaluation as a systematic method of grading a hierarchy of jobs. The study must have given the jobs equal value in terms of the demands made under various headings: for instance, effort, skill and decision-making (EPA 1970, s 1(5); EA 2010, s 80). Although such studies depend on subjective evaluation and are not scientific according to ACAS, the woman's job must be rated at least equal to the comparator's. In *Home Office v Bailey* (2005), the women claimants' jobs were related marginally lower, and the ET upheld their equal pay claims because of the insignificance of the difference and the lack of mathematical exactitude in job evaluation. However, the EAT held that the lower grading did not entitle them to equal pay. If the value of the woman's job is higher than the man's she is entitled to equal pay (*Murphy v An Bord Telecom Eireann* (1988)).

A job evaluation study may be used as a defence by the employer to a claim under the third heading, work of equal value.

Work of equal value

A work of equal value claim can only be made if neither of the other two grounds applies. This is in relation to the woman's chosen comparator. In *Pickstone v Freemans Ltd* (1988) the House of Lords held that, even if there are male employees doing the same work as the woman, she may still claim work of equal value with a man doing different work. Otherwise an employer might be able to employ a token man to do the same job as women in order to avoid the equal value provisions.

This ground is similar to the previous heading, but whereas that applies when the employer itself has undertaken a job evaluation study, this ground is based on the woman herself claiming that her job is of equal value to her comparator's in terms of the demands, made under the same headings. Under the original procedure an equal value case was always referred for a report by an independent expert (designated as such by ACAS), but now that is an option open to the ET, which may decide the matter without such a reference (EPA 1970, s 2A; EA 2010, s 131). The parties are entitled to call their own experts. The independent expert's report is not binding on the ET, although it carries considerable weight (*Tennants Textile Colours Ltd* v *Todd* (1989)).

If there has been a job evaluation study under which the work of the woman and her comparator have been given different values, the ET must find that their jobs are not of equal value unless it has reasonable grounds for suspecting that the evaluation was made on a system which was discriminatory on grounds of sex, or is otherwise unsuitable to be relied on. A job evaluation study discriminates on grounds of sex where a difference, or coincidence between the values given to the demands under the system is not justifiable irrespective of the sex of the person on whom the demands are made. The study will only be a defence to the employer's claim if the woman and her comparator are employed in the undertaking or group of undertakings covered by the study, even if the jobs covered are relevant (*McAuley* v *Eastern Health Social Services Board* (1991)).

(Genuine) material factor defence

Once the woman has shown that there are grounds for applying the equality clause and awarding equal pay, the burden shifts to the employer. Currently, the employer must show that the difference between the woman's and her comparator's pay is due to a genuine material factor which is not the difference of sex (EPA 1970, s 1(3)). The differences in EA 2010 are, first of all, that it is no longer described as "genuine" (but that is because it is implicit and does not alter the defence), but, more importantly, that the position where the factor may be indirectly discriminatory is made explicit and clarified.

The material factor must indeed be genuine, and not a sham designed to provide a mechanism for enhancing basic pay. It must be the cause of the inequality in pay, not simply a justification for it, and it must be significant and relevant. The factor must not involve a difference of sex. The House of Lords rejected the argument that an employer should have to provide objective justification of the difference in pay where there is no allegation of indirect discrimination: it is sufficient to show what the reason was and that it did not involve sex discrimination. In *Strathclyde Regional Council* v *Wallace* (1998) it held that the employer's explanation for the difference in pay between the woman acting as principal teacher and her male principal teacher comparator, which showed that it was based partly on budget and partly on the employer's (mistaken) understanding of the statutory constraints, had been material and sufficient reason which was not based on sex discrimination, even if it did not amount to objective justification.

The factor must continue: once it disappears, the employer's defence also disappears since it is no longer material and relevant (*Benveniste* v *University of Southampton* (1989)).

Economic factors   So long as there is no sex discrimination in the factor it is possible for economic or market forces to amount to a material factor. In *Rainey* v *Greater Glasgow Health Board Eastern Division* (1987) above scale payments in order to attract private sector professionals into a new NHS service was held by the House of Lords to be a material factor justifying, on economic or administrative grounds, the difference between the salary of a new female recruit and one of the private sector recruits.

Indirect discrimination   The interpretation of the material factor defence adopted by the House of Lords does not require objective justification unless there is a suggestion of indirect discrimination. If the factor is "tainted" in this way, the employer must do more than simply explain what the reason was and show it is not direct sex discrimination, but must objectively justify it. This is clear from the ECJ decision in *Enderby* v *Frenchay Health Authority and Secretary of State for Health* (1993), a reference from the UK in an equal value claim from a group of speech therapists, almost exclusively women, comparing themselves with clinical psychologists, predominantly male. The material factor put forward by the employer was that the groups' wages were negotiated in separate collective bargaining agencies and there was no direct sex discrimination. However, the ECJ held that, since there were significant statistics showing a clear gender difference, Art 119 (now 157) required proof that this was justified by objective factors unrelated to sex. Separate collective bargaining arrangements could not be a sufficient justification. Economic factors might operate as a justification, but these would have to be examined carefully by the national court to see the extent and proportionality.

There has been some confusion caused by a decision of the Court of Appeal in *Armstrong* v *Newcastle NHS Hospital Trust* (2006) which appears to suggest that, even in cases of indirect discrimination, objective justification may not be needed, but simply proof of a genuine factor which is the cause of the difference and is not direct sex discrimination. EA 2010 will clarify this by requiring, where the claimant shows that the factor places people of the same sex as her at a disadvantage compared to members of the opposite sex (indirect discrimination), proof that the factor is a proportionate means of achieving a legitimate aim (s 69). This is the defence to indirect discrimination.

Remedy

Claims may be taken to an ET by a worker; a worker or employer may apply to an ET for a declarator of rights; a court may make a reference if it thinks an issue can be more appropriately dealt with in an ET (EPA 1970, s 2; EA 2010, ss 127–128). Claims must be submitted at any time during employment or within 6 months of employment ending, or within 6 months of finding out material facts which the employer had deliberately concealed or, where the worker was suffering from incapacity preventing her claiming, within 6 months of the incapacity ending. Arrears can be awarded for up to 5 years.

Essential Facts

- Sex discrimination in contractual terms is (currently) dealt with in the Equal Pay Act 1970.
- Sex discrimination other than pay is (currently) governed by the Sex Discrimination Act 1975.
- Race discrimination provisions are (currently) set out in the Race Relations Act 1976.
- Disability discrimination is (currently) covered by the Disability Discrimination Act 1995.
- Religious discrimination provisions are (currently) set out in the Employment Equality (Religion or Belief) Regulations 2003.
- Sexual orientation discrimination is (currently) covered by the Employment Equality (Sexual Orientation) Regulations 2003.
- Age discrimination is (currently) regulated by the Employment Equality (Age) Regulations 2006.
- It should be noted that the Equality Act 2010 will replace all of the above when it comes into force.

Essential Cases

Hurley v Mustoe (1981): an employer who dismissed a mother of under-school-age children was held to have directly discriminated against her. He would not have treated a father of under-school-age children in the same way. There was no actual comparator, but comparison with how he would have treated a hypothetical male comparator was made.

Weathersfield Ltd v Sargent (1999): a white employee who was given an instruction not to serve "coloured or Asian" customers resigned as a consequence. Her resignation was a constructive dismissal. Her dismissal was direct race discrimination on racial grounds, even although it was not her own race which had caused the dismissal. This is a form of "associative discrimination".

Azmi v Kirklees Metropolitan Borough Council (2007): a Muslim support worker in a school was ordered not to wear her veil while in class. This amounted to prima facie indirect discrimination since a PCP had been applied which put Muslims, and her, at a particular disadvantage. However, the employer was able to show that the PCP furthered the legitimate aim of enabling communication with the children, and was a proportionate means of achieving it since there had been investigation, consultation, warning and implementation only in relation to the classroom.

Archibald v Fife Council (2004): an employee became physically incapable of doing her job as a road sweeper. She was qualified for other jobs with the employer, which she could do, but after over 100 unsuccessful interviews was dismissed. The House of Lords held that the employer was in breach of its duty to make reasonable adjustments by not transferring her to a job for which she was qualified and which was vacant.

Hayward v Cammell Laird Shipbuilders Ltd (1986): a cook was successful in having her job declared to be of equal value to that of a painter, a joiner and a heating engineer. Her pay was lower, but she had some benefits they did not have. The House of Lords held that the equality clause applied to equalise individual terms within the contract. Thus she was entitled to equal pay with her comparators.

Enderby v Frenchay Health Authority and Secretary of State for Health (1993): this was an equal value claim by female speech therapists using clinical psychologists as comparators. Speech therapists as a group were almost exclusively female, clinical psychologists predominantly male. Their pay was determined by different collective bargaining arrangements. The ECJ held that, where statistics showed a significant gender difference, the employer had to objectively justify the difference in pay. Separate collective bargaining arrangements could not do that. Labour shortage could, but the extent and effect of any shortage would have to be examined carefully.

11 PARENTAL AND ASSOCIATED RIGHTS

The concept of parental rights for employees is a relatively recent one. From 1997 to 2010 it has been one of the stated government aims of reform in employment law to introduce family-friendly measures to assist parents, both mothers and fathers, to balance work and family life. This was also driven by the requirements of EC law and Directives. Until 1999 this law consisted only of maternity rights. Since 1999, parental leave, dependant care leave, paternity leave, adoption leave and a right to request flexible working have been introduced. Maternity rights enable women to combine work with childbirth and the early stage of looking after a baby. Parental rights more generally should enable both mothers and fathers to make arrangements which make work more compatible with family commitments.

MATERNITY RIGHTS

Maternity rights are provided by EC and UK law. The Pregnant Workers Directive (PWD) 92/85, introduced as a health and safety measure, requires specific risk assessments, minimum leave provisions, maintenance of contractual rights and of an adequate allowance during leave. The Equal Treatment Directive 2006/54 provides that less favourable treatment of a woman related to pregnancy or maternity leave within the meaning of PWD 92/85 amounts to sex discrimination (Art 2.2).

The UK law is contained in ERA 1996, ss 55–57 and 66–73 and the Maternity and Parental Leave etc Regulations 1999 (MPLR 1999). Maternity pay and maternity allowance are dealt with in separate legislation.

The limitations and complexities of maternity rights have meant that, in addition to these specific rights, women workers have relied on sex discrimination law, both national and EC, to challenge unfavourable treatment. This remains an important source of rights for pregnant women and women on maternity leave, both for those workers who are not employees and cannot make use of the statutory rights, and also where the terms on which contractual maternity rights are provided amount to discrimination.

Right to time off for ante-natal care

A pregnant employee is entitled to time off for any appointments for ante-natal care which she has made on the advice of a registered general practitioner, nurse or midwife (ERA 1996, s 55). If the employer requests, she must (except for the first appointment) produce a certificate from the general practitioner, nurse or midwife saying that she is pregnant and an appointment card. There is no qualifying service requirement. The employee is entitled to paid time off at the appropriate hourly rate (s 56).

If the employer unreasonably refuses to permit the time off, or fails to pay for it she may complain to a tribunal within 3 months of the date of the appointment. The ET will order the employer to pay the appropriate remuneration (s 57).

Risk assessment

Where an employer has women of child-bearing age amongst the employees, the duty to carry out a risk assessment under the Management of Health and Safety at Work Regulations 1999 (MHSWR 1999) extends to include assessment of the risk to the safety or health of a pregnant woman or her child (reg 16). This arises only where the work is of a kind which could involve risk through any processes or working conditions or physical, biological or chemical agents. The regulation gives effect to the relevant provisions of PWD 92/85, and the processes, conditions and agents referred to in Annexes I and II of the Directive are specified in MHSWR 1999, reg 16.

Failure to carry out such a risk assessment can amount to direct sex discrimination in relation to a specific pregnant employee. However, the duty to the woman must be triggered in the first place. In *O'Neill v Buckinghamshire County Council* (2010) the EAT, following the scheme of MHSWR 1999, regs 16–18, held that the duty arose when the woman had notified the employer in writing that she was pregnant; when the work was of the kind which could involve a risk of harm or danger to the health and safety of the woman or her baby; and the risk arises from processes, conditions or agents in the workplace. In the particular case, the employee was a teacher who claimed that it was the stress of the job which caused the risk, but the EAT did not accept that this was a process, condition or agent as required by the regulation.

Suspension from work on maternity grounds

If there is risk to a pregnant employee, or to one who has recently given birth or is breastfeeding, the employer may be able to implement safety precautions, but if not there is a duty to consider altering working conditions or hours of work if it is reasonable to do so (reg 16). If it is not reasonable, or if it would not be possible to avoid the risk, the employer must either suspend her from work or provide suitable alternative employment. If suitable alternative employment is available, the employee has the right to be offered it (ERA 1996, s 67). The work must be both suitable for her to do and appropriate in the circumstances, and terms and conditions must not be substantially less favourable than those that apply to the job she normally does. In *British Airways (European Operations at Gatwick)* v *Moore and Botterill* (2000) two members of cabin staff were transferred, at their request, to ground staff when they informed the employer that they were pregnant. They did not receive the flying allowances which were part of the package for their normal jobs as cabin staff. Their claim that the employer was in breach of the duty to provide suitable alternative work was upheld, since the difference in remuneration was so substantial.

If there is no suitable alternative employment, the employer must suspend the employee from work on maternity grounds. She is entitled to be paid her full pay during this suspension, unless she has unreasonably refused an offer of suitable alternative employment (s 68). An employee may complain to a tribunal if she is not paid what she is entitled to (s 70).

Statutory maternity pay

The principal legislation governing statutory maternity pay is the Social Security Contributions and Benefits Act 1992 (SSCBA 1992) and the Statutory Maternity Pay (General) Regulations 1986 (SMP(G)R 1986). The employer is liable to pay statutory maternity pay (SSCBA 1992, s 164). Entitlement to statutory maternity pay, unlike entitlement to statutory maternity leave, is subject to service and earnings qualifications. The entitlement to statutory maternity pay does not depend on exercising the statutory right to return to work. The employee must, however, have stopped working because of pregnancy.

Service qualification

To qualify for statutory maternity pay the woman must be an employed earner (a tax concept) with 26 weeks' continuous service with the employer up to and including the 15th week before the expected week of confinement (EWC). She must remain in employment with the employer until the start of the 11th week before EWC, unless she has given birth before then (SSCBA 1992, s 164). An employer who ends the contract of a woman who has worked for him for 8 weeks or more for the purpose of avoiding liability for maternity pay will be responsible to make the payments (SMP(G)R 1986, reg 3).

Earnings qualification

The woman's average earnings in the last 8 weeks must have been not less than the lower national insurance earnings limit (currently £97).

Notice requirements

The employee must give the employer at least 28 days' notice, in writing if requested, of the date she expects maternity pay to start from, or as soon as reasonably practicable (SSCBA 1992, s 164). She must produce a certificate of the EWC (SMP(G)R 1986, reg 22).

Maternity pay period

The maternity pay period is 39 consecutive weeks (SMP(G)R 1986, reg 2). The period was increased (from 26 weeks) in 2007. The Work and Families Act 2006 gave the power to extend the maternity pay period to 52 weeks: to date, the power has been used to extend it to 39 weeks. It starts in the week after the woman stops work, and cannot start before the 11th week before confinement. Although the employee must have stopped work during the period, up to 10 days' work may be done for the employer during the period without losing entitlement to statutory maternity pay (reg 9A).

Rate of maternity pay

The first 6 weeks are payable at the rate of 90 per cent of normal weekly earnings. The remaining 33 weeks are payable at either 90 per cent of normal weekly earnings or the prescribed rate (currently £124.88), whichever is less.

The employer is entitled to be compensated for any statutory maternity pay paid by deducting 92 per cent of SMP paid from PAYE and contributions to the National Insurance Fund. Small employers (those who pay £45,000 or less annually in gross national insurance contributions) will be entitled to additional compensation (Statutory Maternity Pay (Compensation of Employers) and Miscellaneous Amendment Regulations 1994).

Maternity allowance

A woman who is not entitled to maternity pay is entitled to claim maternity allowance, which is a social security benefit payable by the Department of Work and Pensions and is at the same level as the prescribed rate of statutory maternity pay and for the same length of time (SSCBA 1992, s 35). She must have been in employment or have been a self-employed earner, and have paid standard rate national insurance contributions, in 26 out of the 66 weeks immediately before EWC. She does not have to be an employee and does not have to have worked for a single employer. She must work to the 11th week before EWC unless she has given birth before that date. Maternity allowance is payable for up to 39 weeks, and is paid at either 90 per cent of normal weekly earnings or the prescribed rate, whichever is less. Like a woman on maternity pay, a woman will not lose her right to maternity allowance if she works for no more than 10 days during the maternity allowance period.

Right to maternity leave

The maternity leave provisions have been rationalised and are certainly more straightforward than when they were described by the EAT as "of inordinate complexity exceeding the worst excesses of a taxing statute" (*Lavery* v *Plessey Telecommunications Ltd* (1983)). Nevertheless, they are still complex and, as with the rest of the parental rights, only an outline of the basic provisions is provided here.

The right to maternity leave is contained in ERA 1996, ss 71–75D and the Maternity and Parental Leave Regulations 1999 (MPLR 1999). There are three types of maternity leave: compulsory, ordinary and additional. Together, ordinary and additional maternity leave are statutory maternity leave (MPLR 1999, reg 2). The differences in qualification and contractual terms which used to exist between ordinary and additional maternity leave were abolished in 2008 after the High Court held that both forms of maternity leave amounted to maternity leave in terms of the PWD 92/85 so that it was necessary for contractual terms to continue throughout (except in relation to pay) (*EOC* v *DTI* (2007)).

There are no service or earnings qualifications for the right to maternity leave, unlike maternity pay, so that a woman might not qualify for maternity pay, but would be entitled to maternity leave. She must be an employee.

Compulsory maternity leave

For health and safety reasons there is a period of compulsory maternity leave during which an employer must not permit the employee to work. It is an offence for an employer not to comply with this prohibition (ERA 1996, s 72). It applies in respect of any employee who is entitled to ordinary maternity leave, and consists of the 2 weeks immediately after childbirth (MPLR 1999, reg 8).

Ordinary maternity leave

In order to exercise the right to maternity leave the employee must notify her employer (in writing if requested) by the 15th week before EWC, or, if not reasonably practicable, as soon as is reasonably practicable, that she is pregnant, the expected week of childbirth and the date she intends to start her leave (reg 4). When the employer receives this notice he must notify the employee of the date on which her additional maternity leave period will end within 28 days of receiving the notice (reg 7). The employee can vary the date by giving notice at least 28 days before the date varied, or the new date, whichever is earlier, or as soon as reasonably practicable. In that case the employer must notify the end date within 28 days of the ordinary maternity leave starting.

Ordinary maternity leave continues for 26 weeks (reg 7). It normally starts on the date notified by the employee, but no earlier than the 11th week before EWC, or on childbirth if it occurs earlier than the notified date. If the employee is absent from work wholly or partly because of pregnancy in the 4 weeks before EWC, maternity leave starts automatically (reg 6).

Additional maternity leave

Additional maternity leave starts on the day after the end of ordinary maternity leave (reg 6) and continues for a further 26 weeks (reg 7). Thus the total entitlement to statutory maternity leave is 52 weeks.

Employment status when on maternity leave

An employee on statutory maternity leave is entitled to the benefit of the terms and conditions of her employment (other than pay), and is bound by the obligations of the terms and conditions of employment (reg 9).

Work in maternity leave period   An employee on maternity leave may do up to 10 days' work for the employer without terminating the maternity leave. In addition, any "reasonable contact" from time to time between employer and employee, which either party is entitled to make, does not terminate it. The contact might be to discuss the employee's return to work (reg 12A). This provision does not give a right to the employee to work up to 10 days, nor a right on the part of the employer to demand it.

Right to return to job

The right to return depends on whether the employee is returning to work after ordinary or additional maternity leave, and whether the ordinary maternity leave was preceded by some other leave. Where she is returning from ordinary maternity leave, either as an isolated leave or following on from another statutory leave which was not additional maternity leave or additional adoption leave, or parental leave of more than 4 weeks, she is entitled to return to the job in which she was employed before her absence (reg 18). Seniority, pension rights and similar rights must be as if she had not been absent, and terms and conditions must be no less favourable than those which would have applied if she had not been absent (reg 18A).

In other cases, where she is returning from additional maternity leave or from ordinary maternity leave which follows on from a period of additional maternity leave, or additional adoption leave or parental leave of more than 4 weeks, the right is to return to the job in which she was employed before her absence, or, if that is not reasonably practicable, to another job which is suitable and appropriate in the circumstances (reg 18). The same provisions apply in relation to rights and terms and conditions as for ordinary maternity leave.

Redundancy during maternity leave   Where the employee's job becomes redundant during maternity leave, the employee is entitled to be offered alternative employment where there is a suitable available vacancy, under a new contract of employment, which takes effect immediately on the ending of employment under the previous one. The work to be done under the new contract must be of a kind which is suitable and appropriate in the circumstances, and the provisions of the contract as to capacity and place of employment and other terms and conditions must not be substantially less favourable than those under the previous contract (reg 10).

Returning to work during the maternity leave period   An employee may return early from statutory maternity leave, but must give 8 weeks' notice to the employer. If she does not give this notice and attempts to return early, the employer may postpone her return to a date that equates to 8 weeks' notice, but not later than the original return date (reg 11).

Contractual maternity leave

Many employees have a contractual right to maternity leave which is different from statutory maternity leave. The employee may not utilise both rights separately but may take advantage of whichever right is, in any particular respect, the more favourable (reg 21).

Unfair dismissal

All employees, regardless of length of service, have the right not to be dismissed for a number of reasons connected with pregnancy or maternity.

It is automatically unfair to dismiss an employee for a reason connected with her pregnancy, or with the fact that she has given birth, or with a requirement or recommendation for suspension on pregnancy or maternity grounds, or with her taking or seeking to take ordinary or additional maternity leave, or with the fact that she failed to return after ordinary or additional maternity leave when the employer had not complied with its notice duties, or with the fact that she worked or refused to work during the maternity leave period as permitted (MPLR 1999, reg 20; ERA 1996, s 99). It is also automatically unfair to select an employee for redundancy for one of these reasons.

For the reason to be related to pregnancy, it has been held that the employer must know the employee is pregnant. In *Ramdoolar v Bycity Ltd* (2005) an employee, who was dismissed with insufficient service to claim standard unfair dismissal, claimed that her dismissal was an automatically unfair pregnancy dismissal. She had not told her employer that she was pregnant and the reason given for her dismissal was inadequate performance. She argued that her employer should have known she was pregnant because of her symptoms and the reason for her dismissal was connected with that. The EAT did not accept this, holding that the employer must know or believe that the employee was pregnant. This could include suspecting she was pregnant, but this was not the case here.

An employer who refuses to allow an employee to return from maternity leave to a suitable and appropriate job because it is not reasonably practicable, where the reason for this is not redundancy, will have a defence to an unfair dismissal claim if an associated employer offers her a job which she either accepts or unreasonably refuses.

Detriment

An employee also has the right not to be subjected to detriment for the same reasons connected with pregnancy (MPLR 1999, reg 19; ERA 1996, s 47C).

Right to written reasons for dismissal

In a case of dismissal at any other time than during pregnancy or maternity leave, an employee with 1 year's continuous service is entitled to request a written statement of reasons for the dismissal. Where the employee is dismissed while pregnant, or during statutory maternity leave, she is entitled to written reasons without having continuous service and without having to request it (ERA 1996, s 92). The sanction for failure to comply is 2 weeks' pay.

Equality and discrimination and pregnancy and maternity

There have been a number of challenges to the treatment of pregnant women and women on maternity leave which have involved reference to the EC Directives 92/85 and 76/207 (now 2006/54). The ECJ established in *Hertz* (1990) and *Dekker* (1990) that pregnancy discrimination is sex discrimination without any need to make a comparison with a man. This is now expressed in the SDA 1975, s 3A (and is a separate protected characteristic under the EA 2010, s 4). This applies throughout the protected period, that is the period that lasts from pregnancy to the end of maternity leave. Outside this period the ECJ has held that a comparison is relevant. In *Hertz*, the ECJ held that dismissal after maternity leave had finished and the woman had returned to work because of an illness which had its roots in pregnancy was to be treated as a standard sex discrimination case, comparing her treatment with that of a sick man.

During maternity leave, PWD 92/85 permits maternity pay to be less than full pay, so long as it is no less than sick pay. The ECJ, in *Gillespie v Northern Ireland Health and Social Services Board* (1996), rejected a claim that payment of contractual maternity pay at a lower rate than normal contractual pay was sex discrimination, since lesser pay or allowance was permitted by PWD 92/85 (Art 11.2). However, in the same case it was held that in other respects than pay a woman on maternity leave was entitled to equality of treatment, so that in *Gillespie*, although not entitled to full pay while on maternity leave, she was entitled to the benefit of a wage increase which was awarded during that period. This is now an express provision in the EPA 1970 (s 1(2)(d)–(f)); and EA 2010, Sch 9, para 17 and ss 72–76 replicate it by providing for a maternity equality clause.

PATERNITY RIGHTS

During pregnancy and for some time to permit full recovery from childbirth, there is no equivalent requirement for rights for fathers. Special treatment afforded to women in connection with pregnancy and childbirth was expressly excluded from sex discrimination provisions (SDA 1975, s 2; EA 2010, Sch 7, para 2). Once the child has been born, parenting responsibilities are capable of being carried out by men and women, although it is still far more common for women to take the primary responsibility. Statutory paternity rights were only relatively recently introduced, by the Employment Act 2002 (inserting ss 80A–80E into ERA 1996) and the Paternity and Adoption Leave Regulations 2002 (PALR 2002). The provisions concerning additional paternity leave, due to take effect in respect of children born (or placed for adoption) on or after

3 April 2011, introduced by the Work and Families Act 2006, are provided in the Additional Paternity Leave Regulations 2010 (APLR 2010). Paternity pay is governed by the SSCBA 1992, the Statutory Paternity Pay and Statutory Adoption Pay (General) Regulations (SPPSAP(G)R 2002), and the Additional Statutory Paternity Pay (General) Regulations 2010 (ASPP(G)R 2010).

Entitlement

To qualify for paternity leave, a worker must be an employee with 26 weeks' continuous employment ending with the 15th week before EWC or 26 weeks before being notified of being matched with the child in the case of adoption. He must either be the child's father or, though not the father, be married to or the partner of the child's mother, and he must have or expect to have responsibility for the upbringing of the child (if the father) or (if not the father but the mother's husband or partner) the main responsibility (PALR 2002, reg 4). Although called paternity leave, and although most employees exercising the right will be men, it is not a gender-specific entitlement. "Partner" means someone who lives with the mother or adopter and the child in an enduring family relationship, whether of different or same sex, so long as he is not a relative of the mother or adopter (reg 2). Relatives, who are thus not entitled to paternity leave, are the mother's or adopter's parent, grandparent, sister, brother, aunt or uncle.

Paternity leave

When introduced, paternity leave applied only in relation to the birth of the child, and was intended to allow the father to support the mother or look after an existing child around the time of the birth. It could therefore be seen as the equivalent of compulsory maternity leave. As part of a family-friendly approach to employment, additional paternity leave has been introduced to enable a mother to transfer part of her maternity leave on her return to work.

Ordinary paternity leave

Ordinary paternity leave must be taken for the purpose of caring for a child or supporting the child's mother or adopter (regs 4 and 8). It can be taken either as 1 week's leave or as 2 consecutive weeks. It must be taken between the birth and 56 days after birth (or after EWC if the birth was premature); or between placement for adoption and 56 days after placement (regs 5 and 9). The actual week(s) is chosen by the employee.

The right is subject to notice provisions. The employee must give the employer notice of intention to take this leave no later than the 15th week before EWC (or placement for adoption) unless that is not reasonably practicable, in which case as soon as is reasonably practicable. The notice must specify the EWC (adoption equivalent), the length of period of leave being taken and the date chosen by the employee to take leave (regs 6 and 10).

Additional paternity leave

While ordinary paternity leave is a free-standing right, additional paternity leave is secondary to the exercise by the mother of her right to maternity leave. APLR 2010 came into force in April 2010, but will only take effect in respect of children due on or after 3 April 2011. In addition to the father's qualifications for entitlement to ordinary maternity leave, he must remain in continuous employment with the employer until the start of additional paternity leave (APLR 2010, regs 4 and 14). The mother or adopter of the child must have returned to work, although it is not necessary for additional paternity leave to start immediately on this return.

Additional paternity leave must be taken to care for the child. It can take place any time between 20 weeks after birth or placement of the child and the child's first birthday. The minimum period is 2 weeks, and the maximum 26 weeks. It must be taken in multiples of complete weeks, and in one continuous period (regs 5 and 15).

It is subject to notice requirements on the part of the father, including a declaration by the mother or adopter of her return to work and that the father is the only person entitled to exercise additional paternity leave to her knowledge (regs 6 and 16). The notice and declaration must be given to the employer 8 weeks before it is intended to take the leave.

Terms and conditions during leave

During both forms of paternity leave, the employee is entitled to the benefit of all terms and conditions except pay (PALR 2002, reg 12; APLR 2010, reg 27).

Right to return to work

When returning from paternity leave as an isolated period of leave, or as a series of consecutive periods of statutory leave so long as it did not include additional maternity or adoption leave or parental leave of more than 4 weeks, the employee is entitled to return to the job he was employed in before the absence. In other cases, the right is to return to the same job, or, if that is not reasonably practicable, to another job which is both suitable and appropriate in the circumstances (PALR 2002, reg 13; APLR 2010, reg 31).

In both cases the employee has the right to return on no less favourable terms and conditions than if he had not been absent, and with continuity for seniority, pension and similar rights preserved between employment before and after the leave (PALR 2002, reg 14; APLR 2010, reg 32).

Statutory paternity pay

An employee who qualifies for paternity leave also qualifies for statutory paternity pay so long as average earnings were at least at the lower earnings limit for national insurance. It is paid at the rate of either 90 per cent of normal weekly pay or the prescribed rate (currently £128.44). The employee has his own entitlement to this during ordinary paternity leave. During additional paternity leave, if the mother has not exhausted all of her entitlement to statutory maternity pay, he is entitled to be paid for the remaining period at the same rate (SPPSAP(G)R 2002; ASPP(G)R 2010).

Remedy

An employee who is subjected to a detriment because he took or sought to take paternity leave or who was dismissed where that was the reason or principal reason for the dismissal, may complain to a tribunal (ERA 1996, ss 47C and 99; PALR 2002, regs 28 and 29; APLR 2010, regs 33 and 34).

Contractual scheme

Where an employee has a contractual right to paternity leave, he cannot exercise both rights separately but may take advantage of whichever right is in any particular respect more favourable than the other (PALR 2002, reg 30; APLR 2010, reg 35).

ADOPTION RIGHTS

Parents of adopted children were included in the entitlement to parental leave (see below) from its introduction in 1999. Paid and unpaid leave for adopters at the time of placement of a child was introduced by the Employment Act 2002 (inserting ss 75A–75D into ERA 1996) and PALR 2002. Adoption pay is governed by SSCBA 1992 and SPPSAP(G)R 2002. Adoption rights are equivalent to maternity rights.

Entitlement to leave

To qualify for adoption leave the worker must be an employee with 26 weeks' continuous employment by the date when he is notified of being matched with the child. The employee must be the child's adopter (either alone or one of two joint adopters) and have notified the adoption agency of agreement to the placement (PALR 2002, reg 15). Where a couple are adopting together, only one of them is entitled to adoption leave (reg 2). The other adopter would be entitled to exercise paternity rights.

The employee may choose to start adoption leave on the date the child is placed with him for adoption or on a fixed date no more than 14 days before the expected date of placement but no later than the date of placement (reg 16).

The employee must give the employer notice of the intention to take adoption leave within 7 days of being notified of being matched with the child for adoption, or, if that is not reasonably practicable, as soon as it is reasonably practicable. He must specify the date on which it is intended to start the leave. On request, the employee must supply documents confirming the adoption (reg 17).

As with maternity leave, a new adopter is entitled to 26 weeks' ordinary adoption leave, followed by 26 weeks' additional adoption leave. The exercise of these rights is subject to the same provisions as maternity leave in respect of terms and conditions of work and the right to return to work (regs 18–27).

Statutory adoption pay

An employee who qualifies for adoption leave also qualifies for statutory adoption pay so long as earnings averaged at least the lower earnings limit for national insurance. Statutory adoption pay is paid at the lower of 90 per cent of normal weekly earnings or the statutory rate (currently £124.88) for 39 weeks (SPPSAP(G)R 2002, reg 29).

Remedy

An employee subjected to a detriment for taking adoption leave, or dismissed where that was the reason or principal reason for the dismissal, may complain to a tribunal (ERA 1996, ss 47C and 99; PALR 2002, regs 28 and 29).

Contractual schemes

As with maternity and paternity leave, where an employee has a contractual right to adoption leave, he cannot exercise the rights separately but may take advantage of whichever right is in any particular respect more favourable than the other (PALR 2002, reg 30).

PARENTAL LEAVE

A right to parental leave was introduced for the first time in the UK by the Employment Relations Act 1999 (amending ERA 1996). The UK had originally exercised its opt-out in relation to the EC Parental Leave Directive 96/34, but, on the change of Government in the UK in 1997, the Directive was extended to the UK by Directive 97/75. The Directive has been recast in Directive 2010/18. The national law is contained in ERA 1996, ss 76–80 and the Maternity and Parental Leave etc Regulations 1999 (MPLR 1999).

When introduced, the right was given only in respect of children born, or placed for adoption, after 15 December 1999. A challenge to this restriction was referred to the ECJ in *R v Secretary of State for Trade and Industry, ex parte TUC* (2000) as being in breach of the Directive. The restriction was lifted, however, and those disadvantaged given additional rights in advance of any decision by the ECJ.

Framework Directive

The EC Directive is based on an Agreement between the EC social partners, and the MPLR 1999 reflect that in that part of the rights may be agreed collectively. As part of a European social partnership "family-friendly" approach to employment, part of the aim is to encourage workplace agreements about leave. There is a "default" scheme where agreement does not take place, and this too is reflected in MPLR 1999.

Right to parental leave

To qualify for the right to parental leave, the worker must be an employee with 1 year's continuous employment. The employee must have, or expect to have, parental responsibilities for the child, or have been registered as the child's father, and the leave must be taken for the purposes of caring for the child (MPLR 1999, reg 13).

A qualifying employee is entitled to either 13 or 18 weeks' leave in respect of any individual child (reg 14). The right applies until the child's 5th birthday, or, if the child is entitled to disability living allowance, the 18th birthday, or, if the child is placed for adoption, 5 years after placement or until the 18th birthday, whichever is earlier (reg 15). In the case of a disabled child, the entitlement is 18 weeks' leave; for other children, it is 13 weeks' leave.

The default scheme, which applies where there is no collective agreement in force providing for parental leave, states that parental leave may only be taken as a week's leave, or a multiple of a week (MPLR 1999, Sch 2, para 7). In *Rodway* v *South Central Trains* (2005) the Court of Appeal held that a father who had taken a day's unauthorised leave to look after his son could not be exercising his right to parental leave since the period was for less than a week. It rejected the employee's argument that it was permissible to take less than a week's leave, but be deemed to have taken a week. In the case of a disabled child this provision does not apply and a parent would be entitled to leave on individual days.

The default scheme also provides for a maximum yearly entitlement of 4 weeks' leave in respect of any individual child in a particular year (Sch 2, para 8).

There is no statutory entitlement to pay for parental leave. There is nothing to prevent a voluntary scheme providing for pay in certain circumstances.

Continuation of employment during leave

During leave certain contractual terms and conditions continue. The employee is entitled to the benefit of the following terms and conditions of employment: the implied obligation of trust and confidence; notice of termination by the employer; compensation for redundancy; disciplinary or grievance procedures. The employee is bound by the following: the implied obligation of good faith towards the employer; notice of termination to the employer; disclosure of confidential information; acceptance of gifts or other benefits; employee's participation in any other business (reg 17).

Right to return to work

Parental leave can vary from 1 week to 13 or 18 weeks. An employee who takes parental leave is entitled to return to work, the right varying depending on the length of the period of leave. Where the parental leave is 4 weeks or less, the right is to return to the job he was employed in immediately before the absence. Where the parental leave is more than 4 weeks, the entitlement is to return to the job in which he was employed before the absence, or, if that is not reasonably practicable, to another job which is suitable and appropriate in the circumstances. Where parental leave of 4 weeks or less is taken immediately after another period of leave, whether previous parental leave, or maternity leave, the right is the same as if the leave was more than 4 weeks (reg 18).

The terms and conditions relating to remuneration, seniority and other terms should be no less favourable than if he had not taken the leave and the period after parental leave must be treated as continuous with the period before (reg 19).

Procedure

Where there is a collective agreement containing details of a parental leave scheme which is incorporated into the contracts of employment, that is the scheme that is to be followed. Schedule 2 to MPLR 1999 lays out a default scheme for operating paternal leave which applies where there is no collectively agreed scheme. As well as the provisions for minimum and maximum leave already referred to, procedural requirements are provided. The employee may be required to produce evidence of his entitlement to parental leave. The employee must give notice of the period of proposed leave. Normally the notice is at least 21 days; if a father wishes to take leave at the birth of a child he must give at least 21 days' notice of the expected week of childbirth; if an adoptive parent wishes to take leave he must give at least 21 days' notice of the expected week of placement. The employer can postpone leave (except in case of birth or adoption) if he considers that the operation of the business would be unduly disrupted by the leave. However, the employer must permit the leave within 6 months at a time chosen by the employer in consultation with the employee.

Remedy

An employee can complain of refusal or unreasonable postponement of leave (ERA 1996, s 80), and can also complain against detrimental treatment for taking or seeking parental leave (ERA 1996, s 47C; MPLR 1999, reg 19); and against (automatically) unfair dismissal where dismissal is connected with paternity leave (ERA 1996, s 99; MPLR 1999, reg 20).

DEPENDANT CARE LEAVE

The Parental Leave Directive 96/34 also provided for a right to take time off work in emergencies. This right has been implemented in ERA 1996, ss 57A and 57B.

Right to dependant care leave

Dependant care leave is a more limited right than parental leave, and is a right to time off to deal with an emergency. An employer must permit an employee reasonable time off to take necessary action to deal with certain situations. These are: to provide assistance when a dependant falls ill, gives birth or is injured or assaulted; to make arrangements for the provision of care for a dependant who is ill or injured; in consequence of the death of a dependant; to deal with unexpected disruption or termination of arrangements for the care of a dependant; to deal with an incident involving a child which occurs unexpectedly at an educational establishment (ERA 1996, s 57A).

The employee must tell the employer the reason for the absence as soon as reasonably practicable and, unless the information cannot be given until return, how long the absence will last. The right is for the specific purposes in the Act and is not unlimited. In *Qua v John Ford Morrison Solicitors* (2003) the EAT distinguished parental leave and dependant care leave. Dependant care leave is for the temporary purpose of dealing with one of the specific crises in s 57A. It does not entitle the employee to more than reasonable time off to do what is necessary to deal with the immediate crisis. If longer term care is necessary, the employee should either arrange for it to be provided or apply for parental leave for that purpose.

Dependant

Although the right is of more limited scope than parental leave, it applies in a wider variety of relationships and is not restricted to emergencies associated with children. A dependant means an employee's spouse, child or parent. It also includes someone who lives in the same household as the employee (other than as employee, tenant, lodger or boarder). In addition, a dependant also includes anyone who reasonably relies on the employee to provide assistance or make arrangements in case of illness, or in the case of disruption of care arrangements (s 57A).

Remedy

Enforcement is by complaint to a tribunal of unreasonable refusal (s 57B). The employee can also complain against detrimental treatment for exercising the right (s 47C) or (automatically) unfair dismissal (s 99).

PART-TIME WORKERS' RIGHTS

Protection of part-time workers

A majority of part-time workers are women, and part-time work is particularly associated with women who are combining work with family commitments. As a consequence, less favourable treatment of part–time workers raises issues of sex discrimination, in particular indirect sex discrimination. Full-time workers may be paid at a higher rate, or given access to pensions or other benefits which part-time workers are not given access to, or part-time workers may be excluded from opportunities for promotion or training. Much of the case law on indirect discrimination under SDA 1975 and the Equal Treatment Directive 2006/54 (formerly 76/207) has been concerned with the less favourable treatment of part-time workers (*Jenkins v Kingsgate Clothing Productions Ltd* (1981); *Bilka-Kaufhaus GmbH v Weber von Hartz* (1986)). The successful challenge to the hours requirement for qualifying service for unfair dismissal and redundancy in *R v Secretary of State for Employment, ex parte Equal Opportunities Commission* (1994) found the requirements were contrary to Art 119 (now 157) and Directive 76/207 on the ground of indirect sex discrimination.

Although this gave protection to some female part-time workers against unjustified indirect discrimination, part-time workers in general were left unprotected. After lengthy negotiation, during most of which it was opposed by the UK Government, in 1997 the EC Part-time Workers Directive (PTWD) 97/81 was passed, incorporating a Framework Agreement between the social partners. This was given effect to by the Part-time Workers (Prevention of Less Favourable Treatment) Regulations 1999 (PTWR 1999).

Refusal to permit a job to be done part-time or by job-sharing has been challenged as amounting to indirect sex discrimination in a number of cases. In *Glasgow Health Board v Carey* (1987) an application by a health visitor to work part-time over 2½ or 3 days a week was refused: instead she was required to work part-time over 5 days. Because of difficulties with child-care arrangements she claimed that she had been indirectly discriminated against on the ground of sex. Although it was found that the requirement to work 5 days had a disproportionate impact on women (and therefore created a prima facie case of indirect discrimination), the EAT held that the employer's requirement had been shown to be justifiable having regard to the needs of the patients and the service. The PTWD 97/81 and PTWR 1999 do not affect cases such as this. They apply to give protection to those who are already working part-time, but do not give any right to work part-time instead of full-time.

Less favourable treatment of part-time workers

A part-time worker has the right not to be treated less favourably than a comparable full-time worker either in relation to the terms of his contract, or by being subjected to a detriment by the employer (PTWR 1999, reg 5). The ground of the less favourable treatment must be that the worker is a part-time worker and not some other reason. The treatment must be less favourable than the treatment afforded to a "comparable full-time worker". The treatment, however, may be objectively justified by the employer.

On the ground that the worker is a part-time worker

Under the discrimination statutes, the phrase "on the ground of" was interpreted to mean that the protected characteristic must have been an important factor: it does not have to have been the sole factor (*Owen and Briggs* v *James* (1982)). PTWD 97/81, on which PTWR 1999 are based, prohibits less favourable treatment of part-time workers "solely because they work part-time" (Art 4). The Inner House of the Court of Session in *McMenemy* v *Capita Business Services Ltd* (2007) relied on this to interpret PTWR 1999 to mean that the less favourable treatment must be solely on the ground of part-time working. This interpretation has been doubted by the EAT in England (not bound by decisions of the Court of Session) in *Carl* v *University of Sheffield* (2009), which held that it need not be the sole cause, but must be the effective and predominant cause. The approach of the EAT seems preferable to that of the Court of Session as it does not exclude from protection cases where part-time status was an important part of the reason for the discriminatory treatment.

A part-time worker

The PTWR 1999 apply to workers, not only employees. A worker is defined in the same way as under ERA 1996 (Chapter 2) and includes employees, apprentices and those working on contracts to perform work personally (unless the employer is a client or customer) (reg 1). A full-time worker and a part-time worker are workers who are paid wholly or partly by reference to the time they work. A worker is full time if, according to the employer's custom and practice in relation to others on the same type of contract, he is identifiable as a full-time worker. A worker is part time if, likewise according to the employer's custom and practice in relation to others on the same type of contract, he is not identifiable as a full-time worker (reg 2). This means that there may be a range of working hours which are considered to be full-time hours in a workplace. A part-time worker is one who is not considered by custom and practice to be a full-time worker.

A comparable full-time worker

The treatment of a part-time worker must be compared with an actual comparable full-time worker, and not a hypothetical full-time worker. There is no equivalent to the "or would be treated" in the definition of direct discrimination for discrimination law more generally, and the EAT in *Carl* v *University of Sheffield* (2009) could find nothing in the PTWD 97/81 which could compel an interpretation requiring a hypothetical comparator in the absence of words to that effect in PTWR 1999.

A comparable full-time worker is defined in the PTWR 1999, reg 2. Both workers must be employed by the same employer. Both must be employed under the same type of contract. The following are specifically stated to be employed under different types of contract: employees employed under a contract not of apprenticeship; employees employed under a contract of apprenticeship; workers who are not employees; any other description of worker it is reasonable for the employer to treat differently from other workers on the ground that such workers have a different type of contract. In *Matthews* v *Kent and Medway Towns Fire Authority* (2006) the House of Lords made it clear that the last "any other description category" was designed to be a "long-stop", and could not take a contract which was within one of the other categories into another category at the discretion of the employer. Thus, if both are employees employed under a contract not of apprenticeship, the full-time worker is comparable.

In addition, both workers must be engaged in the same or broadly similar work having regard to level of qualifications, skill and experience. The full-time worker should be based at the same establishment as the part-time worker or at a different establishment if there are no comparable full-time workers at the same establishment. The House of Lords has taken a similar view of the concept of the same or broadly similar work as has been taken in equal pay cases. In *Matthews* v *Kent and Medway Towns Fire Authority* (2006), in a claim by part-time "retained" firefighters seeking to compare themselves with full-time firefighters, they stated that the similarities should be emphasised rather than the differences. Particular weight should be given to the extent to which their work is the same, and to the importance of their work to the enterprise.

Workers becoming part-time

Where a full-time worker changes and continues to work as a part-time worker with the employer following either a termination or variation of contract, he does not need to identify a comparable full-time worker but may compare his treatment as a part-time worker with that of his previous treatment as a full-time worker (reg 3).

Workers returning part-time after absence

Similarly, where a full-time worker returns after an absence of less than 12 months to part-time work in the same job at the same level, he will not need to identify a comparable full-time worker (reg 4).

The pro rata principle

The right not to be treated less favourably is determined by applying the pro rata principle unless it is inappropriate (reg 5). The pro rata principle means that the part-time worker is entitled to receive not less than the proportion of the benefit which the full-time worker receives, which the proportion of the number of weekly hours of the part-time worker bears to the weekly hours of the comparable full-time worker (reg 1). Thus, if an employee works for half of the weekly hours of the comparator, the pro rata rate of holiday entitlement would be half of the holiday entitlement of the full-time worker.

However where overtime is worked, unless provided otherwise, overtime pay is not due until the hours of the part-timer exceed that entitling the full-timer to overtime pay. This is expressly provided in PTWR 1999, reg 5, and is permissible according to a decision of the ECJ in *Stadt Lengerich* v *Helmig* (1995) under Art 119 (now 157).

Written statement

A worker who considers that he has been treated less favourably contrary to reg 5 is entitled to receive a written statement of reasons for the treatment from the employer. The worker must request the statement in writing, and the employer must provide it within 21 days of the request (reg 6). If the treatment in question is dismissal and the worker is an employee who is entitled to receive a written statement of reasons for dismissal under ERA 1996, s 92, the employee must use that provision instead.

A written statement is admissible in evidence and where an employer deliberately, without reasonable excuse, fails to provide one, or the statement is evasive or equivocal, the Tribunal may draw any inference it thinks just and equitable, including that the employer had infringed the right in question.

Remedy

A worker may complain to an employment tribunal for breach of PTWR 1999 within 3 months of the treatment (reg 8). A worker may also complain if the employer has subjected him to a detriment because of steps the worker took in relation to the Regulations (such as having brought proceedings or given evidence at a tribunal (reg 7(3)). It is for the employer to identify the ground of the less favourable treatment or detriment.

If the worker is an employee, he may also complain of (automatically) unfair dismissal (reg 7(3)).

RIGHT TO REQUEST FLEXIBLE WORKING

If an employee wishes to alter working arrangements, perhaps to fit in with responsibilities at home, an employer is not under an obligation to agree. However, a refusal by an employer might, in appropriate circumstances, amount to indirect sex discrimination where a female employee is refused, or might amount to direct sex discrimination if a male employee is refused in circumstances in which a female employee would have been successful. In either event this is an indirect way of approaching the issue.

The Employment Act 2002, s 47 (inserting ss 80F–80I into ERA 1996) introduced a right to request a contract variation. This was implemented by the Flexible Working (Procedural Requirements) Regulations 2002 (FW(PR)R 2002) and the Flexible Working (Eligibility, Complaints and Remedies) Regulations 2002 (FW(ECR)R 2002. The original provisions related only to the care of children under the age of 6, and in 2006 they were extended to include older children and adults. The purpose of the legislation is to assist those with family caring responsibilities in balancing work and care. In its original form, there was a narrow child-centred view of caring responsibilities; this has now been expanded. The legislation does not give a right to flexible working, but gives a right to request, and a right to have considered, a variation in a contract of employment.

There is, of course, nothing to prevent an employer and employee reaching an agreement to alter working hours and practices.

Care of a child

In order to exercise the statutory right to request flexible working, the worker must have employee status and have worked continuously for the employer for 26 weeks before the application (FW(ECR)R 2002, reg 3). The employee must be requesting the contract variation in order to enable him to care for a child (ERA 1996, s 80F). The child must either be aged under 17, or be under 18 if disabled: a disabled person is one who is entitled to Disability Living Allowance. The employee must both have responsibility for the upbringing of the child and also be in a specified relationship to the child. This includes being the mother, father, adopter, guardian, or foster parent of the child, or having a residence order, or being married to or being the civil partner or the partner of one of these (FW(ECR)R 2002, reg 3).

Once one application has been made, a further application cannot be made for another 12 months (ERA 1996, s 80F).

Care of an adult

As with the application in respect of a child, the employee must have worked continuously for the employer for 26 weeks before the application, and cannot make another application within 12 months. The request must be made to enable the employee to care for an adult who must be married to the employee, or their civil partner, or their partner (living with as if husband and wife or as if civil partners), or a relative of the employee or living at the same address as the employee (FW(ECR)R 2002, reg 3B). There is an exclusive definition of "relative" in reg 2.

Proposed variation

The employee may apply to have changes made to his terms and conditions of employment in relation to hours of work, times when required to work and where (as between home and the employer's place of business) he is required to work (ERA 1996, s 80F). Some examples of the sort of requests that might be made were given in the original explanatory notes to the 2002 Act. These were: compressed hours; flexitime; homework; job-sharing; teleworking; term-time working; shift-working; staggered hours; annualised hours; self-rostering. (These are examples only.)

Procedure

The procedure for applying for and dealing with the application is laid down partly in the ERA 1996 and partly in the two Regulations, FW(ECR)R 2002 and FW(PR)R 2002.

Application

The employee must submit a written application which must specify the change applied for and the date on which it is proposed it should come into effect. It must also explain what effect, if any, the employee thinks making this change would have on the employer and how this effect might be dealt with. It must also explain how the employee meets the relationship conditions in relation to the person being cared for (ERA 1996, s 80F; FW(ECR)R 2002, reg 4).

Employer's duty

The employer must follow the procedural requirements set out in FW(PR)R 2002. If the employer agrees to the change, it should advise the employee within 28 days, specifying when the change will take place. Otherwise, it must hold a meeting with the employee within 28 days, or longer by agreement (reg 3). The employee has a right on request to be accompanied at any meetings, and for the representative to address the meeting (reg 14). The employer must give the employee a written decision within 14 days of the meeting, and if the decision is refusal, it must state upon which of the statutory grounds the refusal is based (regs 4–5). The employee has a right of appeal which must be heard within 14 days, with the appeal decision being given in a further 14 days (regs 6–9). It is always open to employer and employee to reach an agreement by way of compromise.

Refusal

The statutory right is not a right to flexible working, but a right to make the request and to have the request considered properly. Thus, the employer is not obliged to agree to the request. However, a refusal must be made on one of the specified statutory grounds (ERA 1996, s 80G). These are: burden of additional costs; detrimental effect on ability to meet customer demand; inability to reorganise work among existing staff; detrimental impact on performance; insufficiency of work during periods the employee proposes to work; planned structural changes.

Remedy

An employee who has applied for a contract variation for flexible working may complain to a tribunal on the ground that the employer failed to comply with its duty to follow the statutory procedure, or on the ground that a decision to reject the application was based on inaccurate facts (ERA 1996, s 80H). If the application was withdrawn, or the parties reached an agreement no complaint can be made. When considering an application the tribunal cannot consider whether the refusal was justified. However, they are entitled to hear evidence in order to decide whether a decision to reject was based on inaccurate facts. In *Commotion Ltd* v *Rutty* (2006) an employee became legally responsible for her grandchild and applied under s 80F to reduce her hours from 5 to 3 days a week. Her application was refused on the ground that the change would have a detrimental impact on performance. The ET heard evidence on this subject and found that the decision had been made on incorrect facts. The EAT upheld its decision. The ET had not strayed into considering whether the refusal was either justified or reasonable, which it had no power to do. The evidence showed that the employer had had no evidence to show performance could not be maintained by proper organisation and had made no enquiries to find out if it could cope with the request. This was relevant to a finding regarding the correct factual basis of the refusal.

If the tribunal upholds the complaint it must make a declaration to that effect, and may refer the request back for proper consideration, and may award such compensation as is just and equitable (s 80I). The maximum compensation award is 8 weeks' pay (FW(ECR)R 2002, reg 7). If the breach is in relation to the duty to permit representation at the meeting, the maximum is 2 weeks' pay (FW(PR)R 2002, reg 15).

Detriment and dismissal

Employees are also protected against detriment (ERA 1996, s 47D) and dismissal (ERA 1996, s 104C) in relation to the exercise of their rights.

Essential Facts

- The EC Directive on protection for pregnant workers is Pregnant Workers Directive 92/85.

- The EC Directive on rights for parents to parental leave and emergency time off is Parental Leave Directive 96/34.

- Time off provisions are set out in the Employment Rights Act 1996, Pt VI.

- Suspension from work is governed by the Employment Rights Act 1996, Pt VII.

- Maternity leave, adoption leave, parental leave and flexible working are regulated by the Employment Rights Act 1996, Pt VIII.

- Rules governing maternity leave and parental leave are set out in the Maternity and Parental Leave etc Regulations 1999.

- Prevention of discrimination against part-time workers is dealt with in the Part-time Workers (Prevention of Less Favourable Treatment) Regulations 2000.

- Rules governing paternity leave and adoption leave are set out in the Paternity and Adoption Leave Regulations 2002.

Essential Cases

British Airways (European Operations at Gatwick) v Moore and Botterill (2000): two pregnant cabin crew workers were transferred to ground staff, and lost their flight payment. This was not suitable alternative employment for them under ERA 1996, s 67 because of the reduced pay.

Ramdoolar v Bycity Ltd (2005): the employee was dismissed because of competence. She claimed that this was connected with her pregnancy and that, although she had not told them she was pregnant, her employer should have known because of her symptoms. She was unsuccessful: an employer must know or believe, or perhaps even suspect, that the employee is pregnant but that was not the case here. (ERA 1996, s 99).

Rodway v South Central Trains (2005): the employee applied for time off to look after his son, which was refused. He took the day off and claimed it as parental leave. It was held that parental leave can only be taken in multiples of a week and accordingly this could not be parental leave; nor could the day be deemed to be a week (MPLR 1999, Sch 2, para 7).

Matthews v Kent and Medway Towns Fire Authority (2006): this was a claim under PTWR 1999 by part-time firefighters. The House of Lords held that since both were employed under contracts of employment which were not contracts of apprenticeship they were comparable. They further took a broad view of the same or broadly similar work, emphasising similarities rather than differences.

Commotion Ltd v Rutty (2006): the employer turned down a request for flexible working. The ET found that the employer was in breach of its duty since it had not had evidence on which to base its decision that the proposal was unworkable. ETs are not allowed to examine whether the refusal is justified or reasonable, but they are entitled to see if there was sufficient evidence on which the employer could base its decision.

12 HEALTH AND SAFETY

It is not possible to cover, even in outline, the law relating to health and safety at work in this book. However, it is such an important aspect of the legal relationship between the employer and employee that certain aspects which relate to that relationship will be considered.

An employee who is injured or becomes ill as a result of their work may raise an action of reparation against the employer. This may be based on the employer's breach of the duty of care, or it may be based on breach of statutory duty. As well as this civil liability of the employer, there is an important regulatory framework concerned with the prevention of risk and enforcing the legislation, including a range of administrative powers and criminal penalties. After considering the duty of care and the nature of breach of statutory duty, a brief outline of the regulatory scheme will be given.

COMMON LAW

At common law an employer has a duty to take reasonable care for an employee's safety and to protect him from foreseeable risks. The duty arises under the contract of employment, as an implied term, and also arises out of the relationship of employer and employee under the law of delict.

As an implied term in the contract of employment, it can be enforced in the same way as any other term of the contract. As a breach of contract, it may, if material, justify the employee in resigning and raising an action based on constructive dismissal. In *Waltons and Morse* v *Dorrington* (1997) an employee who resigned because her employer failed to introduce effective measures to protect her from smoking by colleagues was successful in her unfair constructive dismissal claim. The employer had failed to take reasonably practicable steps to look after her welfare.

Where the remedy sought by the employee is damages, an action of reparation may also be raised. There is no difference in the nature of the duty owed by the employer to the employee under contract and delict: the difference would lie in the remedy which could be obtained.

If the action is concerned with obtaining compensation for injury, the key elements in an action based on common law liability are breach of the duty of care, and harm to the employee caused by the breach of duty.

Duty of care

The employer's duty is personal and therefore inescapable. The employer may delegate the carrying out of the duty to someone else but remains responsible for any failure (*Wilsons and Clyde Coal Co Ltd v English* (1937)). This principle was applied by the House of Lords in *McDermid* v *Nash Dredging and Reclamation Co Ltd* (1987). A deck hand employed by the company was seriously injured while working on a boat under the command of a captain employed by another company in partnership with the employer. It was held that, although the responsibility for safety had been delegated to the captain of the boat, the employer could not escape the legal responsibility, which was personal and non-delegable.

The duty is owed to each individual employee, so that if the risk of injury is more serious for a particular employee than an average employee, the employer will owe a greater duty in these circumstances, so long as it knows or should have known of the particular circumstances. In *Paris* v *Stepney Borough Council* (1951) a garage mechanic with only one good eye received an injury to the good eye when a spark flew into it when he struck an axle with a hammer. Although it was not considered reasonably necessary to provide goggles in the ordinary course of this sort of work, the House of Lords held that, in this case, where the employee suffered this disability which the employer knew of, greater precautions were required.

Reasonable care

The duty is not absolute: it is a duty to take reasonable care. In deciding what is reasonable there are a number of factors to take into account. The following statement of principle from an English High Court case in 1968 still encapsulates the key principles adopted by the courts:

> "From these authorities I deduce the principles, that the overall test is still the conduct of the reasonable and prudent employer, taking positive thought for the safety of his workers in the light of what he knows or ought to know; where there is a recognised and general practice which has been followed for a substantial period in similar circumstances without mishap, he is entitled to follow it, unless in the light of common sense or newer knowledge it is clearly bad; but, where there is developing knowledge, he must keep reasonably abreast of it and not be too slow to apply it; and where he has in fact greater than average knowledge of the risks, he may be thereby obliged to take more than the average or standard precautions. He must weigh up the risk in terms of the likelihood of injury occurring

and the potential consequences if it does; and he must balance against this the probable effectiveness of the precautions that can be taken to meet it and the expense and inconvenience they involve. If he is found to have fallen below the standard to be properly expected of a reasonable and prudent employer in these respects, he is negligent." (*Stokes* v *Guest, Keen and Nettlefold (Nuts and Bolts) Ltd* (1968) (Chadwick J))

The foreseeability of the harm concerned is central. The greater the danger, the greater the care that must be taken. The more serious the possible injury, the greater the care that must be taken. Only dangers which are, or should be, known can reasonably be guarded against. To decide what is reasonable in the circumstances, the cost of safety measures may be balanced against the degree of risk.

The standard of care may be assessed in relation to the customary practice of the majority of employers in the relevant industry, though this is not conclusive (*Cavanagh* v *Ulster Weaving Co* (1960)). The employer's duty is not, however, simply to keep up with others in the industry but to apply its mind to safety problems affecting the workforce (*Brown* v *Rolls Royce* (1960)).

An employer that is keeping up to date with relevant developments can be expected to take precautions from the time it is known within the industry that they are necessary, even if they might not be more widely (publicly) known. In *Baxter* v *Harland and Wolff plc* (1990) the company was held to be responsible for industrial deafness caused by its failure to take precautions from the mid-1950s even although a government pamphlet warning about the danger was not issued until 1963. The employer knew that employees were becoming deaf, and there was sufficient legal, medical and scientific knowledge long before then about the dangers and the precautions that could be taken. Similarly, in *Bowman* v *Harland and Wolff plc* (1992) the court went through a similar exercise and found on the evidence that by 1973 a "sensible and reasonably well-informed safety officer and factory doctor between them" would have known of the risks of vibration whitefinger which could arise from the use of pneumatic hammers, so that a duty of care in respect of that risk had arisen then. The employer had argued that the relevant date was 1987 when a British Standard had been issued.

In cases of psychiatric harm, the foreseeability of the harm is subject to special criteria. This is because it can be harder to foresee psychiatric injury than physical injury. In *Hatton* v *Sutherland* (2002) the Court of Appeal held that, unless the employer knows of particular problems or vulnerability faced by an employee, the employer is usually entitled to assume that the employee is up to the normal pressures of the job. Relevant facts in deciding foreseeability would include the nature and extent of the work (including workload) and the signs from an employee of possible impending harm. This could be the employee telling the employer of difficulties, or being off ill with a psychiatric problem, or behaviour giving evidence of problems such that a reasonable employer would be put on enquiry. The principles in *Hatton* were approved by the House of Lords in *Barber* v *Somerset County Council* (2004), with Lord Walker emphasising that, in addition, the employer must give "positive thought for the safety of the employee".

Components of the duty of care

The employer's duty is to take reasonable care for the health and safety of each employee. The extent to which an employer can be expected to do this has been established in four aspects.

To provide and maintain safe machinery, tools and equipment The employer's duty is to ensure that employees are provided with such machinery, tools and equipment as are adequate for the safe performance of the job. There must also be a system of inspection and maintenance (*Davie* v *New Merton Board Mills Ltd* (1959)).

A defence which would have been available to the employer at common law was removed by the Employer's Liability (Defective Equipment) Act 1969, which provides that where an employee is injured in the course of his employment because of a defect in equipment provided by his employer and the defect is attributable to the fault of a third party, the injury shall be deemed to be also attributable to negligence on the part of the employer. This is most likely to apply where the employee has been supplied with defective equipment. In *Ralston* v *Greater Glasgow Health Board* (1987) two cleaners claimed damages for dermatitis contracted after using carbolic soap provided by the employer. The employer's arguments that soap was not equipment, and that it could not be said to be defective, were rejected by the Outer House of the Court of Session, taking the ordinary rather than a restrictive meaning of the statutory words.

To provide and maintain safe premises This applies to all of the premises, including access and egress as well as the working area. It extends to any premises on which the employee must work, but the extent of the employer's responsibility depends on what is reasonable in the circumstances. An employer will have less control over premises that are not its own. In general an employer will not have a responsibility in respect of public roads unless there is some unusual danger. In *Stevenson v Morrison Construction Ltd* (2006) an employee had been injured when a works van which he was driving on a road close to the site was hit by a train at a level crossing. There was nothing unusual about the crossing, and the Court of Session held that the action was irrelevant since there was no general duty on employers to make safety arrangements on public roads which were outwith their own premises.

To provide and maintain a safe system of work

Wherever the work is carried out, it is the employer's duty to provide and maintain a safe system of working. This applies to the job layout, warnings, notices, instructions. A system has been defined by the House of Lords as:

"broadly stated, the distinction is between the general and the particular, between the practice and method adopted in carrying on the master's business of which the master is presumed to be aware and the insufficiency of which he can guard against, and isolated day to day acts of the servant ..." (*Wilsons and Clyde Coal Co Ltd* v *English* (1937))

The maintenance of the system extends to a duty to supervise and enforce. The employer should not let a practice grow of ignoring obvious danger. In *General Cleaning Contractors* v *Christmas* (1952) the House of Lords said that it was not reasonable to expect an individual workman to take the initiative in devising and using precautions: the employer must do what is reasonable to ensure that the safety system is operated.

If the danger is not obvious to the employee, the employer must monitor more carefully (*Pape* v *Cumbria Council* (1991)). An employer must not make it difficult for the employee to comply with safety requirements. In *Crouch* v *British Rail Engineering Ltd* (1988) the Court of Appeal held that a system for obtaining goggles which involved obtaining them from a foreman when it was thought they were needed was not a safe system. However, since in this case the injured employee was a skilled worker, and the potential injury if the goggles were not worn an obvious one, the amount of damages awarded was reduced by 50 per cent for contributory negligence.

To provide competent fellow-workers

Part of a safe system is ensuring that the people with whom an employee has to work are competent and not likely to cause him harm. If a worker's behaviour has shown over time that he could prove a danger to other workers, the employer has a duty to remove the source of danger (*Hudson* v *Ridge Manufacturing Co* (1957)).

Vicarious liability

In the quote from *Wilsons and Clyde Coal Co Ltd* v *English* (above), the House of Lords distinguished between the system of work, for which the employer is personally responsible, and the isolated day-to-day acts of the employee. Thus the employer might devise a system of working with hammers, and the individual employee might drop a hammer regardless of how good the system is. Although the employer is not personally liable for the isolated day-to-day act of an employee, it may be vicariously liable. An employer is vicariously liable for the negligent acts of an employee who is acting in the course of employment. An act by an employee is in the course of employment if it is so closely connected with what he is employed to do that it is fair and just to hold the employer responsible. Prior to *Lister* v *Hesley Hall Ltd* (2001) an employer had been responsible for authorised acts by the employee, even when carried out in an unauthorised way. In *Lister* the House of Lords held that it was fair and just that the employer be held vicariously liable for the acts of its warden when he abused children in its care because of the close connection with what he was employed to do. This would not have been the case under the previous approach.

The employer's vicarious liability can arise when one employee negligently injures another employee, or when a third party is injured by an employee, whether a worker who is not an employee, or a customer or other member of the public.

Occupier's liability

An employer, like any other occupier of premises, owes a duty of care under the Occupiers' Liability (Scotland) Act 1960. For people other than employees, including people working for the employer who are not employees, and people who are working for other employers at the time, the common law duty of care to maintain safe premises will not arise, but the general duty imposed by the 1960 Act will apply. The Act applies to persons who occupy or control premises, and requires them to show such care as is reasonable in all the circumstances to see that someone entering the premises will not suffer injury or damage because of the state of the premises or anything done or not done on them which the occupier is responsible for (s 2). This imposes the same standard of care as common law.

BREACH OF STATUTORY DUTY

The common law duty of care provides a general remedy for all employees in case of negligence by the employer. Legislation provides more specific protection. As the oldest form of worker protection, safety legislation has a long history in the 19th and 20th centuries. Factories Acts, Mines and Quarries Acts and other sector-specific legislation was aimed at prevention of injury and placed criminal liability on employers for breach of the duties imposed. Although there was no express provision of a civil law remedy for injured workers, because the Acts were intended to benefit a specific class of persons (namely, workers) rather than the public in general, a right by people who belonged to that class to raise a civil action was implied. In *Groves* v *Lord Wimborne* (1898) the Court of Appeal held that the Factory and Workshop Act 1878 gave a right of action to a young employee who had lost his arm as a result of an accident in which he was caught in machinery which was unguarded contrary to the Act. In *Butler* v *Fife Coal Co Ltd* (1912) the House of Lords held that the representatives of a miner who died when he inhaled poisonous gases was entitled to raise a civil action based on the duties in the Coal Mines Regulation Act 1887. Such actions are common law actions based on breach of statutory duty.

At the time of these cases, and until its abolition by the Law Reform (Personal Injuries) Act 1948, the doctrine of common employment was a major barrier to an employee seeking to raise a common law action against an employer. The doctrine implied a term into the contract of employment that the employee accepted the risk of injury by a fellow employee. Thus, if negligence by another employee caused the injury, the employer had no legal responsibility at common law. Where a duty was placed on an employer by statute the rule did not apply. This is no longer an issue, but there are still advantages to proceeding for breach of statutory duty rather than breach of the duty of care, the most important being the nature of statutory duties, which in the main are not dependent on proof of negligence, or failure to take reasonable care. A case may be pled on the grounds both that there has been a breach of statutory duty and that there has been a breach of the common law duty of care (eg *Butler* v *Grampian University Hospital NHS Trust* (2002)).

Statute

The Health and Safety at Work etc Act 1974 replaced many of the earlier statutes and introduced a universal health and safety regime. The principal duties imposed under that Act (ss 2–7) cannot be enforced by civil action (s 47). They may found enforcement and criminal prosecution, but not an action of reparation.

In contrast, a breach of duty imposed by health and safety regulations will be actionable, unless the regulations provide otherwise (s 47). The specific requirements of health and safety law (as opposed to the general duties of HSWA 1974) are found in regulations. It is beyond the scope of this book to examine these in detail.

Regulations

There are very many regulations, some of general application, others either sector or process specific. For some years after the implementation of the HSWA 1974 the earlier legislation continued to be in force, and it was the passing of EC health and safety Directives which prompted the issuing of regulations under s 15 of the Act and the replacement of the previous regime.

EC Directives

After the signing of the Single European Act in 1986, health and safety legislation could be passed by majority voting instead of unanimity, thus leading to an increase in Directives in this area. In 1989 the Framework Directive 89/391 was passed which created a general duty on the part of an employer to employees and contains specific directions on how to achieve that. Subsequently, six "daughter" Directives were passed: Workplace Directive 89/654; Work Equipment Directive 89/655; Personal Protective Equipment Directive 89/656; Manual Handling Directive 90/269; Display Screen Equipment Directive 90/270; and Carcinogens Directive 90/394. All of these were given effect to in the UK by the introduction of Regulations. Further Directives, and further Regulations, have followed.

Regulations implementing the EC Directives

The seven sets of Regulations passed to give effect to the first Directives are among the more generally applicable legislation and will be summarised. Of the many Regulations, these are the only ones that are going to be referred to specifically. The first is the Management of Health and Safety at Work Regulations 1999 (originally 1992). These important Regulations provide for a framework for the implementation of health and safety procedures. They impose duties: to carry out a suitable and sufficient risk assessment; to carry out preventive and protective measures according to specified principles; to make appropriate arrangements for effective planning, organisation, control, monitoring and review of safety measures; to provide health surveillance; to appoint competent safety officers; to establish appropriate procedures in case of serious and imminent danger; to ensure contact with external services; to provide employees with safety information; to co-operate with other employers in a shared workplace; to advise temporary or visiting workers of risk; to provide adequate health and safety training. There are also duties in respect of new or expectant mothers (see Chapter 11) and specific duties to ensure the safety of young employees. Duties are also imposed on employees to use machinery, equipment, substances, transport equipment, means of production or safety devices in accordance with training and instructions. Initially these Regulations did not give rise to civil proceedings, but since 2003 employees have had the right to rely on them in civil actions. Other workers and third parties, however, may not rely on them. All of the other Regulations referred to below confer civil liability.

The Workplace (Health, Safety and Welfare) Regulations 1992 implemented Directive 89/654. They impose duties: to ensure that any building a workplace is in is of appropriate stability and solidity; to maintain the workplace, equipment, devices and systems in efficient working order and good repair; to ensure sufficient ventilation of every enclosed workplace; to ensure reasonable temperature, suitable and effective lighting, that the workplace and furnishings are clean, that rooms are of sufficient space, that workstations are suitably arranged, that floors and traffic routes are suitable, that areas where there is a danger of falling are securely fenced; and to ensure the suitability of windows, traffic routes, doors and gates, escalators, sanitary conveniences, washing facilities, clothing accommodation, facilities for changing, facilities for rest and meals; and there is a provision that areas used by disabled persons should be organised to take account of them.

Like all legislation which is passed to give effect to the requirements of EC law, the Regulations must be interpreted to give effect to the relevant Directive. In *Donaldson* v *Hays Distribution Services Ltd* (2005) the Inner House of the Court of Session had to decide whether these Regulations applied to third parties, in this case a customer, as well as workers. A customer had been injured, while picking goods up, by a lorry in a loading bay at a store. She argued that references in the Regulations (reg 17) to persons and pedestrians were wide enough to cover people affected other than workers. The Court did not agree and held that it was necessary to interpret the Regulations by reference to their history and context of implementation of Directive 89/654, which suggested that they were intended to apply to workers only: there was nothing else to suggest otherwise. Thus the customer would have to rely on the Occupiers' Liability (Scotland) Act 1960 and the common law.

Third, the Provision and Use of Work Equipment Regulations 1998 (originally 1992) implement Directive 89/655. They impose duties: to ensure that equipment is constructed or adapted to be suitable for purpose;

to maintain equipment in efficient working order and good repair; to inspect it according to the regulations; to restrict the use of equipment which poses specific risks; to give information and training in its use; to control access to dangerous machinery; to protect against specified hazards; and a number of provisions relate to controls, stability, lighting, markings and warnings.

Fourth, the Personal Protective Equipment at Work Regulations 1992 give effect to Directive 89/656. They impose duties: to ensure that suitable such equipment is provided unless safety is adequately controlled by other means; to ensure compatibility where more than one such equipment has to be used at once; to assess whether equipment is suitable; to maintain and replace equipment; to provide suitable accommodation for such equipment when not in use; to take all reasonable steps to ensure that any personal equipment provided is properly used. Duties are placed on employees to use equipment as trained to do, and to report any loss or defect to the employer.

Fifth, the Manual Handling Operations Regulations 1992 implement Directive 90/269. They impose a duty on an employer so far as reasonably practicable to avoid the need for employees to undertake manual handling operations involving a risk of injury; and, where it is not reasonably practicable to avoid them, place a duty to assess them and take appropriate steps to reduce the risk of injury; and to give necessary information to employees. They also place a duty on employees to make full and proper use of whatever system is provided.

Sixth, the Health and Safety (Display Screen Equipment) Regulations 1992 give effect to Directive 90/270. They impose duties: to analyse workstations to assess health and safety risks; to ensure the workstations meet requirements specified in the Schedule; to plan work to ensure periodic interruptions; to provide appropriate eye and eyesight tests are carried out on request; and to provide adequate health and safety training and information.

Seventh, the Control of Substances Hazardous to Health Regulations 2002 (CSHHR 2002) (originally 1994) give effect to Directive 90/394. They impose duties: to carry out an assessment of the risk to the health of employees before exposing them to such substances; to prevent exposure to hazardous substances or, if that is not reasonably practicable, to ensure it is adequately controlled; to maintain, examine and test control measures; to monitor exposure; to carry out health surveillance; to give information and training to those who may be exposed; and to ensure there are arrangements to deal with accidents, incidents and emergencies.

"Reasonably practicable"

Many of the duties imposed by the legislation are absolute: that is, they state a result that has to be achieved and do not qualify this by providing that it should be done so far as is reasonably practicable. Many other duties, however, do impose duties which are qualified by being to achieve the end so far as is reasonably practicable, or so far as is practicable. These qualify the duty concerned so that it is less strict. The concepts pre-date HSWA 1974 and the Regulations, and there is established case law on what reasonably practicable means. In *Marshall v Gotham Co Ltd* (1954) the House of Lords interpreted reg 7 of the Metalliferous Mines General Regulations 1938 which imposed a reasonably practicable duty to ensure that the roof and sides of every working place in a mine were secure. A miner had been killed when a roof collapsed. Usual procedure had been followed in securing the roof and it had appeared to be sound, but was in fact subject to an unusual condition which had not appeared in the mine for 20 years. The House of Lords held that the mineowners had done what was reasonably practicable, defining the concept as depending upon a consideration whether the time, trouble and expense of the precaution which might be taken are disproportionate to the risk involved. More modern cases would be likely to look for gross disproportion. Thus, like the common law concept of reasonable care, economic considerations are relevant.

However, foreseeability is not part of the concept of reasonably practicable. In *Neil v Greater Glasgow Health Board* (1996), a case under s 29 of the Factories Act 1961, an employee was injured when a machine tipped over. The employee had raised an action based on the common law duty and on breach of statutory duty. The common law claim failed because the incident was not reasonably foreseeable. However, the claim based on breach of statutory duty succeeded, since foreseeability was irrelevant and it was reasonably practicable to clamp the machine to the floor. Thus the statutory duty had been breached. In *Dugmore v Swansea NHS Trust* (2003), a case under reg 7 of CSHHR 1988 (predecessor to the current 2002 version), the same approach was taken. A nurse with an allergic reaction to latex raised an action based on breach of the common law duty of care, and breach of duty under the regulations, when she had such an extreme reaction that she suffered anaphylactic shock and was unable to return to work. She was unsuccessful in the common law action because the employer could not have foreseen that she was at risk. However, the Court of Appeal held that foreseeability was not relevant to liability under CSHHR. Regulation 7 required that the employer ensured exposure to hazardous substances was prevented, or, if that was not reasonably practicable, controlled. When prevention is not reasonably practicable, therefore, it must be controlled. The duty to prevent, or, if appropriate, control is absolute.

The employer's knowledge may, however, be relevant to reasonable practicability. If the employer could not have known of the existence of a particular hazard, there are no reasonably practicable steps that could be taken. In *McLean* v *Remploy Ltd* (1994), another case under s 29 of the Factories Act 1961, a worker was injured when she tripped over yarn set up as a practical joke by a fellow-worker. The employer did not know it had been set up, and the yarn had been up for such a short time before the trip occurred that it was not reasonably practicable for the employer to have taken steps to make it safe.

A duty so far as is practicable is stricter than one so far as is reasonably practicable. It therefore cannot be qualified by the economic considerations which have been held to be relevant in reasonable practicability. It does not mean "possible", but has been held to mean "possible in the light of current knowledge and invention" (*Adsett* v *K and L Steelfounders and Engineers Ltd* (1953)).

Challenge by European Commission

There is no reference to reasonable practicability in the Directives on which the Regulations are based, and to which they are subject. In *Commission of the EC* v *UK* (2007) the European Commission took enforcement proceedings to have the UK declared to have failed in its obligations under Directive 89/391, with particular relevance to s 2 of HSWA 1974. The challenge was unsuccessful: the ECJ held that the Directive does not require no-fault liability. However, there was no support for the cost–benefit approach of reasonable practicability, but a finding that the Commission had not been clear in its interpretation of the duty imposed by the Directive. The compatibility of the current approach to reasonable practicability with the Directives is far from clear.

Burden of proof

In criminal prosecutions, in offences of failing to comply with a duty to do something so far as is reasonably practicable, or practicable, it is for the accused to prove that it was not reasonably practicable, or practicable, to do more than was done, or that there were no better practicable means of complying with the duty (HSWA 1974, s 40). There is no equivalent statutory provision for civil proceedings, but the courts have held that the same principle applies. The burden is on the person who has the duty to act so far as is reasonably practicable to prove that it was not reasonably practicable to have done more to comply with the duty. Before the burden shifts to the employer, the pursuer employee must prove that the employer owed the duty and that the duty had not been complied with. The House of Lords held in *Nimmo* v *Alexander Cowan & Sons Ltd* (1968) that it was not necessary for the injured employee to prove that his employer had failed to do all that was reasonably practicable to keep his workplace safe. This was a case which arose under the old Factories Act 1961, s 29, but the principle is the same. The majority in the House of Lords held that, in order to attain the object of the legislation, namely to keep the workplace safe, such an interpretation was necessary, since the means of achieving that object in specific cases was more likely to be in the employer's knowledge than the employee's.

An unsuccessful challenge was made to the statutory burden of proof in *R* v *Davies* (2003) on the grounds that it breached the presumption of innocence and therefore was not compatible with Art 6(2) of the ECHR. This related specifically to s 3 of the HSWA 1974, which imposes a reasonably practicable duty. The Court of Appeal held that the imposition of the burden of proof on the employer was no more than was justified, necessary and proportionate. The Act regulated a sphere of activity which the employer chose to operate in, the prosecution had to prove that the duty was owed and that the breach had occurred before the burden shifted, while, as a regulatory offence, conviction did not involve the "moral obloquy" of a truly criminal offence and imprisonment was not possible. These arguments apply with at least equal force to civil liability for breach of statutory duty.

HEALTH AND SAFETY AT WORK ETC ACT 1974 AND REGULATION

Apart from its role as source of the power to make the Regulations which form the substance of workplace health and safety law, HSWA 1974 creates the framework for regulation. The duties contained in ss 2–9, in particular ss 2 and 3 which impose general duties on employers to employees and others respectively, are the cornerstone of an employer's legal responsibility. They cannot be enforced by an employee, or other person, as a breach of statutory duty, but they, and the generality of statutory health and safety law, are enforced by a system of regulation and prosecution. It is beyond the scope of this book to examine this in detail.

Self-regulation

A central objective of the Robens Report (1972) on which HSWA 1974 was based was the establishing and encouraging of self-regulation and co-operation between employers and employees. The general duties of the employer towards employees in s 2 include a duty to prepare and revise a health and safety policy. The provisions of the Management of Health and Safety at Work Regulations 1999 are also concerned with the arrangements made by the employer to ensure safety.

The general duties include the duty to consult with safety representatives and to establish a safety committee. Where there is a recognised trade union, it may appoint safety representatives (Safety Representatives and Safety Committees Regulations 1977). If there is no recognised trade union, the employer must consult with the employees directly or with their elected safety representatives (Health and Safety (Consultation with Employees) Regulations 1996). The employer's duty is to consult representatives with a view to making arrangements to enable effective co-operation in promoting measures to ensure the health and safety at work of the employees and in checking the effectiveness of these measures. If requested by the representatives, the employer has a duty to establish a safety committee to keep health and safety measures under review. There are detailed provisions governing election, meeting and powers of inspection.

Safety representatives and members of safety committees have the right not to suffer detriment or to be dismissed for exercising their functions (ERA 1996, ss 44 and 100).

Regulation

The body with the statutory task of carrying out the general purposes of HSWA 1974 is the Health and Safety Executive (HSE). This body replaced two predecessors in 2008: the Health and Safety Commission and the Health and Safety Executive which dealt with policy and enforcement respectively. The general purposes are: securing health, safety and welfare of persons at work; protecting persons other than those at work against risks to health or safety arising out of the activities of persons at work; controlling the keeping and use of explosive or highly flammable or otherwise dangerous substances; and generally preventing the unlawful acquisition, possession and use of such substances (s 1). The HSE has a number of statutory powers, including the power to conduct investigations and inquiries, and the power to issue Codes of Practice.

The key responsibility is enforcement. As well as the HSE, local authorities are the designated enforcing authority for certain purposes, and there are a number of specialist enforcing authorities. Every enforcing authority may appoint inspectors, who have a wide range of statutory powers (s 20).

Inspectors may issue enforcement notices in appropriate circumstances. These are either improvement notices, where the inspector is of the opinion that there is a breach of legislation (s 21), or prohibition notices, where the inspector is of the opinion that activities give rise to risk of serious personal injury (s 23). In the former case the notice orders remedy of the breach, while the latter orders that the article or substance cease to be used immediately and the danger be remedied. In both cases the employer may appeal to an employment tribunal against the notice. An inspector may also seize and render harmless any item believed to be a source of imminent danger (s 25).

Criminal law

There are various criminal offences created by the Act (s 33). They include breach of ss 2–9, breach of regulations, preventing an inspector exercising his powers, and contravening an improvement or prohibition notice. Trial of offences may be by summary procedure or on indictment. While in England and Wales the HSE is the prosecuting authority, in Scotland it is the Crown. Penalties were increased by the Health and Safety Offences Act 2008 in an attempt to provide a greater deterrent to employers against breach of the legislation. For the more serious offences after conviction on indictment, an unlimited fine can be awarded. The highest fine awarded to date was the £15 million pound fine imposed on Transco after its conviction of a breach of s 3 of the HSWA 1974 in the Larkhall gas explosion which killed a family of four.

Essential Facts

• The Health and Safety at Work etc Act 1974 provides the framework for health and safety law.
• The EC Directive creating general health and safety duty on employer is Framework Directive 89/391.
• The "daughter Directives" of Framework Directive 89/391 are:
  – Workplace Directive 89/654
  – Work Equipment Directive 89/655

- Personal Protective Equipment Directive 89/656
- Manual Handling Directive 90/269
- Display Screen Equipment Directive 90/270
- Carcinogens Directive 90/394.

• The Management of Health and Safety at Work Regulations 1999 provide the framework for health and safety procedures in the UK.

• The EC daughter Directives are implemented in the UK by virtue of the following regulations:

- Workplace (Health, Safety and Welfare) Regulations 1992
- Provision and Use of Work Equipment Regulations 1998
- Personal Protective Equipment at Work Regulations 1992
- Manual Handling Operations Regulations 1992
- Health and Safety (Display Screen Equipment) Regulations 1992
- Control of Substances Hazardous to Health Regulations 2002.

Essential Cases

Wilsons and Clyde Coal Co Ltd v English (1937): this case both establishes that the employer's duty of care to an employee is personal and non-delegable, and also provides an explanation of what is meant by a "safe system of work", distinguishing between the practice and method of carrying on the business and isolated day-to-day acts.

Stokes v Guest Keen and Nettlefold (Nuts and Bolts) Ltd (1968): Chadwick J gives a comprehensive explanation of the key principles involved in the duty of care, looking at the conduct of the "reasonable and prudent" employer and what should weigh in such an employer's mind when dealing with safety.

Hatton v Sutherland (2002): this Court of Appeal case established the approach to determining liability of the employer for psychiatric injury to the employee, particularly arising out of overwork. It was approved by the House of Lords in *Barber* v *Somerset County Council* (2004).

Lister v Hesley Hall Ltd (2001): in this case the House of Lords broadened the approach to common law vicarious liability. A residential home was held to be liable for the acts of its warden abusing children in their care. His acts were so "closely connected" to his employment that it would be fair and just to hold his employer responsible.

Commission of the EC v UK (2007): the ECJ did not find that the Commission had established that the UK was in breach of its obligations under Directive 89/391 by creating obligations qualified as being so far as is reasonably practicable. However, it did not support a cost–benefit approach towards the concept and has left the situation of the UK legislation unclear.

Nimmo v Alexander Cowan & Sons Ltd (1968): the House of Lords held that in a civil action for breach of a statutory duty to take care so far as is reasonably practicable, once the pursuer has proved that the employer owed the duty and the duty has not been complied with, it is for the employer to prove that it was not reasonably practicable to have done more to comply with the duty.

INDEX